CASE STUDIES IN
CULTURAL ANTHROPOLOGY

GENERAL EDITORS
George and Louise Spindler
STANFORD UNIVERSITY

THE HUMAN DILEMMA:
A DECADE LATER IN BELMAR

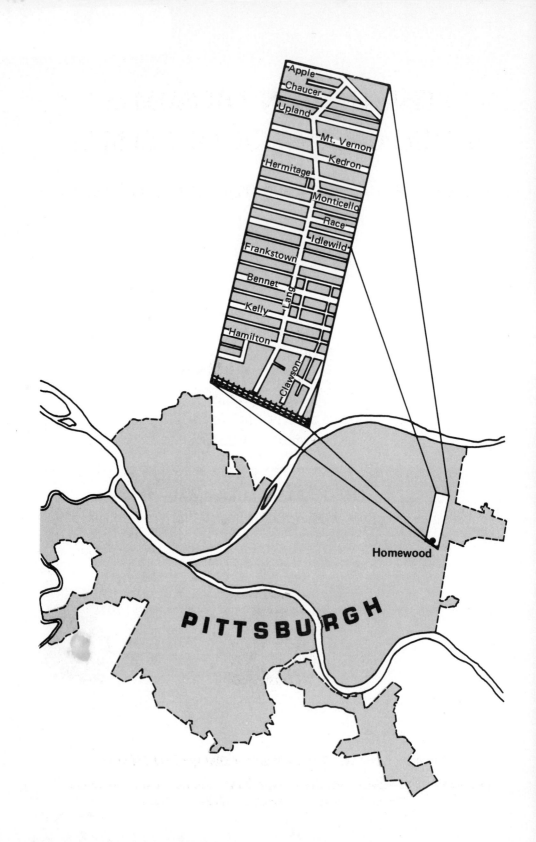

Apple
Chaucer
Upland
Mt. Vernon
Kedron
Hermitage
Monticello
Race
Idlewild
Frankstown
Bennet
Lang
Kelly
Hamilton
Clawson

Homewood

PITTSBURGH

THE HUMAN DILEMMA: A DECADE LATER IN BELMAR

(A Revision of *On the Street Where I Lived*)

by MELVIN D. WILLIAMS

University of Michigan
Ann Arbor

Harcourt Brace Jovanovich College Publishers

Fort Worth   Philadelphia   San Diego   New York   Orlando   Austin   San Antonio
Toronto   Montreal   London   Sydney   Tokyo

Publisher	Ted Buchholz
Acquisitions Editor	Chris Klein
Project Editor	Catherine Townsend
Production Manager	Thomas Urquhart
Manager of Art & Design	Guy Jacobs

Library of Congress Cataloging-in-Publication Data

Williams, Melvin D., 1933–
   The human dilemma : a decade later in Belmar / by Melvin D.
Williams.
      p.   cm. — (Case studies in cultural anthropology)
   Rev. ed. of: On the street where I lived. c1981.
   Includes bibliographical references.
   ISBN 0-03-031594-8
   1. Afro-Americans—Pennsylvania—Pittsburgh—Social life and
customs. 2. Belmar (Pittsburgh, Pa.)—Social life and customs
3. Pittsburgh (Pa.)—Social life and customs. I. Williams, Melvin
D., 1933– On the street where I lived. II. Title. III. Series.
F159.P69N49   1991
974.8'86—dc20   91-32798
                                              CIP

ISBN: 0-03-031594-8

Address editorial correspondence to: Harcourt Brace Jovanovich, Publishers, 301 Commerce
Street, Suite 3700, Fort Worth, TX 76102

Address orders to: Harcourt Brace Jovanovich, Publishers, 6277 Sea Harbor Drive, Orlando, FL
               32887
               1-800-782-4479, or 1-800-433-0001 (in Florida)

Printed in the United States of America

6 7 8 9 0 1 2 016 9 8 7 6 5 4 3 2

To Big Man, Bob, Hannah, Leonard, Mattie and Tobias

Foreword

ABOUT THE SERIES

These case studies in cultural anthropology are designed to bring to students, in beginning and intermediate courses in the social sciences, insights into the richness and complexity of human life as it is lived in different ways and in different places. They are written by men and women who have lived in the societies they write about and who are professionally trained as observers and interpreters of human behavior. The authors are also teachers, and in writing their books they have kept the students who will read them foremost in their minds. It is our belief that when an understanding of ways of life very different from one's own is gained, abstractions and generalizations about social structure, cultural values, subsistence techniques, and the other universal categories of human social behavior become meaningful.

ABOUT THE AUTHOR

Dr. Melvin D. Williams is professor of anthropology at the University of Michigan, Ann Arbor, and Ombudsman of the College of Literature, Science, and the Arts. He held the Olive B. O'Connor Chair in American Institutions at Colgate University in 1976–1977. He has been the organizer and president of a citywide chapter of the National Association for the Advancement of Colored People. He is the author of *Community in a Black Pentecostal Church and The Black Middle Class and Social Transformations: The Reproduction of Social Inequality*. He has been chairperson of the Project Area Committee of the Urban Redevelopment Authority in Belmar. He has published articles in professional journals and was active in community affairs in Pittsburgh, where he was born and educated.

ABOUT THIS CASE STUDY

In this ethnographic account of a Black neighborhood in Pittsburgh, Dr. Williams describes the pain and pleasure of being poor and Black, and the various life styles that accompany these conditions in one neighborhood. He states, "I intend an intimate look at the trials, tribulations, and joys of a street and neighborhood scene that can probably be found in places like this all over the United States." Dr. Williams allows people to speak for themselves in telling us how it is and uses his lifelong experience to explain what it is all about. What emerges is a vivid picture by an African-American anthropologist of a small Black world that looms large in America.

This is one of several studies in this series, Case Studies in Cultural Anthropology, which focuses on a segment of North American society. When we started the series in 1960, with five titles concerned with the Palauans, Cheyennes, Tepozlan,

Tiwi, and the Bunyoro, we declared our intention of including studies of our own society. The concepts and methods of cultural anthropology should be applicable anywhere. Since then many anthropologists have "come-home" to study America.

This case study by Dr. Williams has particular meaning for us as teachers of anthropology, for its argument is a significant part of the central thesis of a course we developed at Stanford, "Anthropological Perspectives on American Culture." Since its first publication in 1981 we have authored and published *The American Cultural Dialogue* (1990) which carries further the major themes of this course. Dr. Williams contributes a chapter in that volume. We have been significantly influenced in our thinking by his observations and interpretations. Dr. Williams interprets what he terms the "genuine" Black life style as a reaction to and confrontation with mainstream norms, expectations, and models, as well as a development in its own right. We interpret "American culture" not as a single set of norms, values, or behavioral patterns, but rather as a complex interaction of groups that in itself exhibits certain regularities. One of the important regularities is in the conflicts and accommodations between mainstream segments and others who, by reasons of economics, oppression, access to power, history, and culture, are not full participants in the mainstream. These conflicts and accommodations take predictable forms. Dr. Williams' "genuine" and "spurious" typologies, developed in the introductory pages of this case study, are versions, original with him, of forms of adaptation exhibited in other settings in American society. The many individuals whom the reader will meet on these pages give life to these categories.

This new edition of *On the Street Where I Lived* exhibits clearly the anguish that Dr. Williams feels as he views the inner city and its miserable circumstances. He shares with us the reasons for this anguish and frames his analysis in a perspective that is both passionate and reasoned.

Everywhere in the inner city black communities in America the traditional institutions of family, religion, education, and social cohesion have been eroding as the middle class moves out to the suburbs, the shops, clinics, restaurants, and even the churches disappear, and the drug culture moves in. Belmar, the particular community of Melvin Williams' focus, has lost most of its business establishments. He describes it as a "scene of blight". The empty buildings and vacant lots attest to a "process of abandonment". And yet there is social life. People belong to a neighborhood that belongs to them, partly because "no one else wants it". Williams describes this social life in telling detail. He puts himself in the setting in his telling, and goes further to speak of what it is like to be a Black in America outside the deteriorating inner city.

This case study is essential reading for anyone who wants to understand contemporary America and the problems we all must squarely face if we are to maintain a viable society.

George and Louise Spindler
Series Editors
Ethnographics
Box 38
Calistoga CA 94515

Acknowledgments

This revised volume is the culmination of a three-year study and fifteen years of revisits for anthropological observations of a Pittsburgh neighborhood, beginning in 1973. Much of this time was spent residing in the neighborhood, visiting the homes of neighbors, intensively interviewing a selected group of *residents,* conducting a survey and leading a citizens' neighborhood organization.

The research was supported in part by funds from the Social Science Research Council. *I am grateful.*

I am indebted to the residents of Belmar who accepted me in their neighborhood in spite of my often peculiar behavior and unique role. This long Belmar sojourn has brought us to the brink of the twenty-first century. It has taught me that the problem of the twenty-first century is the problem of the human line—*the challenge to eliminate* boundary decisions about who belongs within the human community at any given time (see fig. P 1-4). The Belmar residents await the end of the *social* lag in our cultural evolution when we humans will "catch-up" in *our social and political relationships* in the *Ecological Revolution.*

Writing endeavors are usually the result of much support and assistance. Most of it remains unmentioned. I mention David P. Boynton, who discovered me and my original manuscript in my office in Pittsburgh in 1978. Rachel Cohen in the anthropology department of The University of Michigan typed the manuscript into the computer system. She is a rare young woman. Dianna S. Campbell, a pleasant and able colleague at Michigan, read the manuscript and advised me *on revisions.* Dr. Ralph D. Story, another colleague, provided me the administrative support that enabled me the time to write. *Early in my academic career Marise Melson taught me the value of a concerned and able editor. I regret that I was not wise enough then to appreciate it.*

Finally, there continues to be my supportive family—Faye, Aaron, Steven and Craig. To them I must now add my grandson, Christopher.

My efforts here continue to be designed to contribute to the complex process of unraveling the conceptualization of the urban African American. This time that process seems inseparable from the total human dilemma.

Contents

1 / Introduction

In 1981, I wrote:
I suggest that the song "We Shall Overcome" is fast becoming obsolete among the young of these disillusioned poor, and unless this society commits itself to a more equitable distribution of resources and justice, the tactics of urban guerrilla warfare will soon replace the song. Denial, defiance, and defilement will reach an apex of violence in "genuine" life styles in response to that violence in the wider society and the world.

Humans create meaning, and ultimately culture, from the material and institutional resources available to them. If we restrict and differentiate these resources among populations, we differentiate the nature and meaning of the world for them. We set the stage for subcultures. If we want to integrate Americans, we must provide similar ecological niches for them. We must destroy the Belmars in America by an equitable distribution of national resources, whatever the economic device. If we do not want to integrate America, we must recognize, validate, legitimate, and accept the expressive life styles of these slum dwellers. We must assign them equal merit within the scheme of things, whatever the sociocultural device. To do neither in a world destined for economic retrenchments is to further isolate them from this society. It is to recall the violent energies that reemerged during the New York City blackout of July 13, 1977, and the Miami riot of May 17, 1980. It is to hasten the last ray of sunshine in these Western skies. It is to encourage the articulation of ghetto institutional patterns into cohesive movements whose poor Black identities are aligned with the Third World to the extent that they cast their lot and their allegiance with the majority of mankind. (p. 141)

Now, ten years later, we have had the homeless crisis; the teenage-gang phenomenon (including "wilding") in the inner cities of Los Angeles, Washington, D.C., and others; more riots in Miami, the MOVE murders in Philadelphia, and still cries of "and we are not saved." We are witnessing a pervasive growth in an underclass without hope, drug subcultures, Black male incarcerations, and single-female parents in an America that is still not sufficiently motivating us to take the necessary social and political action (see Branch 1988, Lemann 1991 & Williams 1990).

We can no longer pretend to contribute to the well-being of the poor and the Black by studying them. We have overstudied them "and they are not saved." Many books and papers about the Black and poor, economics and social policy, and government action and spending priorities are designed to promote the authors and their supporters, not those in poverty. This volume's revision is justified only because I believe I have some new and different solutions to these social problems.

On a level of abstraction above social action, any treatment of Blacks as a separate and distinct category of human being reinforces the oppression of all

Blacks. We should study the white churches that shun Black members, white leaders who shun Black input, and the rich and powerful who tolerate and exploit oppression, not the Black and the poor. As Hylan Lewis (1971) stated:

> My own view is that the most important research into this area now should focus not on the culture of poverty but on the culture of affluence—the culture that matters more and that is far more dangerous than the culture of poverty. Jean Mayer has put the thrust and the focus succinctly:
>
> There is a strong case to be made for a stringent population policy on exactly the reverse of the basis Malthus expounded. Malthus was concerned with the steadily more widespread poverty that indefinite population growth would inevitably create. I am concerned about the areas of the globe where people are rapidly becoming richer. For rich people occupy much more space, consume more of each natural resource, disturb the ecology more, and create more land, air, water, chemical, thermal and radioactive pollution than poor people. So it can be argued that from many viewpoints it is even more urgent to control the numbers of the rich than it is to control the numbers of the poor (Mayer, 1969, p. 5).

The concept, conspiracy, and mythology of a Black middle class does violence to the African-American dream of community and pushes the mythological treatment of race to its extreme (see Majors 1976 as an illustration, Williams In Press). The "genuine" Black is threatened as the carrier of Black culture in a system in which the ultimate goal is to be white and upper class. How can Blacks trust or follow the Black middle class? Culturally secure Blacks are "genuine." African Americans whose livelihoods are imperiled because economic circumstances have allowed them to fall through the societal safety net are the Black "underclass," to the extent that the term is useful. The others are Blacks aspiring to be something else. Langston Hughes, Marcus Garvey, and E. Franklin Frazier understood that.
  In 1981, I wrote:

> Humankind is on the threshold of new experiments in human societies. The old models have run their course and appear inadequate to deal with the social problems they have inherited and created (see Nisbet 1975). My material may suggest new life styles and new orientations toward living once we destroy old preconceptions about material excesses and obsessions with possessions, property, prestige, power, fame, money, wealth, and competition. We are beginning to appreciate the nature of our limited world and the potential of human satisfaction without the waste of manpower and materials (see Dubos 1976, McHarg 1972). The crisis of our times is such that we begin to think the unthinkable and attempt to achieve the impossible. The alternative is to end it all in human folly—the present petty goals and successes that fill our daily lives. This simple and modest work about a poor Black neighborhood may present a timely and important message about humans everywhere. There has never been a people as patient with an oppressor as the poor Black in America. His final recourse to violence will not be an isolated event, but it will be one of the last signals that this culture and society are no longer capable of providing the cognitive orientation necessary for every human group within it. His call for justice is a call for salvage of a potentially great American society (Harrington 1976, Hall 1976, Heilbroner 1976, Lekachman 1976, Mead 1975, and Nisbet 1975). Such a society can then be an example to a world awaiting solutions to similar problems. (Williams 1981:140)

Now, ten years later, I offer you the new approaches to which I alluded in that earlier volume. "New life styles and new orientations toward living" are difficult to formulate within an acceptable form. People who control the instruments of communication are not easily convinced of the merits of new ideas. As one director of a press at a prestigious American university told me, "I want to get on the map, not on the mat."

The pervasive problems of discrimination and oppression of human populations have historically been treated population by population, nation by nation, when the phenomena are panhuman (see Williams In Press b). We have sought piecemeal explanations and remedies when something far more was required. The human conditions that foster and perpetuate racism are the same conditions that create many of our other social problems. We must no longer treat the symptoms of those conditions, but we must alter the conditions, change the present course of civilization, and establish a new and necessary respect for life and planet. We must not only recycle the products of human culture, but also recycle human culture (values, attitudes, and myths about being human) itself. As Montagu, repudiating the innate aggression of man, said:

> What, in fact, such writers do, in addition to perpetrating their wholly erroneous interpretation of human nature, is to divert attention from the real sources of man's aggression and destructiveness, namely, the many false and contradictory values by which, in an overcrowded, highly competitive, threatening world, he so disoperatively attempts to live. It is not man's nature, but his nurture, in such a world, that requires our attentions. (1968b:16)

The law of survival requires no less in the next century. We must somehow convince a fragmented world that has been forced into a global society that what Kenneth Clark said is true:

> The truth of the dark ghetto is not merely a truth about Negroes; it reflects the deepest torment and anguish of the total human predicament. (1967:xxv)

In his preface to *Black Bourgeoisie,* Frazier stated:

> Another criticism which deserves attention was that this study did not reveal anything peculiar to Negroes. This was a criticism offered not only by Negroes who are sensitive about being different from other people, but by white people as well. Some of them were the so-called liberal whites who, when any statement is made which might be considered derogatory concerning Negroes, are quick to say that the "same thing is found among whites." Other whites pointed out what is undoubtedly true: that this book dealt with behavior which is characteristic of middle-class people—white, Black, or brown. Some of my Jewish friends, including some young sociologists, went so far as to say that the book was the best account that they had ever read concerning middle-class Jews. (1968:13)

This classic book remains the best example of the myth of Black solidarity as many Blacks struggle to separate and distinguish themselves from their poor brothers and sisters. But as Frazier suggests, this is not a Black problem; it is a human problem. And that is how we must approach the solution. So this revised volume is merely another example of the human dilemma, not just the American dilemma.

My studies of the "genuine" African American who denies, defies, and defiles American values (dddav, pronounced "did-did-dav") have culminated in my concept of DDDAK (pronounced "did-did-dac," see Williams 1990, In Press b) for humankind. These have been adaptive human emotions. Since the beginning of human culture, humans have denied, defied, and defiled their animal kinship. That energy and that vector created culture and, eventually, modernity. But the technological sophistications of modernity no longer permit this approach to humanness. They threaten the endangered Earth. DDDAK is the human (with his/her unique perceptive ability) response (including fear) to his/her animal heritage and destiny (death). Humans fear what they are (animals) and what may happen to them—hunger, violence, homelessness, meaninglessness, loneliness, illness and death. Thus, humans substitute myth (including superiority) and power (to enforce and validate myth) for their history, their present and their future. Superiority requires comparisons and contrasts (see Veblen 1987), so humans create "inferior" ("lower") animals and "inferior" people (races, classes, genders and "devils"). The people of Belmar are some of the victims of this human origin and cultural evolution of myth and power. The other victims are the remainder of humankind. Together, they are in the human dilemma created by cultural evolution and DDDAK. Similarly, African Americans have created their own distinctive subculture by denying, defying, and defiling American values. One of the few avenues for subgroup separation, identity, and association among humans is to disavow the values of "others." The "hippies" and "flower children" of the '60s, the separatist religious groups, animal-rights activists, "skin heads," and even the radical environmentalists of the '80s and '90s attest to this. The behavior (dddav) of the "genuine" Black combats the hegemonic value system in America and appropriates and transforms the discourse into "genuine" Black collective identities.

Dddav created a viable subculture for African Americans, as this volume demonstrates, but like DDDAK and its obsolescence for humankind—and the parallelism is no accident—modern life in American Black ghettos can no longer tolerate this approach to subculture.

Many American cities are predominantly Black. Most have large Black populations. Mayors, police, judges, and city bureaucrats are African Americans. African Americans have access to sophisticated weapons, drugs, and local power. The traditional dddav that we describe below is no longer sufficient in modern cities. African Americans have control of many of their neighborhoods and now must create communities among themselves based on an approach broader than dddav. Just as DDDAK may create human extinction, dddav may create Black inner-city destruction:

$$\frac{\text{DDDAK}}{\text{Human extinction}} = \frac{\text{dddav}}{\text{Black inner-city destruction}}$$

or

$$\frac{\text{D}}{\text{HE}} = \frac{\text{d}}{\text{Bid}}$$

We have created human categories and multiplied them since the agricultural revolution. For instance, one of the unique inventions in the New World was the creation of the category, race. Race, which is almost meaningless outside of political designs, has become pregnant with political interpretations and beliefs (see Montagu 1952). We attempt to assign all humans to a race, to give races a rank, and to deny the depravity of this process. Notwithstanding our denial of their existence, racial classification and ranking persist. And most nations of the world reflect this persistence in their respective minority problems. The Ibo of Nigeria, the Luo of Kenya, the Blacks, Colored, and Hindu of South Africa, the Tamil of Sri Lanka, the Hutu of Ruanda, the Kurds of Iraq, the Ukranians of the Soviet Union, the Armenians of Turkey and the Soviet Union, the Jews of Nazi German, the Eta and Ainu of Japan, the Indians of the Americas, the barbarians in China, the Catholic Irish in Britain, the African Americans and Hispanics in the United States, and the Indians of Canada are all examples of race classifications (or similar categories) used to separate peoples, often for oppressive ends (see Berreman 1972).

BELMAR, 1990

I have returned to the Belmar section in Pittsburgh several months every year for the past decade to observe the social and physical transformations in the neighborhood. The economic decline in Belmar that I described in 1981 continues ten years later. It will not reverse itself until the values change in America and in Belmar. Black "leaders," poverty programs, public policy agents, government intervention, private investments, housing code enforcement, school desegregation, and political realignments in Belmar and Homewood (the larger region containing Belmar) are cosmetic factors that do little to address the problems of the neighborhood. Houses continue to decay and to be replaced by lots full of debris. Pool halls are replaced by

Carnegie Library on North Lang Avenue

drug streets, street corners, and houses (crack houses) while other activities, for instance, at the library, taverns, with store-corner groups, "wino" groups, street-mechanic groups, street and schoolyard game groups, "huffy" bicycle groups, and at the swimming pool seem to wane in the face of major economic enterprises in street drug traffic. Even vandalism, burglary, and robbery appear to have decreased as money seems more available in the drug traffic. The rubbish and garbage that the residents remove from their property in the early morning after the busy night's transactions reveal new and more-expensive eating and drinking habits of those who work and litter there.

The alterations in family, church, and neighborhood life had a major impact on educational goals, single-parent families, teenage pregnancy, and the un-employables. The spirit and the activities seem dominated by the young men and women who ply their trade and participation in drugs. The children are surrounded and sometimes inducted into these drug activities. They see and know the dealers and their cars. They admire their clothes, shoes, money, cars, loud car stereo systems, and business acumen. One 21-year-old male dealer called to a nine-year-old neighbor as he stored his drugs into the trunk of his parked-car-business location, "Milton watch my stuff. Don't let anybody mess with it. If you see anybody messing with it, let me know who it is."

The neighborhood continues to lose its "core members" (those who invest in their community without expectations of immediate returns). Even Deacon Griffin (Williams 1981:55, p. 55 below), who was "mainstream" and "resigned to live out his days" in Belmar, has moved. If he could see the traffic in front of his former house today, he would have no regrets. The neighborhood seems alive with young adults, and many older residents appear overwhelmed by the drug networks, activities, control, noise, and the dominating impact on them and their children.

This process of blaming and debating about the victims diverts attention from

A winter marketplace under the kitchen window of an irate neighbor

the problem—"inferior" people created by those who require "inferior" people to sustain their own mythical superiority. That problem has reached gigantic proportions—infant mortality, the AIDS epidemic, the homeless, the "underclass," the health care debacle, environmental disaster, and irrational economic greed—that can no longer be ignored. There are no superior people or other, less-important forms of life. We are all in this web together. And together we must begin the Ecological Revolution.

The human inferiority complex created by DDDAK has forced us to assume a mythical superior status and role on Earth. But we humans are animals that perspire, and perspiration has its odor. We secrete mucous from the eyes, hair, lungs, bronchial tubes, skin, sexual organs, and the colon. We salivate, masticate, expectorate, regurgitate, urinate, defecate, masturbate, fornicate, gestate, exudate, suppurate, lacrimate, lactate, fight, kill, sleep, hemorrhage, die, and decay. Yet we reject our animal kinship and even subordinate other arbitrarily defined humans to prove our superiority (see Degler 1991). This is the problem, and it has become so severe that it threatens an endangered earth as well as Belmar. Shakespeare illustrates the problem:

> What a piece of work is man! How noble in reason! How infinite in faculties! In form, in moving, how express and admirable! In action how like a god! the beauty of the world! the paragon of animals! (*Hamlet*, Act II, Scene II)

As long as humans use artificial categories to conceptualize arbitrarily identified human populations and to place other forms of life outside of the human community and to define these forms as inferior to humans, then there is little to prevent circumstances that allow human populations to be shifted about in terms of significance and even to be regarded as nonhuman (for example, Jews in Nazi Germany) and, thus, outside of the concentric circles of the human community (see Fig. 1.3). This concentric circle conception of the human community is an abiding threat to all humans. At any time, genocide, homelessness, war, or some other human circumstance may place any of us on the margins or outside the human community with other "lower" forms of life.

ORGANIZATION OF THE VOLUME

The new introduction attempts to cast the American dilemma (African Americans) into the broader human dilemma. The "genuine" Black and the human race are both at risk from two formerly adaptive strategies—DDDAK and dddav. DDDAK came into existence once humans had evolved from primates. Dddav emerged in African-American slavery. Both have become obsolete. With their elimination, the commonalities and panhuman qualities of social, economic, ethnic, religious, and racial discrimination will end. We will begin to truly respect all forms of life on Earth and our own kinship with them. We will end the human process (DDDAK) that results in the people of Belmar and populations throughout the world being denied equitable resources and a recognized, validated, legitimated, dignified, and accepted way of life.

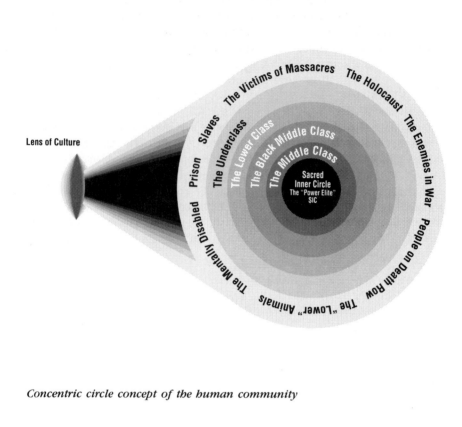

Lens of Culture

Concentric circle concept of the human community

Most of Chapter 2 (History) from the earlier edition will be eliminated here to provide space for new material. The remaining materials from that chapter will be placed in Chapter 3 (The Place). Chapter 2 (The "Genuine" Black in an Inner-City Neighborhood) in the present volume contains the material from Chapter 1 of the former case study, with additional materials on recent changes in the Belmar neighborhood.

Chapter 4 (Household Styles) and Chapter 5 (Landlords and Tenants) retain their former descriptions with updates. Chapter 6 (Activities in Belmar) has new materials on church services. Chapter 7 (World View in Belmar) has new discussions of religious healing and perspectives of African-American women.

As a result of the critiques of ethnography (see Agar 1986, Fetterman 1990, Rose 1990, and Wengle 1988), anthropologists are more aware of the limitations of that social science approach to understanding human behavior. But we must extend that attitude, critique, and examination to the values that humans harbor about the Earth and all of its creatures because such values are pervasive and they distort the perspectives in all of our sciences, humanities, and policy decisions (about war, populations, and ecosystems).

Just as we have attempted to meet the challenges for the limitations in ethnography, we must rise to the challenges that are created by the distortions of DDDAK. Until the social scientists come to grips with DDDAK in themselves and others, their research perspectives will be flawed. Human perspectives and observations will improve in most respects when we discard our myths about our position, prestige, and place in the nature of life on Earth.

Last, reflexive ethnography has been a major addition to anthropology in the past decade. In a different kind of book, its influence would have encouraged me to insert a chapter on the ethnographer's perceptions and observations. But this is a series for beginning college students, and for them, my perceptions and observations may be better understood by a closer look at the author, his childhood, adulthood, attitudes, and values. I have attempted to provide that sketch in Chapter 8 (Human Inferiority Feelings: The "Spurious" and the "Mainstream"). This may give the interested reader some insights into my assumptions about the world, African Americans, and, indeed, Belmar. "Inferior" people of the world will unite in the Ecological Revolution. And we shall be saved.

PART ONE

THE PLACE

2 / The "Genuine" Black in an Inner-City Neigborhood

Belmar is a Black neighborhood in Pittsburgh whose middle-income residency (Black and white) was invaded in the 1950s by low-income Blacks, who were displaced in the Pittsburgh Hill District by the redevelopment project to expand the central business district. Demographic analyses have documented these population movements (Health and Welfare Association of Allegheny County 1963, Lowe 1968, Lubove 1969, Windell 1975), but they fail to capture the trials, tribulations, and disorientations of those who moved to Belmar when their homes, with their Hill District community, were demolished, and of those who lived in the stable, predominantly middle-class Belmar before it was invaded. This volume, an ethnographic account, examines the impact—the nature and dilemmas of some of their lives. It looks at the diverse life styles of contemporary residents—a diversity which, to some extent, is forced upon the neighborhood by urban redevelopment, the myths of ritual race pollution, and economic deprivation.

The Black residents of Belmar live daily with certain conditions in the neighborhood (see Williams 1980). I will attempt to identify the complexity of character and behavior of the people who live under these conditions. The material presented is not a definitive statement about Blacks in America or the various people described. Rather, it highlights the variety and complexity of the people. As the sole investigator, I have not given attention to all its residents or even equal attention to those I have studied. On the contrary, I have lived on North Lang Avenue in Belmar, and I have known my immediate neighbors best. I have interviewed those whom I have known, and in most cases, they were cooperative. This book is a selective description of Belmar, its economic decline, some of its people, and their activities and world view. As such, it is a look at part of America. This effort is focused on selected people and activities rather than on a well-defined political or geographical area. I try to capture some of the variety and complexity of people often described in the literature in terms that suggest a homogeneity and commonality that belie my data. My material suggests that there is no single Black culture or subculture (Blackwell 1975, Green 1970, Hannerz 1969, Johnson and Sanday 1971, Lewis 1971, Rodman 1963, 1971, Young 1970) among these poor people; rather, several identifiable life styles, behavior patterns, and conflicts can be identified to suggest multiple cultures and subcultures. Yet, there is some consensus, some common historical experiences and phenotypes that most of them accept or react to. Much of this consensus is expressed in their world view (Chapter 7). My intention is to discuss those aspects I have observed—household style, landlords, tenants, street activities, verbal communications—and offer some explanations when I am able.

This study draws upon the scholarly tradition of American studies by Abrahams (1964), Anderson (1978), Aschenbrenner (1975), Clark (1967), Davis et al. (1941), Dougherty (1978), Drake and Cayton (1962), DuBois (1896, 1961), Hannerz (1969), Hippler (1974), Keil (1966), Keiser (1979), Kennedy (1980), Kunkel and Kennard (1971), Ladner (1971), Liebow (1967), Lynd and Lynd (1937, 1956), Powdermaker (1939), Rainwater (1974), Stack (1974), Valentine (1978), Warner et al. (1963), West (1945), Whyte (1955), Williams (1974), and others. It is motivated by the belief that the endurance, strength, and faith of some of the people of Belmar are not only important to them, but also important to students of human behavior (see Clark 1967). The residents of Belmar are victims of a dumping ethos and phenomenon in Pittsburgh (see Rainwater 1967, Szwed 1972). Since 1881, Belmar and Homewood have been the site for locating the undesirable in Pittsburgh. This has created a steady decline in real estate value and commercial enterprise. It is the economic process of manipulating and exploiting people and places for profit that creates Belmar and other economic wastelands in our increasingly polluted and resource-ravaged world. So this is a timely study of the social life and economic death of a Black neighborhood. Yet the spirit of many residents has not been broken.

The physical setting of the research is an area in the Belmar section of Homewood, Pittsburgh, Pennsylvania. This neighborhood is bounded by Apple Street, North Lang Avenue, North Homewood Avenue, and Frankstown Avenue. It is populated by welfare recipients, pimps, entrepreneurs, skilled and unskilled laborers, domestics, government employees, retired people and "hustlers." It has an elementary school, four grocery stores, one restaurant, three dry-cleaning establishments, four taverns, one home remodeling company, one "jitney station" (illegal taxis), and three churches.

North Lang Avenue, where I lived during the study and concentrated by research efforts, was a thriving business community 25 years ago. It boasted a supermarket, a drugstore, three grocery stores, a gasoline station, two beauty parlors, three barber shops, a nightclub, a laundromat, a candy store for the children (with a few hardware items), a magazine store, a bakery, two taverns, an elementary school, a Chinese laundry, a dairy store with a beer license, two dry cleaners, and a real estate office. Today, only the taverns, the school, and the cleaning establishments remain.

The city rezoned North Lang Avenue in 1965 from C3 (commercial) to R2 (two-family residential), and it is destined to become totally residential in the future. The remainder of the area, excluding Homewood Avenue, has been residential for over 50 years. Thus, the neighborhood gave me the opportunity to reach Blacks who have established their residence since at least 1940, as well as those who recently moved into the area. By means of a questionnaire, intensive interviewing, censuses, and participant observation (taking up residence in the immediate neighborhood), I attempted to determine to some extent the ideology and subsequent behavior of members of this population.

When I began this research on Belmar, I compiled 500 questionnaires for the neighborhood, and with the aid of my research assistant, who is a Black female resident, I distributed them throughout the area. My assistant and I began to enter homes to discuss the questionnaire with the residents of Belmar. With those who had taken the time to fill them out, we went over their responses. Most people had not filled them out, so we sat down and assisted them in answering the questions. During this process, however, I realized that getting information by questionnaire would damage my ability to perform participant observation in the neighborhood. Information gathered by questionnaire was in most cases given reluctantly, and in many cases, the veracity of the information was dubious. In almost all cases, people were uncomfortable about having detailed information about them written on a piece of paper in questionnaire form, in spite of the fact that the questionnaire's use was thoroughly explained; there was no reason for me to believe that its use would eventually cause them problems. Because of the drawbacks of this technique, my research assistant and I discontinued the collection of questionnaires. Our experience convinced me that continued questioning would eventually stigmatize me in the neighborhood. It would give me a profile related to a questionnaire procedure which I believed had negative connotations and would result in counterproductive attitudes. Indeed, I felt that my position as a viable participant observer and resident in the neighborhood would be threatened if I continued to be perceived by the residents as "that man who fills out those papers."

This decision does not reflect the nature of the survey and questionnaires, only the impact of the experience itself. Yet, the experience was one of the methods used to make contact with the Belmar residents, and many of them seem to appreciate, understand, and forgive the mistake. Thus, the content of this book is primarily the result of residing in the neighborhood, visiting in homes of neighbors, intensively interviewing a selective group of 36 of them, and leading a citizens' neighborhood organization for three years.

There has been considerable discussion concerning the personal or qualitative approach in anthropology and the other social sciences (see Bennett 1976, Berreman 1968, Gulick 1973, Honigmann 1976, Kerri 1974, Maquet 1973). This approach, in spite of its limitations, seems especially pertinent to the study of the Black ghetto. Clark states the case:

A few years ago a highly respected friend, who is a psychiatrist interrupted a humorous but somewhat serious discussion by observing that I would not permit "the facts to interfere with the truth." At the time we laughed in appreciation of the wit inherent in the seeming incongruity of the observation. Since then I have many times recalled that remark with increasing appreciation of its profound significance. Throughout my involvement in the study of the ghetto, in the collection of the data about Harlem, in the exposure to currents and cross-currents of the community, it became increasingly clear to me that what are generally labeled as the facts of the ghetto are not necessarily synonymous with the truth of the ghetto. In fact, there are times when one feels that "facts" tend to obscure the truth. *Dark Ghetto* seeks to more, as far as it can, beyond a narrow view of fact, beyond the facts that are quantifiable and are computable, and that distort the actual lives of individual human beings into rigid statistics. Probably such facts reflect or suggest some of the truth; delinquency and infant mortality rates do tell us that some people get in trouble with society and that others die early in life. But such facts do not relate the truths of the parents' emotions when confronted with the blight of defeat or death nor do they reveal the individual delinquent, his struggle for self-esteem, his pretense at indifference or defiance of his fate, his vulnerability to hurt, his sense of rejection, his fears, his angers, or his sense of aloneness. These are rejected as facts by most social scientists because they are not now quantifiable. (1967:xxiii)

I affirm the position of Clark (1967), Geertz (1973), Honigmann (1976), Kroeber (1935), Maquet (1973), and others by my efforts in this book.

As Hannerz has said so well (see also Blackwell 1975, Green 1970, Johnson and Sanday 1971, Kapsis 1978, Lewis 1971, Rodman 1963, 1971, and Young 1970), the variety of life styles in Black ghettos is complex:

There are many who are in the ghetto but not of the ghetto in the sense of exhibiting much of a life style particular to the community. (In some ways, of course, everybody in the ghetto has special problems to cope with by virtue of his residence there.) There are people in the ghetto who have good, stable jobs, help their children with their homework, eat dinner together at a fixed hour, make payments on the car, and spend Saturday night watching Lawrence Welk on TV—to their largely mainstream way of life we will devote rather little attention. This neglect may distress those who profess their friendship for the people of the ghetto, yet feel that conformity to mainstream standards is a prerequisite for full citizenship. For my "bias of exoticism"—which is perhaps typical of anthropologists (cf. Naroll and Naroll 1963)—they might want to substitute a bias of togetherness, an emphasis on the ways in which ghetto dwellers in general, and some of them in particular, are "just like white folks." Perhaps those who feel this way are motivated by an understanding of what may be the culturally authoritarian demands of the American majority. To this the only answer is that some differences cannot be swept under the rug and that it has always been one of the duties of anthropology to show that whether a way of life is like your own or not, it is a reasonable and understandable combination of common human themes with the experiences of a unique past and present. (1969:15)

My participant observations are highly selective, as mentioned above. I have had most contact with those who are expressive and communicative and whose spirits exemplify harmony, balance, and self satisfaction—the "genuine" (see Sapir 1966). They often speak for themselves in these pages.

LIFE STYLES

Sapir describes *life style* as that which consists of "those general attitudes, views of life, and specific manifestations of civilization that give a particular people its distinctive place in the world" (1966:83). He places the emphasis upon the significance that their behavior and beliefs have in their total existence. The "spirit" and the "genius" of a people take on identifiable form. But the "adequate interpretation" of this form "*is beset with difficulties* [emphasis mine] and . . . is often left to men of letters."

Sapir labels *life style* as one of three different conceptualizations of culture. He postulates that this particular conception of culture may have an ideal form— "genuine culture." It is contrasted with "spurious culture." Sapir explains:

> The genuine culture is not of necessity either high or low; it is merely inherently harmonious, balanced, self-satisfactory. It is the expression of a richly varied and yet somehow unified and consistent attitude toward life, an attitude which sees the significance of any one element of civilization in its relation to all others. It is, ideally speaking, a culture in which nothing is spiritually meaningless. (1966:90)

I have borrowed Sapir's terms "genuine" and "spurious" to discuss the "spirit" and "genius" of Black people in Belmar. The terms are used as indicators of the level of integration of African Americans into the values of American culture.

There are "mainstream" (after Hannerz) Blacks in Belmar who are difficult to distinguish behaviorally from their white counterparts anywhere in America. There are poor Blacks with "mainstream" aspirations who seldom forget or forgive their "outrageous fortunes" ("spurious"). There are poor Blacks ("genuine") who live harmoniously with their economic situation. This complexity and variety impedes the quest for community in Belmar (see Smith 1965, 1969). This volume will concentrate upon the "genuine" and the "spurious," and I will try to identify them, although this categorization will oversimplify the varied characteristics of complex human beings (see Spindler 1955, Spindler and Spindler 1971). These categories are depicted in Figure 2.3. The scheme is designed merely to give some social context to my concept of the "genuine" Black.

The "spurious" Blacks in Belmar are on welfare or have menial jobs, and they detest the noise, the dirt, and the decay around them, but they do not possess the resources to leave. Their incomes make it impossible to maintain "mainstream" appearances, but they try. They arise with their children and prepare them for school. Often, they walk some distance with them and wait for them after school. They belong to the P.T.A., and they confer with their children's teachers. They are members of a church (although not part of a church community, see Williams 1974), and they send their children to Sunday school. You will not find them on "the avenue" or in the bars. They are very selective of the neighbors they befriend and often "keep pretty much to themselves." They complain about "conditions" to whomever will listen. But they are aware of the hopelessness of their complaints. Their incomes, education, mannerisms, and social networks deny their acceptance by the "mainstream," and they would not defile themselves by associating with the "genuine." The "spurious" live interspersed between "genuine" and "mainstream" residents in quiet desperation with a lean and hungry spirit, anxiously awaiting any opportunity to escape their poverty.

Yet they have a few avenues of escape. They can become part of a church community and immerse themselves in church life (see Williams 1974). But their aspirations are usually higher. They can acquire better jobs, more education, political appointments, community action positions, and, thus, change their social networks. But such opportunities are rare. From these ranks emerge the vocal "community leaders" who devote all their energy necessary to become exposed and visible when an opportunity arises. More than any other group, these poor Blacks are "invisible." So they join fraternal organizations to aspire to leadership. They are the ambitious strivers wherever you find them, but their racial and economic characteristics are persistent obstacles to upward mobility.

Frustrated, the "spurious" often withdraw from their neighbors, social networks, and neighborhood gatherings. The Cat Lady, whom we will meet in Chapter 4, withdrew to her private world of pet animals and seldom ventured into human company. In 1985, she moved to the suburbs. Her son chose first a world of fantasy—comic books, basketball, sport periodicals—then became a spectator sports enthusiast, and, finally, discovered a job and a church (Seventh Day Adventists) to absorb him completely. Another widow resident, labeled by the neighborhood children as the Food Lady, withdrew to her job as a driver for a truck rental company, and after retirement, she fed abandoned dogs and semiabandoned children in the neighborhood. She shopped daily, and most of her income was consumed in "service" to the neighborhood needy. From her, the refuse collectors, as well as municipal or utility employees working in the area, could get a hot cup of coffee on cold mornings. As a result, the Food Lady was held in special regard in Belmar, and she always received special consideration from municipal and utility employees as well as constant attention from stray dogs and children in Belmar. Aged and ill, she remains in the neighborhood and communicates with a few selected residents.

These, then, are the "spurious." However, the focus of my work (see also Roberts et al. 1982) is on the "genuine." Their subculture is the keystone of Black culture in the urban North. "It is not of necessity either high or low; it is merely inherently harmonious, balanced, self-satisfactory" (Sapir 1966:90). Sapir also warns us not to be purists, and he accepts the propensity for such harmony as valid or "genuine." Similar to the phenomenon that Sapir discusses, the "spirit" and "genius" of urban American Blacks continue to escape "adequate interpretation." His discourse provides a useful point of departure for describing that behavior in Belmar which I have discovered to be the "genius" and "spirit" of Black culture here.

The "genuine" life style is an ecological adaptation to the urban desert that is Belmar. Other people have attempted different responses to their perceptions of an oppressive, prejudice-ridden culture and society (for example, beatniks, street people, communes, flower children, religious cults, gangs, runaways, hippies, and the like). But no other American has articulated and developed an alternative life style to the extent of the "genuine" Black.

I have followed Hannerz's (1969) use of "mainstream" as appropriate for describing similar life styles in Belmar. But his use of "partying" seems inappropriate here because many people ("genuine," "spurious," and "mainstream") "swing" occasionally and try to give the impression that they do so more frequently than is true. His "street families" come close to my category of "genuine," but neither his term nor his discussion is adequate for people who are the keystone of Black culture in urban America. His "streetcorner men" (and those of Liebow 1967) are merely congregations or communities of "genuine" men in Belmar who exploit the area for its opportunities for social and, to some extent, commercial interaction. Both Hannerz (1969) and I recognize the limitations of the categories, and within these limitations, I attempt to describe some of the people of Belmar.

Racism, with its economic, social, and geographical restrictions, has encouraged behavioral adaptations and creations within the confines of Black ghettos. The residents are faced with serious obstacles to moving upward in a society whose values emphasize that mobility as one important basis for self-esteem. They are also handicapped by phenotypic features that are considered symbolically inferior by the wider society, and they are denied access to many institutional resources in the larger society that represent and socialize in "mainstream" behavior, values, and resourcefulness. "The declining significance of race" (Wilson 1978) can be a scapegoat for the middle-class Black and white who would rather believe discrimination is due more to the vicissitudes of class than to the inheritance of phenotypes (see Clark 1978 and p. 65 here).

In this social and economic environment, poor Blacks have responded in a variety of ways. The "genuine" ones have defied pervasive influence of "mainstream" values and have persisted in demonstrating a style that often defiles and denies those values. Thus, their behavior is distinctively expressive rather than instrumental, in terms of the goals and rewards in "mainstream" society. The "spurious" have become a sort of "man without a country." They seem to belong nowhere. Uncomfortable with the "no good" characteristics of the "genuine" and denied the resources, networks, and stylistic codes of the "mainstream," they linger in a "no-man's land." They are often bitter about both the behavior of "genuine" Blacks who, they rationalize, "keep us down," as well as the attitudes and institutional restrictions of the "mainstream" that keep them out. They refuse to be the one and cannot be the other, so they are marginal or isolated, but the tolerant bosom of the ghetto provides a place for them in spite of themselves. The "spurious" are often the hard drug addicts, amateur poets and novelists, or chronic prison inmates who fail to "beat the system." Sometimes, they find release in various religious sects (see Williams 1974); at other times, they live out their lives with a suppressed rage or a marginal isolation.

"Spurious" Blacks who are "bearing down hard" upon the "mainstream" often consist of families in which the husband does two menial jobs, the wife does domestic work, and the older children work after school. Yet the family is often too large; their spending habits, patterned after the "mainstream" which they imitate, are too extravagant; and their income, in spite of their efforts, is just not adequate. This dilemma is often compounded by the threat and execution of layoffs. These Blacks struggle from day to day to maintain their impossible life styles. They coerce, advise, and nurture their children in "mainstream" values and attitudes. They shun their "genuine" neighbors and are excluded by their "mainstream" ones. Their children are often humiliated as they reach beyond their "genuine" neighbors for playmates. Some "spurious" families have fallen from former financial grace. They have lost the necessary resources and much of the hope of participating in "mainstream" life styles. They isolate themselves in poverty and humiliation. Some of the children dare to be "genuine," and the price is often a severe one as "genuine" children force them to prove their commitment again and again and demand that they rebel against their previous "mainstream" training. To "spurious" Blacks, "genuine" is not only a life style, but it is also the lowest class in America. Yet the "spurious" belong to the same lower class. The "genuine" have adapted to it and have learned to live with their situation; the "spurious" have not accepted it.

The "spurious" are often involved in neighborhood projects, political activities, volunteer programs, and large church congregations (see Williams 1973a) in order to remain close to opportunities and possibilities for upward mobility and, therefore, closer to "mainstream" patterns of behavior. Those "spurious" who come precariously close to being "genuine" are often members of small Pentecostal sects. They too have learned well how to cope with their lives. They do not pine to be "mainstream," but they refuse to be "genuine." Although they differ from the "genuine" primarily in creed-restricted behavior, they see themselves as distinctive, different, and superior to the "genuine" (see Williams 1974). They attempt to harmoniously integrate their world but choose to ignore their counterpart as evil and transitory.

The "genuine" Black is the one most socialized in distinctive subcultural patterns that differ from values and norms in the wider society (see Johnson and Sanday 1971). His perception of the world and his concomitant behavior are to some extent determined by isolation and long-term restrictions in poor Black ghetto ecological niches. Depending upon the limitations and successes of his contacts with "mainstream" Americans, he may be a human unable to function within ecological niches characteristic of "mainstream" America or one who (though uncomfortably) is able to make temporary and limited adjustments for employment, travel, shopping, bureaucratic agency contacts, and other restricted interactions. With a limited value-stretch (Rodman 1963) or a biculturalism (Hannerz 1969) that is far more adequate in its subcultural component, the "genuine" Black constantly fails and violates the standards that operate within "mainstream" society. He resides in an America that has few "places" for him, that has a very limited range of tolerance for his styles and mannerisms, and that excludes him from the institutions that socialize in "mainstream" behavior as well as from the opportunity to participate in them fully, regardless of socialization. Worst of all, he lives in an America that does not know him. With Black and white flight from the inner cities, there are too few connections to the culture at large for the "genuine" isolated there in the 1990s.

He often begins this pattern in youth with truancy to avoid the hypocrisy in the schools. If the schools are ghettoized, he attends but learns little which will prepare him for social mobility (see Kozol 1967, Ogbu 1974). If the schools are not ghettoized, he will escape their regime regardless of the costs. Those costs usually are constant involvement in a law enforcement system that is designed to break the human spirit into resignation and conformity or to confine the human body in perpetuity. Those who continue to attend ghettoized schools fear departing at graduation time for they sense what awaits them—the diploma but not the training or the contacts. There is no "place" for them to go. They are already in their "place." The females go on welfare with their babies. The males go into the streets or menial jobs.

There are occasional cases where a "genuine" Black acquires enough contact with "mainstream" behavior during the period of early childhood and adolescence to participate further in "mainstream" institutions; but even in business courses, liberal arts colleges, secretarial jobs, and clerical or civil service employment, he suffers the handicaps of "genuine" Black socialization. One alternative is to reward the behavior he learns and to make American institutions receptive to his experiences throughout his lifetime. We might begin by using or incorporating "genuine" styles and behavior in the classroom learning process and later—not only on the football fields, basketball courts, entertainment stages, and in boxing rings, but also in the full range of prestigious life styles that privileged Americans inherit.

The "genuine" can be self-employed and earn enough to be potential members of the "mainstream" as professional pimps, gamblers, pool sharks, prostitutes, and "pushers." But being "mainstream" would undermine their "hustles." They make money but save none. They spend money, but their spending habits are not as wise as "mainstreamers" would demand. They are "kings among the rats," and they must be "rats" to be "kings." I have known some who "went mainstream" when their incomes were more structured and certain, as well as large, but most are addicted to the "life" and remain "genuine" as long as they live. They depend upon the "genuine" to make their livings. They have usually grown up "genuine," and they know that world well. Occasionally, they marry "mainstream," or their "genuine" wives have a change of heart with such large and stable incomes; but when the wife "goes Black society," the husband often "hangs on the avenue." He accompanies her reluctantly to social events, but his heart belongs to the ghetto. Most of them channel their incomes back into the same social network to which they belong. They seem to have a fear of accumulating too much money. It would disrupt their life styles. They "blow" money with a passion and are recognized and given high status for such behavior, often among those who benefit from such escapades. They buy Cadillacs, expensive clothes, furs, rings, and entertainment, not stocks, bonds, real estate, and futures. Their clothes often match the color of their Cadillac, and they are sometimes famous stars in their ghetto. They carry large rolls of money in their pockets and are not mugged. They make grand entrances at most major "genuine" social affairs in their ghetto. I have seen one of them throw $1500 in small assorted bills on the floor in public (in a small confectionery store) and walk on it to demonstrate that he was "king for a day" by defying, defiling, and denying "mainstream" values. They have seen other "genuine" Blacks go "mainstream," who are "up today and down tomorrow." Among the "genuine," you may fall from your high perch and, yet, be fully accepted by your associates.

There are major changes occurring among the "genuine" in Belmar in the decade of the '90s. The whites and the Black middle class have practically all moved out of the neighborhood. The dddav that was essential to maintain African-American identity in the presence and dominance of these populations now operates in a context (vacuum) where it is destructive. There are fewer and fewer people remaining in Belmar to maintain the social and physical superstructure. The sewer basins must be cleaned. Zoning laws must be enforced, and refuse must be collected on a timely basis. Streets must be repaired and cleaned. Schools and their teachers must be encouraged and supported. Houses and appurtenances must be maintained. Residential yards and vacant lots must be cut, trimmed, and cleaned periodically. The laws must be enforced. The peace and security must be kept. But many of the people who were vigilant about these matters have moved. The "genuine" remain, and dddav was not designed to perform these tasks; on the contrary, it was designed to assert that these were not the only essential aspects of African-American essence.

Today, the young adults and the teenagers are exploited by the advertising industry and other economic interests. They must wear expensive jewelry, shoes,

Teenage boys waiting for a day's work—the old scene

and clothing to be normal and accepted. These items are not available to them with their levels of legal income. The result is the sale of drugs.

The society has always encouraged illegal activities in African-American neighborhoods where the political "elite" could procure clandestine partnerships, payoffs, conspiracies, and sexual favors. Prostitutes, gambling dens, "speakeasies," jitney and number stations, and the trade in stolen goods have been traditional enterprises. As a teenager, I witnessed it all. I have observed the payoffs to police and other city officials as a cleaning and errand boy for a gambling establishment. I can yet remember the displeasure of cleaning the spittoons. Crack and other drugs have merely replaced what sexual diseases, the state lotteries, and dislocation of Black communities have done to destroy other illegal enterprises.

Observations of these drug-selling groups ("gangs") soon destroy the myths of their ignorance, laziness, and lack of ambition. They work day and night, in the rain and the snow, seven days a week, including holidays. They haul chairs, towels (to lie on the streets and sidewalks), and food to their street and street-corner business locations where they ply their trade. They use the money to buy more drugs and the American dreams. They devise ingenious schemes and methods of hiding, hawking, and retrieving their wares, evading the police, and accommodating potentially irate residents. Free enterprise has come to the ghetto, and these "genuine" Blacks are trying to institutionalize it.

There were teenage "gangs" in my neighborhood 50 years ago. Teenage "gangs" are not new; only their drug businesses and the media's fascination with sex, violence, and death in any form are new. Teenagers in the ghetto socialize in the streets within groups. These are often primary groups for them, in which they learn to become adults. The difference between today and yesteryear is the abandonment of the African-American communities; that is, the human and finan-

Teenagers waiting for customers—the new scene

cial resources that create a community are gone (Williams 1990). Teenagers can no longer work in their neighborhoods as soda jerks, stock boys and girls, theater ushers, ticket and confections salespersons, grocery clerks, shoe-store salespeople, shoeshine boys, fish market workers, and the myriad of other jobs in retail establishments that existed when I was a teenager in my Black community. Today, even most fast-food restaurant jobs require Black commuters. Meanwhile, the athlete's shoes and apparel, the expensive stereo equipment, and the vehicles that all "normal" teenagers possess, especially those which are portrayed on television are coerced upon these children. Of course, the goods that are sold by these drug venders in Belmar are like most of the goods sold in America. They destroy people, the environment, and the future.

Blacks in America have alternative life styles as subordinates in this society. Some ("spurious" and "mainstream") are striving for the goals and standards of the larger culture and society; others ("genuine") are creating their own goals and standards as reactions and responses (denying, defying, and defiling "mainstream" values) to those of the wider society.

The members of this subculture, "genuine" Black, wear cultural glasses whose lenses have been ground into bifocals by socialization. They have a two-dimensional cultural perspective or are "bicultural," as Hannerz (1969) prefers. Only the "genuine" have a distinctive subculture (see Fig. 2.3). Some of this distinctive way of life is a response to the nature of oppression in the larger society. It is a partial response to "mainstream" values in the face of inadequate economic resources. Some of the distinctiveness is the result of the denial, defiance, and defilement of those values as well as emphasis upon the expressive, rather than upon the allusive instrumental. This rebellion is reinforced by "spurious" Blacks who, from the "genuine" perspective, pine to be white (and "phony") and repudiate "genuine" life styles. The "spurious" adopt "mainstream" values and see their own inferiority within the context of those values. They compensate with the contemptuous attitudes toward the "genuine." They imitate "mainstream" behavior as far as financially possible. There is little authenticity among them or "mainstream" Blacks. The "mainstream" Blacks think white, notwithstanding the sociological and economic barriers that restrain them from participating in the "mainstream" white culture (see Fig. 2.3). The variety of Black styles creates conflict, fear of contamination, and ambiguity about racial identity among "mainstream" Blacks. "Mainstream" Blacks, who already have a propensity to be expressive, resort to expanded, exaggerated expressive symbols of "mainstream" values to assuage their fears; thus, they reinforce the values which contribute to the oppression of all Blacks, who are identified with the "genuine" stereotype (see Frazier 1965). "Spurious" Blacks have a similar attitude but are economically barred from the

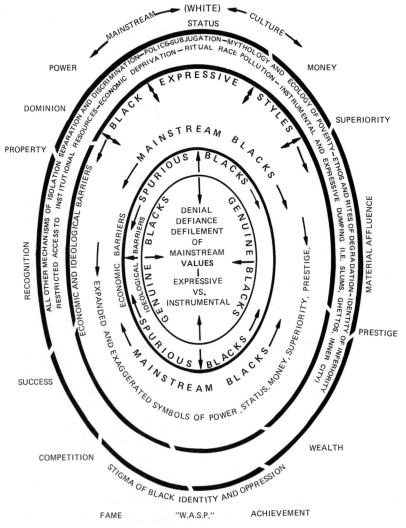

The "genuine" Black within American culture

symbolic behavior. Few Blacks get beyond the sociological and economic barriers (see Fig. 2.3) into "mainstream" white culture (full participation); but even those who do carry with them the stigma of Black identity created in their people's oppression—an identity which is based upon "genuine" styles and is mythologized to include all Blacks. So John Hope Franklin (see *Chronicle of Higher Learning* 1978) and Clifton R. Wharton, Jr. (see *Jet Magazine* 1977) are more the popular subject of that stigma than they are of their expertise. In American society, Blacks are equated with being poor as well as "genuine" (and poverty is full of degrading images; see p. 35). Both are perceived as inferior and as the rationale (to escape) for a life of hard work and sacrifice. Only the "genuine" Black defends himself against these attitudes with any behavioral fortitude, and he is not equal to the task.

In this sense, all Blacks (except the "genuine") subscribe to the values which make victims of them all. Especially victimized are the "genuine," who constitute a living contrast to all that represents achievement and success in this society. As long as Blacks are effectively socialized by negative attitudes toward "genuine" Black subculture, they will be a part of the oppressive process. Witness the effectiveness of "genuine" rhetoric and antics of social action during the 1960s, when Blacks of all life styles found it fashionable to take the part of "genuine" Blacks. There was a growing acceptance of "genuine" behavior which increasingly undermined oppression as well as the stigma of being Black in America.

There are rites, ceremonies, and episodes of degradation that have become a persistent way of life among the "genuine" and "spurious" in Belmar. The degradation is derived from attitudes and values in the wider society. Thus, certain aspects of these values are repudiated by the "genuine" in their creative adaptation to subordinate status in the wider society. "Genuine" life styles reinforce the attitude of the national culture that this Black subculture is inferior because these styles are defined as inferior in the wider society. The circle is vicious.

"Mainstream," "spurious," and "genuine" are categories that represent various degrees of integration of Blacks into the larger society (see Spindler 1955, Spindler and Spindler 1971, 1990). But the stigma of "genuine" Black behavior follows all Blacks, even those few who manage to reach full participation in white "mainstream" society (as the live-microphone insult of Senator Brooks in 1976, by Nelson Rockefeller and Carl Albert, indicates). This stigma will continue as long as Blacks at any level of integration accept society's definition of inferiority associated with "genuine" Black subculture. Social subjugation and economic exploitation are rich with daily rites of degradation in the Belmars of this country. And all Blacks are forced to live in the cognitive space and time of this discrimination. We are not all poor, but we are contaminated with poverty. We are not all "dropouts," but we are tainted with the assumption of ignorance. We are not even all "Black," but we are tainted with the phenotypic evidence of some African genes. So it is that Blacks who do not enjoy the "genuine" subculture are yet victims of oppression.

The "mainstream" and "spurious" Blacks have persistently attempted to ritually cleanse themselves by exaggerated expressive symbols of a "mainstream" life style that only compound this American dilemma (Frazier 1965). They seek to disassociate themselves from "genuine" Blacks. But they cannot escape by this route. Class, race, and ethnicity will not separate for them (see Clark 1978 and Wilson 1978).

They must all unlearn generations of persisting institutional patterns and ignore ever-present symbols of Black inferiority. They might begin by recognizing "genuine" subculture as a successful adaptive strategy. Further anthropological study can help this process. I have identified three Black life styles in Belmar. There are others, but they await further research.

THE "GENUINE" LIFE STYLE

Poor "genuine" ghetto Blacks whom I have observed in Belmar have developed and accentuated some of the following behavioral characteristics:

1. A defiance of social distance among themselves.
2. Defilement of mainstream symbols of value.
3. Body expressiveness for identity and interactional cues.
4. Public interaction within large groups and with loud oral communication.
5. Reciprocal distribution of scarce goods.
6. Mutual humiliation for group pleasure.
7. A propensity for physical contact (touching, "the press of flesh").
8. The proclivity to soothe oneself and others in a social context, notwithstanding wretchedness and despair.
9. A will to be involved in intensive social processes but little concern with the manipulation of such processes for predetermined ends.
10. Acceptance of and satisfaction with the expressive symbols of status and power.

Street salesmen

Defiance of Social Distance Why must poor "genuine" ghetto Blacks minimize social distance among themselves? Historically, social distance has been the characteristic of the master and his "finks." It threatens collusion with the enemy and indicates a feeling of contempt for the "genuine" style. "Genuine" Blacks are so cut off from the wider society that they must create and sustain their own in-group in order to retain some sense of identity. Any evidence of social distance within this group would make other members suspicious of that person's social orientation.

> . . . Exposed to the values of mainstream America via television, radio, employment, schoolteachers, landlords, bill collectors, social service personnel, and other networks that extend into the wider society, the Black ghetto dweller must exert tremendous energies to maintain a viable in-group perspective.
>
> One traditional means of maintaining this group solidarity has been to defy, defile, and deny certain standards of mainstream mobility. Social distance is a pervasive characteristic of social organization in the United States. So one feature of the poor Black subculture, where mobility is rare, is the effective control of disruptive levels of social distance within groups that tend to cohere and persist. (Williams 1974:167)

Techniques used to reduce social distance are uninhibited laughter (which is used as a social lubricant and interactional catalyst) and the mouth-to-mouth sharing of bottled drinks, cigarettes, and food. The defiance of social distance is evident in people's demonstrative greetings.

> This often takes the form of a stylized "handtapping." One person offers his hand, palm upwards. The other lightly taps it. Generally this ceremony follows a verbal exchange where one party has "won a point." It is the latter who has the option of offering up his hand. (Suttles 1970:125)

In interacting, a repertoire of "insults" and other examples of social license provide intermittent guarantees that the "genuine" can afford to take such liberties (Suttles 1970). Social distance is a luxury of substantial economic resources, but it is a threat to economic reciprocity in a social network with a precarious subsistence base. Last, the degree of social distance is a pervasive cue and code for distinguishing the various styles ("genuine," "spurious," and "mainstream") in Belmar.

Defilement of "Mainstream" Symbols of Value The defilement of "mainstream" symbols of value takes many forms in Belmar. Often, it is accomplished by extending, emphasizing, and elaborating upon styles of clothing, manners of speech, walk, stance, and demeanor (Suttles 1970).

> Whether rapping, jiving, running it down, copping a plea, signifying, or sounding (Kochman 1970), poor ghetto Blacks manipulate defiant signs and symbols—oral, anal, and genital—which defy, defile, and deny certain standards of mobility in the wider society (see Abrahams 1964, 1969).
>
> To protect his redistributive social network from the disruptive symbols of social mobility of the wider society the poor Black attempts to level any tendency of hierarchy among his group with the use of defiant symbols with oral references—"suck," "sucker," "suck out," "eat," "eat my," "blow," "tongue," "kiss," "kiss my," "gum," "teeth" (defiled), "mouth" (polluted), symbolic lips (defiled), and symbolic tongue (polluted)—in his daily inoffensive communication. He also manipulates genital symbols—"fuck," "fucker," "sack," "make," "some," "get over on," "stuff," "cock," "pussy," "hole," "cat," "poontang," "poodle," "a little bit," "grinding"—in the same manner. And anal

signs and symbols too—"ass," "asshole," "butt," "sweet," "nice," "punk," "faggot," "girl"—are basic conversational vocabulary (see Gover 1961).

The poor Black will also nickname his children for food—"Sugar," "Peanuts," "Peaches," "Beans," "Butter," "Duck," "Cookie," "Honey." He will publicly manipulate his anal and genital zones, he will use terms that are polluted and value-laden in the wider society—"mother," "sister," "father," "brother"—as common expressions of greetings and communications as well as verbal games ("dozens"). These are not historical accidents so much as mechanisms of survival and adaptability. Oppressed groups will organize, utilize, and manipulate signs and symbols to defy the values in the symbol system of the oppressor (see Abrahams 1962; Bailey 1965; Berdie 1947; Boas 1966; Dillard 1972; Dollard 1939; McDavid 1951; Stewart 1965, 1966). I have found similar evidence in prisons, ghetto schools, detention homes, and among the Black Muslims, where defiance becomes an instrument of solidarity for those whose lives are oppressed (Williams 1974:169).

Body Expressiveness for Identity and Interactional Cues   There is considerable interactional body expressiveness. I have already mentioned the "handslapping" mode of greeting and interacting. Suttles (1970) elaborates further:

> Apparently no one is willing to accept another at face value, and extreme proofs of one's identity and sincerity are required. Effusive greetings, name dropping, "woofing," "rapping," and other verbal trials are only some of the more direct ways of doing this. Dress, grooming, decorum, stance, and even one's way of walking can be enlisted to eliminate doubts and suspicion. Among the Negroes in the Addams area, the major identities that have to be avoided are those denoted by the labels "country," "savage," "nigger," and "Uncle Tom." Thus, to show their sophistication, some girls go to school in high heels, "fix" their hair into fantastic shapes, and in recent months have shortened their skirts to a perilous level.
>
> In contrast to the girls, the Negro boys in the Jane Addams Projects face a somewhat more ambiguous dilemma. If the boys completely repudiate the image of an "Uncle Tom," they risk being mistaken for a "savage." In this Scylla and Charybdis, two alternatives are open. On the one hand he can become a "gauster," by wearing the "rag," "shaping" his hair, belonging to a gang, adopting the "pimp's walk," and wearing a belted coat and baggy trousers. On the other hand, he can become "Ivy" by wearing a button-down collar, tight pants, and always keeping himself in immaculate order. The "gauster," however, runs the risk of being considered a "savage" while the "Ivy" may be suspected of being "sissy." In either case, "keeping cool" may preserve a questionable identity when others would be discountenanced (Suttles 1970:126).

Public Adult Interaction   "Home" for "genuine" Blacks in Belmar is "just a stopping-off place." It is a "motel" where you sleep, eat, and "hide, if you have to." But it is not one's "hearth," "castle," or showplace for entertaining. The street corner, the tavern, the "speakeasy," a favorite stoop, or the neighborhood "greasy spoon" are where people, especially men, "hang out." This variation of location is referred to as "down the way," "up the way," "hit the street," "over the way," and the "avenue." Most "genuine" Blacks have never had the consistent resources to furnish and maintain a home, so they spend most of their interactional time out of the house.

Part of the mystique of out-of-home interaction is the potential for including large numbers of people. One of the techniques is loud communication. Thus, all within hearing distance are welcome to interact and respond to "what's going on."

Reciprocal Distribution of Scarce Goods   One of the comforts of ghetto life in Belmar is that everyone knows that subsistence resources are very scarce. One is expected to pay $10 for a cabaret ticket, but no one is surprised when one runs out of sugar, bread, or bologna. One can borrow clothes, "Pampers," cigarettes, and food in Belmar without apology or stigma. One middle-aged man leaves his station wagon in the same parking space, despite the fact that it is frequently "stolen" and returned by someone he thinks he knows. Reciprocal allocations of scarce goods are part of the Belmar scene.

Mutual Humiliation for Group Pleasure   The phenomena of "rippin'," "dozens," and laughing are part of a syndrome of creating enjoyable interactional contexts at the expense of someone in the group. The victim usually rotates among the members, but often, one of them becomes particularly attractive as the buffoon. This practice sometimes results in violence when a victim becomes irritated or a perpetrator extends the humiliation to physical aggression.

Very early, children learn to prey upon one another, criticizing one in the group with the accompaniment of laughter among the others until the person being victimized often is in tears. There are so few resources that the major resource becomes yourself. And then, you are used, even for group pleasure. Some of the games "genuine" Blacks play are typical of that (see Chapter 6 for example, hide the belt). There are many examples not only of how "genuine" Blacks are socialized, but also of how individuals continue to practice that behavior even in adult life. And I think to a large extent that socialization accounts for a great deal of the violence in ghetto areas, violence which for the most part is Black upon Black.

Propensity for Physical Contact   From greeting church members with a holy kiss to the smothering embrace of Grandma, physical contact is pervasive in Belmar. Children's and adults' games usually involve touching, and interacting groups of all kinds are often crowded together in physical contact. Back-slapping, shoulder-slapping, and arm-slapping laughter is common, and unfortunately, even violence is perpetuated with direct physical contact. The "genuine" people here enjoy and execute the feel and press of flesh.

The Proclivity to Sooth Oneself and Others in a Social Context   Groups or individuals singing or listening to hymns or moaning prayers or the blues tend to soothe and recreate their spirit in spite of hardships. Wailing is a release and a comfort. It identifies and reassures that suffering is pervasive, but there are the means and resources, meager though they be, to survive "to these 350 years."

Involvement in Intensive Social Processes   There are intensive social relationships between women of all ages, which protect them against the charges of "sin" from the outside morality. Women live with their men in and out of wedlock (and have done so before the present fashion), regardless of whether or not they are "no count," "shiftless," and "just a big front" by the standards of the wider society. The man-woman relationship is so intensive that there is no deference to him. She can love him or kill him with the same intense passion. The interaction between men, young and old, is ceremonially solidified as they treasure one another's expressive "bullshit."

There are not merely a scheming, devious, manipulative, designing, and contriving people who exploit intensive social interaction for preconceived ends. They are people who derive abiding pleasure, reassurance, and identity from such interaction. Intensive interaction "shields and redeems those human spirits" confined to such areas as the urban Black ghettos of America.

   Acceptance of and Satisfaction with the Expressive Symbols of Status and Power   No one knows Miss Ann (the white female employer) better than Pearlie Mae (the Black female employee). Pearlie Mae thinks Miss Ann's house, children, and life style would all be in shambles if not for her quality maid care. Pearlie Mae knows Miss Ann's problems, predicaments, failures, frustrations, and vanity in spite of it all (see Coles 1977, Grinker 1978, Simon and Gagnon 1976, Stone and Kestenbaum 1975, Wixen 1973). Yet, Miss Ann ignores all of this and asserts her class position, prestige, recognition, and status to all the world. Through generations of contact and intensive exposure to the white upper class in America, Blacks have learned some of the tricks of that expressive trade from their most powerful role models of the wider society. Miss Ann pretends that the substance of status and power are the symbols of the good life. Pearlie Mae pretends that the symbols of status and power are the substance of it.

   Power and status are elusive among these poor, notwithstanding their focus and emphasis in the larger society. So the "genuine" Blacks of Belmar, denied the substance (instrumental), accept the expressive symbols—Cadillacs, stereos, "good liquor," "rolls" (of money), razors, switchblades, and "Saturday-night specials." The children commit violent acts to obtain fashionable shoes and apparel. The Black media are saturated with oppressive illustrations of fictive status and power. These characteristics help "genuine" Blacks maintain self-esteem, secure necessary social membership, and mitigate against the disruptive economic differentiation in the context of their already unstable social, economic, and residential confinement (see Abrahams 1964; Williams 1975:112). The expressive behavior must be emphatic and intensive to convince others (and even oneself) that it is authentic in a society where alternative instrumental actions have greater meaning and rewards from a "mainstream" perspective. The "genuine," consistent in their denying, defying, and defiling "mainstream" values, must integrate harmoniously, even if this behavior is bizarre and exotic to "mainstream" America. They must enforce their subcultural codes, often with their own demise (a fight to the death over a dime) or be bombarded and convinced by "mainstream" cues—"you *are* inferior." This expressive behavior reminds me of how, as young boys, we ridiculed the Hassidic Jews with their long beards and distinctive black garb. Today, I understand their loud and clear message. In summary, the "genuine" Black is more concerned with expressive symbols than with instrumental action because he can control only his expressive world.

   Even among "mainstream" Blacks, there are variations of orientations. Some are situated precariously within the bounds of that category and are threatened constantly by the potential to slip back into the "spurious." There are families (see Blackwell 1975, Frazier 1965) making their final effort to keep themselves separate and distinct from "genuine" Blacks, but their economic resources are not large enough to do so in comfort. There are important church members of large churches who can barely support this expensive association simultaneously with the support of their "mainstream" habits. There are the self-employed who usually are service oriented—barbers, caterers, small business entrepreneurs, beauticians, painters,

plasterers, wallpaper hangers—who pride themselves in their economic indepen-
dence and who often feel superior to "genuine" Blacks but whose income is not
sufficient to put them within a safe range of "mainstream" life styles.

Those who are secure within "mainstream" life styles often enjoy the income
from both spouses—postal employees, school teachers, secretaries, government
community-program employees, and other civil servants. Upper-class "mainstream" Blacks (see Blackwell 1975) consist of the professionals and the "Black
aristocracy." So here, within "mainstream" life styles, there is a range of class
patterns—lower-middle to upper class.

ATTITUDES TOWARD THE POOR

Once we have forthrightly confronted the myth of poverty in this society, we will
know it for what it is—a materialistic monster. This economic demon is dreadful
partly because of our mania for tinsel goods and money and not always because it is
so terrible to be poor. We must decondition ourselves about the poor and the
mythology surrounding them before we can adequately analyze social conditions in
this culture and society. I reaffirm what I wrote earlier:

> Poverty and its ideology, then, are an intrinsic part of our economic system. And though
> we all suffer from the social and human ramifications of that phenomenon, we contrive to
> superimpose all the expressive disadvantages upon the poor. Yet the instrumentalities are
> grave for a society and culture which assume that somehow the good, the true, and the
> beautiful are related to one's command over material goods and property rights. The
> quest for fame, wealth, status, material possessions, recognition, prestige, and power
> leaves its devastation everywhere. Why concede those ill effects only among the poor?
> (1974:185)

Most Americans seem to perceive and identify the poor not as those people who
have an income near or below the national subsistence level, but as Black, culturally
and socially deprived, lazy, dirty, a national burden, a minority group, slum-ghetto
dwellers, inferior, oppressed, ignorant, polluted, powerless, criminals, drunks,
drug addicts, failures, welfare recipients, miserable, wretched, odor ridden, pest
ridden, rat infested, contaminated with disease, oversexed, undermotivated, violent, uncouth, crude, and immoral (see Rainwater 1974). (These descriptions are
those of my students, collected over a ten-year period; in class after class I had
requested "gut reactions of what poverty means to you.") On the other hand, the
good, the true, and the beautiful are perceived as American values to which the poor
or the Black have little or no access. Power, fame, recognition, status, money,
wealth, property, prestige, material possessions, symbols of superiority, and success are considered out of the reach of most Blacks and deservedly so. Achievement
in the upwardly mobile segment of society is conceptualized in terms of the above
values, and all such movement is recognized as "progress." The American dream is
a nightmare in which no one ever attains all the worldly goods he or she needs, but
in which everyone must continue to strive lest he slip back into the ranks of the poor
or Black or be outdistanced by his mythical competitor. Thus, many of the most
wealthy, powerful, and famous people spend their "last days" on earth grubbing

around for a larger piece of the American pie. Poverty in the "culture of poverty" concept is hopelessly culture bound in America regardless of refinement (see Rodman 1977). Meanwhile, our ideals—liberty, freedom, God, friendship, trust, faith, fellowship, truth, beauty, goodness, neighborliness, good will, hope, charity, love, joy, peace, brotherhood, and peace of mind—are those values which we reach for but never fully achieve. How do poor Blacks in Belmar adjust and survive in this hostile and painful environment? The categories "genuine" and "spurious" assist with the answers.

DISCUSSION

The range and variety of life styles in Belmar—some of which I have tried to conceptualize by the categories "mainstream," "genuine," and "spurious"—have ramifications for the people that live here—ramifications such as transience, un-certainty, conflict, distrust, and economic decline. Like most complexities of human behavior, the characteristics for each of these behavioral categories merge, overlap, and often are not separate and distinct for certain individuals in particular populations. The categories, like any category pertaining to human beings, are not precise and do not delimit behavior as the concept of *category* would imply. Yet for me, they are heuristic and provide a framework for discussion of the range and variety of life styles here.

The "genuine" expressive orientation and the lack of instrumental action is an adaptive strategy in an acquisitive society which requires material wealth as an indication of upward mobility. It maintains self-esteem and bolsters identity in an oppressive society where man has little control except over his expressive destiny. Yet, this expressive orientation appears to generate a cycle of poverty and a persistent way of life (a so-called "culture of poverty;" see Rodman 1977).

This is especially attractive theorizing to explain the "genuine" who have learned to "live" in spite of their poverty and oppression. But the cycle is mandated from oppressive institutions in the wider society; this is demonstrated by the "spurious" who have no subculture but who come from the same background of generations of poverty. Furthermore, the "genuine" are bicultural. They will dis-sipate ("blow") or distribute sudden large financial resources into their networks for future reciprocity. These are resources which would disrupt their networks and life styles if not treated accordingly. In other words, they will incorporate substantial incomes into "genuine" life styles and networks if these incomes are from uncertain sources—prostitution, gambling, "hustling," poverty programs, and the like. But given a stable, legitimate, and long-term income that will support a "mainstream" life style, they will abandon their precarious "genuine" existence to "go legit," be a "muck-t-muck," "live high on the hog," go "top shelf," or move "out" or "up." These values are within the range of values (the "stretch") that the "genuine" possess as intrinsic components of their subculture. Furthermore, stable, long-term, and substantial income destroys "genuine" networks and intensive relationships. It enables one to be independent of resources distributed in the network of "genuine" relationships and encourages one to hold onto one's own resources that are now too large and continuous to ever be reciprocated. One is financially secure, knowing that tomorrow will come and one knows how one is going to live. This is not the "stuff" of "genuine" existence. The values of the larger society pull one into "mainstream" life styles, whereas the values of the "genuine" press one out of the fraternity. To remain there, one must be "a fool," "a sucker," or "crazy." The "genuine" expect one to "move up in the world when your chance comes." It is all a part of their perceptual bifocals.

I am sympathetic to Rodman's thesis that the "culture of poverty" concept has had "bad press." If we could appreciate the concept as a focus on positive adaptive strategies among the poor, then it might be conceptualized as similar to "genuine" Black behavior in Belmar; but as I have tried to point out, the concept is inundated in culture-bound mythology. Furthermore, the concept could not account for distinctive Black life styles.

We need data on the "culture of affluence" to expose the myths of well-being associated with money (see Coles 1977, Grinker 1978, Johnson 1978, Nader 1974, Stone and Kestenbaum 1975, Simon and Gagnon 1976, Wixen 1973). We need to demysticize affluence. I suspect that the plight of the affluent in human terms is just as great as that of the poor. As I wrote in 1974:

> Knock on any American door and you will find incidents of despair and frustration. I have yet to be convinced that poverty is an independent variable. (p. 184)

Perhaps the culture of poverty, like the culture of affluence, has its problems and despair (see Commoner 1971, 1976). We have hastened to document those of the one and, as expected in our culture-bound discipline, we have with appropriate rationale avoided those of the other (Lewis 1971, Nader 1974).

In the Belmar of the '40s and '50s, this variety of Blacks had established patterns of residence and interaction. "Mainstream" Blacks and whites dominated the area. The "spurious" liked that arrangement, and the few "genuine" "walked soft" (see Chapter 3) and patronized their own "hangouts." But the influx of "genuine" Blacks in the '60s disrupted the neighborhood, and the dust has never settled.

In 1967, Kenneth Clark, talking about himself, wrote:

> More than forty years of my life had been lived in Harlem. I started school in the Harlem public schools. I first learned about people, about love, about cruelty, about sacrifice, about cowardice, about courage, about bombast in Harlem. For many years before I returned as an "involved observer," Harlem had been my home. My family moved from house to house, and from neighborhood to neighborhood within the walls of the ghetto in a desperate attempt to escape its creeping blight. In a very real sense, therefore, *Dark Ghetto* is a summation of my personal and lifelong experience and observation as a prisoner within the ghetto long before I was aware that I was really a prisoner. To my knowledge, there is at present nothing in the vast literature of social science treatises and textbooks and nothing in the practical or field training of graduate students in social science to prepare them for the realities and complexities of this type of involvement in a real, dynamic, turbulent, and at times seemingly chaotic community. And what is more, nothing anywhere in the training of social scientists, teachers, or social workers now prepares them to understand, to cope with, or to change the normal chaos of ghetto

communities. These are grave lacks which must be remedied soon if these disciplines are to become relevant to the stability and survival of our society (1967:xv).

Much of what he said about himself is applicable to me (born and reared "spurious," I am now "mainstream"). Thus, my three years and subsequent of fieldwork in Belmar are just another sojourn in a lifelone "trip" in other Pittsburgh ghettos. The world should hear their people's voices and know their secrets, their meanings of a life with few worldly goods and ceaseless denial from access to institutional resources in the wider society. These residents create their own social meanings (Chapter 7) and activities (Chapter 6), often from unstructured neighborhood contexts. They create structure from human and meager physical resources. Denied access to the institutional structures of the wider society, they become adept at manipulating and devising their own kind of structure. Such manipulations and creations are perceived by many as "soul" or "Black culture."

We must attempt to understand the strategic instrumentalities of the neighborhood's institutional and structural characteristics for their socializing and transmitting qualities—the "jitney" stations, street-corner taverns, neighborhood bars, ghetto schools, afterschool and school vacation activities, drug networks, "hustler" lifeways, church groups, beauty parlors, and barber shops. Then, when we discover the nature of the social networks, the symbolic language, and the distinctive world views of this population, we will be in a position to determine the social isolation of some residents who live here but who do not adhere to the "genuine" norms.

Even I am sensitive to the value-laden connotations of my three categories. But my basic assumptions about American values encourage me to make my point accordingly.

Last, Clark again speaks for me in Belmar when he says:

> To understand Harlem, one must seek the truth and one must dare to accept and understand the truths one does find. One must understand its inconsistencies, its contradictions, its paradoxes its ironies, its comic and its tragic face, its cruel and its self-destructive forces, and its desperate surge for life. And above all one must understand its humanity. The truth of the dark ghetto is not merely a truth about Negroes; it reflects the deeper torment and anguish of the total human predicament. (1967:xxv)

3 / The Place

... For the average Negro who walks the streets of any American Black ghetto, the smell of barbecued ribs, fried shrimps, and chicken emanating from numerous restaurants gives olfactory reinforcement to a feeling of "at-homeness." The beat of "gut music" spilling into the street from ubiquitous tavern juke boxes and the sound of tambourines and rich harmony behind the crude folk art on the windows of store-front churches give auditory confirmation to the universal belief that "We Negroes have 'soul.' " The bedlam of an occasional brawl, the shouted obscenities of street corner "foul mouths," and the whine of police sirens break the monotony of waiting for the number that never "falls," the horses that never win, place, nor show, and the "good job" that never materializes. The insouciant swagger of teen-age drop-outs (the "cats") masks the hurt of their aimless existence and contrasts sharply with the ragged clothing and dejected demeanor of "skid-row" types who have long since stopped trying to keep up appearances and who escape it all by becoming "winos." The spontaneous vigor of the children who crowd streets and playgrounds . . . and the cheerful rushing about of adults, free from the occupational pressures of the "white world" in which they work, create an atmosphere of warmth and . . . intimacy which obscures the unpleasant facts of life in the overcrowded rooms behind the doors, the lack of adequate maintenance standards, and the too prevalent vermin and rats.

This is a world whose urban "folkways" the upwardly mobile Negro middle class deplores as a "drag" on "The Race," which the upper classes wince at as an embarrassment, and which race leaders point to as proof that Negroes have been victimized. But for the masses of the ghetto dwellers this is a warm and familiar milieu, preferable to the sanitary coldness of middle-class neighborhoods and a counterpart of the communities of the foreign-born, each of which has its own distinctive sub-cultural flavor. The arguments in the barbershop, the gossip in the beauty parlors, the "jiving" of bar girls and waitresses, the click of poolroom balls, the stomping of feet in the dance halls, the shouting in the churches are all theirs—and the white men who run the pawnshops, supermarts, drug stores, and grocery stores, the policemen on horseback, the teachers in black-board jungles—all these are aliens, conceptualized collectively as "The Man," intruders on the Black Man's "turf." (Drake 1965:777)

The streets and "the avenue" are the only things that seem to be permanent to the "genuine" Black. He usually owes money for rent and payments on his utilities. He must often move to have a "nice" place to celebrate the holidays, to have heat after the seasonal gas shut off when winter approaches again, to get telephone service after various names and aliases have run their course, to escape a belligerent mate, to evade the car repossessor or other aggressive creditors, and generally to manage life on an income that is inadequate. Moving is one technique that "genuine" Blacks employ to secure the subsistence subsidy that they require to live.

New low income housing on North Lang Avenue

But the streets and "the avenue" do not change much. They continue to be dirty and the places where people meet and interact in Belmar. There one learns the local news from colleagues, the national news from the bar T.V., and the prison news from shuttle inmates. There one finds love, liquor, or work for a day, and always companionship. There one meets people whose problems are similar to one's own, regardless of how severe, and whose solutions the wider society unanimously condemns. It is the reason to rise every morning in spite of the lack of a job, agenda, and "future." It is the evidence of their subculture that must exist for these people to escape mainstream values, "failure," and quiet desperation.

Pittsburgh is an ethnic city (see Lorant 1975, Lubove 1969). Its ethnic enclaves and neighborhood boundaries create a plethora of villagelike districts with concomitant group identity. With its college and university population, humanistic and civic programs, and central business area, Pittsburgh offers a unique opportunity for citizens to enjoy its activities without the feelings of massive isolation and anomie which are typically metropolitan (see Lowe 1968).

Waste containers that overflow into vacant lots

Belmar is one of Pittsburgh's ethnic neighborhoods. North Lang Avenue, where I lived during the study, extends into Homewood South (see Windell 1975 for a complete description) as well as into Belmar. Portions of Belmar are within the area defined as Homewood South and other portions border upon it. Thus, the following information on Homewood South is also pertinent to my study of Belmar.

> For purposes of this report, Homewood South shall be defined as the area encompassed by 1970 census tracts 1303 and 1304. The area is located in the northeastern portion of the City of Pittsburgh, approximately six miles from the City's Central Business District. . . . A portion of the boundary of census tract 1304 also forms the boundary between the City of Pittsburgh and Wilkinsburg. . . . As shown in Diagram 3, the area is bounded on the south by the Penn Central Railroad tracks, and on the north by the former Port Authority Transit car barns. Coinciding with other definitions, the western boundary is somewhat arbitrarily set at North Murtland Avenue. Oakwood Street, which roughly traces the base of the first of the East Hills, forms the eastern boundary. The area is approximately 0.4 square miles with a 1970 population of 8,876. Density is, therefore, approximately 20,000 persons per square mile, as compared with an overall City density of about 9,422 persons per square mile. (Windell 1975:15)

Much of the area southwest of Belmar is commercial, institutional, and light industrial. To the east, the area is primarily residential with a few small commercial operations. The north and east are predominantly Black residential areas. A mile or more beyond Belmar, in any direction, the areas become more populated with whites, and the standard of living rises to middle- and upper-middle class. Thus, Belmar specifically and Homewood generally (the Thirteenth Ward) sit in a pocket surrounded by middle-class whites with a sprinkling of middle-class Blacks. Serving this latter population are three shopping districts within a two-mile radius of the area: East Liberty to the west; East Hills to the east; and the business area of the Borough of Wilkinsburg. Twelve bus lines serve Belmar. Ten of these routes reach East Liberty and the areas beyond it; one enters Squirrel Hill; two enter Wilkinsburg; and one enters Oakland and continues to the central downtown business district of Pittsburgh. As illustrated by its location, Belmar is still a prime residential area in terms of its access to the business and cultural (that is, Oakland) areas of the city. Its advantageous location is overshadowed, however, by problems such as the low-income level of its residents, the dwindling pride in the neighborhood, and the aging of most of the housing and other structures there. As Windell states about the overlapping and contiguous neighborhood:

> A series of events over which the area has had little or no control has transformed Homewood South from a relatively stable working-class, residential neighborhood into one possessing many of the socio-economic characteristics of the classic inner-city "slum." During the 1950s, Homewood was subjected simultaneously to (1) the push exerted by land clearance in the Lower Hill in conjunction with the migration of Southern Blacks into Pittsburgh, and (2) the pull of decreases in the cost of transportation which permitted many of the working-class residents to leave Homewood South in favor of more suburban residential areas. The result has been a deterioration of the physical structures and an accumulation in Homewood South of subsectors of the population without sufficient income to purchase the goods and services necessary to maintain themselves and resolve the problems which they encounter. (1975:34)

But, geographically, Homewood South is not an "inner-city" neighborhood.

Indeed, portions of its border demarcate the limits of the City of Pittsburgh. Furthermore, the area does not have an overabundance of underemployed males, as do the Hill District and portions of the Central Northside. Thus, the immediate problems of Homewood South are somewhat different from those in the typical urban ghetto (see Williams 1980).

But the roots of the problems in Homewood South are similar to those in the Hill and in Central Northside. The peculiar discrimination to which the Black residents have been subjected restricts their socioeconomic opportunity structure and places an extraordinarily high level of stress, evidenced by the high rates of separation and divorce, on the primary interpersonal relations.

Thus, the long-term solution to the problems in Homewood South depends, as it always has, upon changes in the broader social structure. But, just as the Civil Rights Movement resulted in the destruction of the Homewood shopping district and, simultaneously, in the foundation and construction of the Neighborhood Health Center, the consequences of national and regional events also depend upon the use which is made of the mobilization of people that can be, or is, generated at the local level.

Today, Belmar is a patchwork of various life styles. The "genuine" reside next door to the "mainstream" and those who aspire to the "mainstream" ("spurious"), yet most are deprived of adequate "mainstream" socialization. Their orientation is expressive, not instrumental. The homes of "genuine" newcomers (see Epstein 1969) to the neighborhood are obvious: new aluminum siding, vinyl replacement windows, bright new awnings, new concrete-block porches with wrought iron supports, window air conditioners, and new cars—newness encouraged by easy loans and high-pressure, home-remodeling salesmen. But the new style is tinsel and

Remodeled apartment building on North Lang Avenue

superficial—"sterile externality." There is no "mainstream" ethos to cut back the weeds, maintain the lawn, paint the trim, point the chimney, repair the flashing, clean the gutters, and sweep the front walk. The interiors are also neglected, not in furnishings (on the contrary, furniture is often elaborate, including stereos, color television sets, and bars), but in the maintenance of floors, walls, doors, windows, kitchen and bathroom fixtures, basements, attics, and general housecleaning. This is not a criticism, as one may suspect. It is not necessarily a disadvantage that these residents have never been socialized by the property fetish and "Mr. Clean" neurosis infecting the traditional middle class (white and Black). Lacking the impetus to clean and maintain, they just do not see the weeds, the dirt, or the path running through the lawn. They are not conditioned. Their orientation is different (that is, expressive). Perhaps it is another way to dddav. After all, there are few television commercials about high status Blacks pointing the chimney and cleaning the gutter. These Belmar residents know what they have learned from advertisements and each other—buy the glitter and the new, and it shall make you "big."

Before 1940, most of the houses in Belmar were built to show that the owner had ample money or that the house was taken care of by servants. These structures, as with much American housing, had only a remote functional relationship to human living. The houses were built for the middle class, who were aspiring to imitate the rich and who were anxious to exhibit as many characteristics of the wealthy as possible. In their own ways, they imitated the sprawling estates of the rich, although they laid claim to only one small lot. Most of the residents seldom used the numerous large rooms, the grand entrances, and the stylistic gingerbread features that characterized those Belmar houses. In the early days, the women remained at home to manage the full-time job of caring for them if they could not afford servants. Today, however, many of the women must work to help pay for the

New enterprise on North Lang Avenue

house, leaving little time for managing the household. Many houses show the results of neglect, age, or both. Some owners attempt to salvage them with flimsy building materials currently available; but these old structures require continual care and inspection, and most residents are either unaware of the upkeep requirements, too tired to implement them, or too poor to pay for them. After approximately 80 years, Belmar's boarded-up buildings, burned-out shells, and empty lots foreshadow its doom as a residential area for Blacks.

Many houses in the neighborhood are 90 to 120 years old, and their aging condition reveals their owners' ignorance of such essentials as glazing compound, spackling compound, caulking, mortar, roofing cement, roof coating, plaster, rock lath, flashing, coating membrane, tinner's red, weed scythes, weed killers, house maintenance tools, and commercial repairmen. With such ignorance persisting, most of the dwellings in the neighborhood will soon be maintenance nightmares, requiring too many expensive repairs and becoming ripe for the wrecker's ball.

During my research, I lived near one home owner. She completely remodeled the house with aluminum siding, a new roof, a new porch, new vinyl windows, interior paneling, two window air conditioners, a new natural-gas line from the curb to the interior, new gutters and downspouts, and a new picture window. She also bought a new car to complete what she felt was a total new style of living. However, she overlooked the porch roof, which began to leak soon thereafter, and she never noticed the five-foot weeds and weed trees growing around the foundation of her house and in the rear yard. In fact, the weeds were impeded only by the path worn in the yard from the rear door to the alley. A guest of mine, while admiring the house, once asked me why she did not take care of her grounds and paint her rusty and neglected refuse containers. My response then, and now, was that she did not see them, and what one does not see is not annoying. This characteristic plagues the next-door neighbors, who do all the "right things" to their homes and property. The neighbors can only put up a fence, clean up their own homes more thoroughly and more often, and hope and pray that the building is torn down quickly when it becomes gutted by the overcrowding which undermines any improvements, especially the tinsel ones of remodeling "racketeers."

The development in entertainment and educational facilities somewhat parallels that of housing in Belmar. "Belmar Theatre was built in 1912" (*Homewood Needle* 1942). It was closed by 1969. "Belmar School was built on Hermitage Street at Lang Avenue. Although the contract was let in May of 1900, the dedication was not until February, 1902" (*Homewood Needle* 1942). By 1965, the population had outgrown the school, and a "portable" addition was planned. George Westinghouse High School was opened on Murtland Avenue in Belmar in 1922 (Van Trump 1973). Today, after a distinguished reputation in Pittsburgh for over 50 years, it is known as "the house," "the toughest Black school in the city."

Here in Belmar one observes the phenomenon of Blacks' anger at other Blacks because of differences in life style and values. The whites are gone. The few who remain—the old, eccentric, and drug or alcohol addicts—would not be welcome by most. Thus, "mainstream" Blacks feel isolated and persecuted in this urban wasteland, and sometimes they are. Poor "genuine" Blacks can be most intolerant of other Blacks who "act white," and "ain't for real, down to earth, and with it." On the other hand, "mainstream" Blacks cannot stand idle, watching their hard-won material gains become dissipated. Neither group understands the other, at least not enough to tolerate its behavior.

Furthermore, many Belmar residents (the "spurious") cannot translate into action their ethos of neighborhood care and concern. They are poor, haunted by the historic dumping phenomenon and the specter of powerlessness. Others (the "genuine") have never developed the ethos in the first place, a tragic indictment of the society in which we live. So the quest for community fails here in Belmar. Living in a neighborhood of "mainstream," "spurious," and "genuine" Blacks creates the instability and conflict characteristic of a pluralistic society (Smith 1965), where there is a cultural and social pluralism (Smith 1969). We pretend to desire "good" and responsible citizens until it is time to produce the resources that create them. Perhaps, then, it is true that "the poor you will have with you always" because they are the best measure of the wealth and illusive well-being of others. Thus, we perpetuate our human yardsticks and the institutions of guilt that feed upon them— Salvation Armies, United Funds, Goodwills, welfare, food stamps, day-care centers, halfway houses, and other rehabilitiation and poverty programs. Name your own charities or public- and private-poverty programs; somehow, they never seem to solve the problem. It will, therefore, require massive changes in our social system for urban deserts like Belmar to grow and thrive in the "wholesome" American way (Anderson 1976).

Nevertheless, the ambitious and concerned "mainstream" Belmar citizens have not yet given up. Neighborhood groups attempt to clean and maintain the area (for instance, Operation Better Block, Homewood-Brushton Renewal Council). Other neighborhood groups (Project Area Committee of Urban Redevelopment, Interagency Council, and others) function to revive the commercial district and community spirit. These groups have successfully cleared the old "Homewood Shops" (streetcar barns) in order to provide land for new construction (a low-rise apartment for the elderly is being built). They have secured a $1,600,00 state grant for site improvement and incidentals necessary to attract an investor into the area, who will take on the responsibility of redeveloping the commercial district. They have remodeled two large buildings, one for residential apartments, and the other for a local community college. Indeed, some residents still hope that the area can be revived, but in these days of high unemployment, frightening crime rates, and general business decline, it is doubtful that private investors will make the massive investments required to revive the commercial district or stabilize the residential areas. The confidence to restore places like Belmar has been undermined by these conditions in "mainstream" America. Only a few of the residents believe in the restoration, and their faith will probably not move mountains, or in this case, abandoned buildings. Outsiders who claim faith in the area are usually on a community agency payroll and in local government. Many "mainstream" residents have already put their houses on the market and would sell tomorrow, if they could get buyers. Some of them are elderly and can no longer sustain the duties of home ownership; others are disenchanted with the neighborhood and would like to escape to rural or suburban areas. And, of course, there are the "genuine," who do not want to leave. They have adapted and adjusted to the screaming sirens, the boisterous laughter, the cars with their blasting radios and screeching tires, and the excitement of the streets (fires, altercations, and loud conversations). Here the faces are familiar. Besides, they "wouldn't live where they're not wanted." They would feel ill at ease, not at home amidst the cleanliness fetish, sanitation neurosis, and lawn anxiety.

Thus, we outside of Belmar can realize some important aspects of the people's character and dilemma vis-à-vis the middle-class ideals of home management and neighborhood pride. The uncertainty here precludes commercial or residential investments. The information I have collected encourages me to examine the mechanisms available to revitalize urban Black slums and to know more about the impact of housing upon the nature of hope among poor Blacks. That is, how much does housing contribute to the welfare and well-being of the people described here? We already know that housing and neighborhoods are critical for mental and physical health. They are strategic in the growth and development of the mind, but the key to this development is the enrichment of social relations, not the adherence to physical standards, such as cleanliness and neatness. Nevertheless, these standards are crucial in determining the outlooks, styles, perspectives, and attitudes of those socialized in Belmar only because our society as a whole is so intolerant of variation.

As things stand today, no outside investors are likely to invest in the property in this neighborhood. And most home owners in Belmar who have the means feel that further investments in their own property would be too risky because of the neighborhood's dubious future.

Yet we must bear in mind that, in spite of all the problems, Belmar is considered the most favorable area for Blacks in the Homewood-Brushton area. In 1973, Van Trump stated:

Vacant land in Belmar

. . . The "best" residential section is currently Belmar. Here on the site of the old racetrack, the long streets running parallel to Frankstown—Race, Idlewild, Monticello, Hermitage, Kedron, and Mount Vernon—are filled mostly with small Edwardian "reception hall" houses and a minor sprinkling of row housing. Most of the residents here own their own homes and can afford to keep them in seemly fashion. For the most part the aspect of these streets is trim and bright. Above, the once half-rural north wall of the valley is becoming covered with housing developments.

At the same time, let us not forget that, in spite of the physical setting, people manage to survive here. Indeed, the people in this area are most adept at living. On any spring afternoon, for example, the school yard and the surrounding area in Belmar appear to be the scene of a spring carnival: People wash and wax their cars; boys with bats, balls, and footballs meander toward the ball field; and new mothers in bright colorful outfits walk in the sunshine with their babies wrapped in sparkling new blankets. Little children are everywhere, playing with balls, performing acrobatics, and conversing with one another on street corners. Cars cruise with convertible tops down and radios "sounding." Children and adults ride bicycles. Entire families and couples take walks together. The air resounds with laughter, and the observer is a witness to the greatest human show on earth. No scene in any neighborhood in the world can surpass this one, and one realizes that, to some extent, the attitudes in the wider society toward the so-called "Black ghetto" are a cruel distortion of the truth. This ghetto scene makes all seem well in the world.

The major street corners of Belmar often seem to be the focal points of the seasonal Black fair. People are walking, talking, standing, and interacting with each other. At the bus stops, some people wait for the bus, whereas others exploit that setting for a captive audience. Jitney drivers sit in chairs or on boxes at vantage points for viewing the scene. Here, they interact among themselves as well as with pedestrians and drivers as they await "trips." The street scene is a satisfying distraction during the long days and nights.

A vast array of automobiles move through the streets. There are new custom-made Cadillacs, assorted custom-made vehicles, and abused "heaps" that seem barely able to run. There are bicycles, motorcycles, buses with people yelling out the windows, and motorists, bus drivers, and police who stop their vehicles in the middle of the street to converse with someone.

There is a variety of clothing styles. Some are designed to be chic, others to be outlandish. The costume jewelry, the hair styles, the foot gear, the stylish gaits, and the unrestrained laughter give these corners a distinctive character of their own. The streets and sidewalks are cluttered with debris, but no one seems to mind. The stores are often sparsely stocked with high-priced goods, and the restaurants are seldom rated highly by restaurant critics. But all of this is familiar.

Teenagers huddle in their own groups of interaction, and their friends pass in cars and honk. No one appears to be hurrying, and the screech of "rubber" is only for attention. There is touching and dramatic threatening. There are teenage mothers who do not seem to be much older than their babies and old men and women who seem to be much older than they are. The teenage boys attempt to imitate the street-corner men, and the teenage girls flirt with these masculine symbols of their

Black world. The school traffic dominates the Belmar scene twice a day, five times a week.

But these scenes disguise the poverty and undernourishment, the dropouts, alcoholics, drug addicts, the health problems, the lack of recreation and aspiration, the shoes that distort feet, the merchants who exploit meager incomes, the landlords who offer poor housing, the automobiles no one can afford, the shoddy goods the residents are forced to buy from the few credit merchants who will serve them, the unemployment, the high crime rate, teenage illegitimacy, and the potential despair in every tomorrow which is hidden from those who do not want to see.

No one perspective or single conceptualization will ever communicate to us what Belmar is. It is many different kinds of places to many different people at various times and under a range of circumstances. So the author is under no delusion that he can describe to you what Belmar is. What I can do is to attempt to communicate some feelings, give you some glimpses of what I and others see at given moments in time—snapshots of a complex process. I can hope that the way I compile these pictures approaches the human substance and content of which my informants and I have been a part. As Maybelle expresses:

I don't mind the dirt, rats, bugs, roaches, plaster [falling], leaks, killin', stealin', bums, and no privacy so much. I'm old now and I've just about lived my life. But damn, I don't want to look down the road and see that's all that's there for my grandchildren. Jist give 'em a chance, jist a chance! If they don't make good of it, then that's on them. But my God, give 'em a chance. Everybody ain't no fool. We know, and so does everybody else, our schools ain't no good. And we get the teachers that nobody else wants. You ought to see 'em walking around like hippies, tryin' to look like they like the ghetto and makin' it home to the suburbs when school is out. They here because they can't do no better and they ain't foolin' nobody.

And you sure can't fool these kids. They know what's waitin' for 'em. They see it every day after school in the streets. They know what their chances are by the way they get treated in school. You can't fool kids. That's why they're always singing and dancing and playin' basketball and football. They know where the action is. But it should be in school too and in decent jobs. Not jist that one or two Blacks up front, but in all jobs. You can't fool kids. If there's a chance, they will know it somehow and go after it. That's why they practice on that field [basketball court] to two o'clock in the morning and sometime all night. You can't fool kids. I use to work for a white lady who had plenty of money but no time for her kids. She was always kissin' 'em and huggin' 'em between social things, club meetings and charity work. She was always telling 'em how much "mother loves you." She tried to catch 'em before they went to sleep and before they went to school for that make-believe love. But she wasn't foolin' them kids. You don't have to tell kids you love 'em. They know it if you do. Those kids cried when I quit that job cause they knew the only one who loved *them* was leavin'. I cried too, but the woman's husband had been poor and he loved that woman's money more than he did the family. So he made things hard for me so I would quit. He thought she was too nice to me. The fool didn't know what I brought in that house you couldn't pay for. I felt sorry for the kids, but the longer I stayed the harder he made it for me and the lady. So you can't fool kids. They'll know when they really got a chance. Jist give our children a chance. Stop lyin' about the "equal" stuff. You can't fool people always and you can't fool God at all.

Another "genuine" resident expresses differently:

It's cuttin' and shootin' and cussin'. It's being beat up or beatin' somebody else up. It's laughin' because it's funny or crying because it hurts. There ain't no in between. It's raw, baby.

It's being chased or runnin' after someone. It's talkin' about people or being talked about. It's workin' and screwin' and dyin'. It's touchin' people and people touchin' you. You got to take the press of flesh.

It's action, baby, and when it's over you get the blues til it starts all over again, if you ain't dead yet. So we go out on the avenue after work or on weekends to see and be seen, to be in the happenings because that's where it's at if you ain't sanctified [a dedicated church worker] or a turkey ["mainstream" or "spurious"]. If that street could talk, it would tell you about the blood, sweat, and tears, the piss and the spit that ran there, dried up, and blowed away like we do. The fight, the fuck, the fun, it all happens here; the pimp, the faggot, the wino, the drug addict, and the prostitute come by here. It's the greatest show on earth. This is the ghetto, man, and this is how we have to make it here. Kennedy and Rockefeller want to be president, Howard Hughes wants to be left alone, Mellon wants more money, Nixon wants to be king, and you, you want to be God [understand everything]. I just want to watch the world go by, feeling little pain as possible. But then I can't do no better. I'm on the bottom rung of the ladder, and the next step up is outta sight. If it wasn't, I would be reaching just like the other suckers.

This doom affects the spirits of residents who are exposed to aspire to middle-class neighborhoods. As "spurious" Winston explains:

One bad thing about going to the show [movie theater] is going home after it's over. You sit there in the show and see big houses, fine lawns, and pretty streets, and then, you go home and walk through your streets to your house and what do you get? Garbage and rubbish in the streets. Dog shit and guys pissing on the sidewalk and in doorways; empty houses boarded up with the boards ripped off so garbage and rubbish can be dumped in them. As you walk by, the funk [foul odor] almost kills you. Empty lots are full of junk cars, rubbish, garbage, funk, and weeds that grow up to the sky. The streets are dark and cramped, and the sidewalks are so bad and dangerous too that you have to walk in the

Waste containers that hide drugs

Remodeled house on North Lang Avenue

street. Then you look at the houses and even the good ones are shit when you think of the ones in the movies, much less the shacks.

Boy! It makes you feel bad! It makes you think you're not much in the world. It makes you scared, you may never get out of all this. It makes you think you are like the place—the garbage and rubbish and funk and high weeds. It makes you want to steal and lie and cheat and, yeah, even kill to get out, to get away, to breathe a little clean air, to taste a little freedom. And when you think that this is what your children are going to have too, why not? What do you have to lose?

But Winston is a "cog" in the "mainstream" perspective. The spirit and the style ("genuine" culture) of Golf-stick George (p. 52) are not part of Winston's cultural orientation (see Fig. 2.3).

Some of Belmar, of course, is a scene of blight. The empty buildings and vacant lots attest to a process of abandonment. Yet beneath this economic facade, there is a social substance. Many people who live here still feel a sense of belonging to this neighborhood. The young and old men who man the corners, day and night, monitoring all activities within their vantage points, regard Belmar as their turf. The residents who patronize the few remaining business enterprises and converse with and engage their proprietors finally sense that this neighborhood belongs to them because no one else wants it. The informal atmosphere of the local bank with its long lines attests to this. This has now become not only a place to transact business, but also a place to meet and interact with one's neighbors. The atmosphere here is different from any other bank in Pittsburgh. It has a distinctive Belmar characteristic. People sit in chairs and wait for patrons. People stand outside the entrance and engage those who enter and leave. Peddlars and solicitors stand at the entrance and attract attention to their wares and causes. Even the Black tellers and officers relate to and interact with, as well as serve, their customers. To many of these welfare and food-stamp customers, this is a new experience. They have become important and this bank's most numerous patrons.

This style, demeanor, and atmosphere are pervasive among the few businesses that remain in Belmar (see Freedman 1971, Grensch and Staelin 1970). Much of this appears unattractive to "mainstream" orientations but is the very character that makes these enterprises belong to the people that live here. The plumber's shop, stocked sparsely and with no apparent rationale; the restaurant, so small that takeouts are obligatory; the fruit and vegetable market, where most of the produce seems to be on the sidewalk; the Justice of the Peace office; the hardware store; the drug store, where nothing is accessible to the reach of customers; the variety stores; and the many taverns are evidence that this place—Belmar—exists, notwithstanding how the people in the wider society perceive it. Belmar belongs to the people now, but given the economic scheme of this society, it is an urban desert. It is discouraging to observe that, rhetoric of political and community "leaders" notwithstanding, little has changed in the quality of life for the residents of Belmar from 1976 to 1991.

So these residents, who for most of their lives have lived in neighborhoods in which they could not feel a membership, now discover a new sense of importance in Belmar. This neighborhood is theirs to do with as they wish and are able. They now possess a neighborhood completely, but it is one that most others have abandoned. Some of the residents are unaware of the pervasive impact upon Belmar of the economic sense of things. Belmar, or places similar to it, is all they know. This is their place, their cradle and tomb. They will live here and die here, unless they are routed again (see fig. 6.12 and 6.13).

PART TWO

PEOPLE IN BELMAR

4 / Household Styles

Most Belmar residents have not completed high school, and as one would expect, there is a paucity of them employed in prestigious professional and managerial positions. Most of them are employed in low-income jobs. Windell (1975, see Williams 1980:25–29) demonstrates that concomitant with these characteristics are corresponding high rates of separations, divorces, matriarchal households, and fertility. The area also has a high concentration of women in the labor force.

These statistics reflect the nature of the urban wasteland, exploitations of money and power, denials of goods and services, ravages of racial discrimination, and the other inequities in American society. But there is much more to discover by meeting and living among the people.

This section presents a selection of the people of Belmar and the restrictive opportunities in their lives. The descriptions are not intended to form a comprehensive analysis, but they do indicate the range of life styles existing within this neighborhood. The people, as well as their lives, are products of our social system. The fact that their lives are meaningful, substantial, and significant is in part an achievement of our society, but their pain, suffering, and hopelessness are also products of the American way.

"Home" in Belmar is a place of security, refuge, family gathering, nourishment, entertainment, and commercial enterprise. Some homes are used for selling illegal merchandise or operating weekend taverns where wine drinkers ("winos") traffic at all times because a group of their comrades live here and maintain a distributing center for their alcoholic friends. There are the very old who live alone, often in fear of their safety and security, and there are the very young who are recently emancipated from their parents and live with their young adult visitors an exaggerated life style of freedom and boisterousness to validate their new-found adulthood. There are middle-class ("mainstream") families and lower-class ("genuine" and "spurious") families often living next door to each other. The complexity of life style and attitudes here defies a community spirit.

Nevertheless, humans are ingenious for discovering others like themselves with whom to interact. So, throughout Belmar, groups of residents form interactional networks among themselves. Teenagers use the school grounds day and night to congregate and converse. Street-corner men and women assemble in and around the Belmar taverns. Drug addicts and pushers have their own Belmar street corners, as well as a network of houses and cars in the neighborhood where they gather and visit in conspiratorial style. Spring weather and sunshine bring new mothers and their newborns out of their homes to chat on their designated corners of the school grounds, trading compliments. Little children, of course, play everywhere.

GOLF-STICK GEORGE

Golf-stick George is a "genuine" Black. He has lived in Belmar for 20 years. He is 57 years old. He lives in a rather well-maintained house with a small lawn, formerly a large, nine-room, single-family home. The owners have divided the home into apartments, and George lives in two rooms on the third floor. George is often seen sitting nude at his third-floor attic window (not exposed to the street, however) when he is trying to keep cool in the heat of summer.

One's first impression is that George lives a very lonely life. He has no spouse and no children. Twenty-five years ago, he abandoned his family in a northern city; he is reluctant to talk about this part of his past and the members of his former family. Seldom, if ever, does George receive visitors in his two attic rooms. Thus, to a newcomer in the neighborhood, George appears to be a recluse in a third-floor attic, a welfare recipient with no family and no friends (see Gazaway 1969).

In reality, however, George is not lonely, for once one discovers, observes, and analyzes George's behavior over a long period of time, one is able to discover that George has a very viable social network within Belmar. When he is not at his corner tavern, he walks the streets of Belmar swinging a golf club, a symbol, to some extent, of the style that he is extremely successful at demonstrating; he makes a conscious effort to swagger or "swing" as he walks rapidly up and down the streets of Belmar. This is how he spends most of his time, visiting his network of other taverns in Belmar or visiting a few of his street-corner buddies at their homes. George's style is perspicuous. As he walks along the streets of Belmar, he invariably speaks to everybody, whether the person is standing at a window or in the doorway, sitting on the porch, driving down the street in the car, or walking on the sidewalk. Indeed, it is not unusual to see George stop a car in the middle of the street and carry on a conversation with the driver by leaning through the open window. Furthermore, it is common for George to borrow cigarettes from the drivers he stops or for George's comrades driving down the street to stop and summon George to ask him for a cigarette or just exchange some minor thoughts or opinions. George interacts with almost everybody in Belmar, and he very clearly lets everyone know that he is well-known. His style of interaction is distinctive. He talks loudly to make sure that not only the person who is listening hears him, but that everyone on the block also hears him and recognizes that he is engaging in conversation with someone in the area. He is boisterous, but most of the time he is pleasant. He is an interesting human being who greeted me frequently even before I knew him because he had seen me in the neighborhood, and he recognized that I was staying there. He still hails me as I drive by the street-corner tavern where he loafs. He hollers across the street when he sees me standing in front of my residence. He has something pleasant to say, but it is always said loud enough so everybody in the vicinity can hear what he is saying. This is his way of indicating that he knows everybody. In fact, most people in Belmar do seem to know George. He feels very comfortable as he interacts with females, males, and children. They can recognize him from almost a mile away, his swinging golf stick is his hallmark. Thus, Golf-stick George who lives alone is not alone after all. He does not have a family, but he has a group of people that he interacts with consistently and distinctively.

George's stylistic gait and attire are also part of his attention-getting demeanor. Dressed in the youthful fashions of the day, George steps quickly, his golf stick swinging as he sways from side to side with his head held high in a princely manner. When beards were in, George grew a beard. He has a variety of hats which leave no doubt that he is "down with it" even when it comes to clothing styles. He knows the latest hair styles, and he does his best, within the confines of his income, to demonstrate clearly that he knows "where it's at."

In fact, George does not act his age. He behaves as a man 20 or 25 years younger than his age of 57, and he interacts with people who are much younger than he. He gets along well with that age group and often identifies with them. Probably the only thing that exposes George's age is gray hair in his beard and on his head. He admits he would dye his hair if it were not for the fact that the graying makes him look distinguished. He also follows a pattern: On certain days, he dresses in his fineries. Typically, he dresses upon the days that he receives his check or a day or so after (as long as large portions of the income from the check are still at his disposal), or on certain holidays, such as Easter, Christmas, Memorial Day, and the Fourth of July. He recognizes these holidays as a means for him to expressively display his best clothes, and although he does not have many expensive clothes, there are not many holidays for which he has to compete with the fashions. Furthermore, on certain days when George dresses better than on other days, he is even more persuasive, more seductive, and more vocal than he is on the days when he is not feeling his expressive best. When he is feeling his best, George makes a point of demonstrating to all those who see him that he is capable of interacting very intensively with the women of the neighborhood. In reality, these interactions, to one who has observed George closely, are only casual. Women speak to George only because he almost insists they do; he can embarrass women easily with his persistent, loud mannerisms no matter if they choose to respond or not. After all, George's obstreperousness is his claim to fame, and to protect this claim, his mod appearance gives no clue that he lives alone, on welfare.

Thus, for the purpose of further observation, we can call George a street-corner man. He spends most of his day in the street, on the street corner, or in the street-corner tavern. A large part of his time, as I mentioned before, is spent moving through the bar network, interacting with people who frequent the street-corner taverns in the neighborhood. George, like many street-corner men, exhibits an articulate style of conversation. He is very capable of carrying on long arguments about sports or some other subject that may be of interest at the moment. He takes a great deal of pride in his ability to argue, to persuade, and to influence by means of regular conversation or a shouting match. Moreover, from my conversations and association with George, I know that he is one of the more intelligent of the street-corner men. In George's exchange of thoughts and ideas with others, I am convinced that he receives more material goods from the people in his network than he provides. George is not only receptive to the members of his social network for resources, such as liquor, beer, and loans, but he also cajoles the females for sexual pleasures. Often, George is seen on the corner trying to persuade a female for favors, and he is frequently successful. He is "a good talker." With a great deal of practice in persuasive conversation, he has a "good line," and many females "fall for it."

I will not detail the life style of street-corner men because that has been done adequately elsewhere (Liebow 1967, Williams 1974). The point I wish to make is that George is a resident of Belmar who, upon close observation, has a meaningful pattern of life in this neighborhood. First, as a source of sexual stimulation, for example, George spends many evenings at the street-corner tavern where he interacts with men and women. Often, they all reach a point of intoxication at which inhibitions are lowered and sexual appetites are stimulated, so they retire to one another's homes two at a time, three at a time, four at a time, and even in groups, to enjoy even further intensive interaction. These people know each other well; they see each other daily, day in and day out, in the context of the streets, of the street corner, and of the taverns on those street corners. Second, George shares financial resources with these same people. When their Social Security checks come in, people share their finances with others by means of lending money, "clipping" (robbing the intoxicated or unaware), setting up a bar, and sharing their drinking habits with those who happen to be congregated at the tavern at the same time. This reciprocity takes place because, when the recipients of these gifts receive their own welfare income, employment income, or lottery income, they will also provide resources to those who formerly gave to them. Last, George's popularity in the neighborhood gives him, as you can imagine, all kinds of privileges as a source of information in the community. He possesses the privilege of communicating with females; chastising children; being consulted when information is needed about something or someone in the neighborhood. Indeed, Golf-stick George can give information about almost anyone who lives in Belmar. He knows the intimate details of their lives, and details are discussed and exposed in street-corner conversation and tavern interaction in social network messages. To this extent, George is a message center in Belmar. Thus, we see that Golf-stick George is a member of a group we can call the "street-corner subculture."

It is not difficult, then, to understand why George is so buoyant. He has found a niche in which he can interact with most others. George, in a sense, has discovered a good life as an individual who has the capabilities to enjoy most of the people who operate within his social network.

Furthermore, we have to admit that George is a pleasant human being. It is a pleasure to talk to someone who does not tell his troubles, who shouts that life is great, who bobs and weaves forward and backward, from side to side, as he exhibits his "down" (ghetto sophisticated) behavior. George is "with it." George knows "where it's at." George is not a "jive cat" (unaware). He walks and talks "his stuff." He is good at it, and he knows it. George has lived in the same two-room attic for 20 years. His expenses are low, and he is intelligent enough to get along well from his income and his "hustle." One has to admit, as one sees George walk the streets of Belmar day in and day out with his flamboyant style, his quick pace, and his pleasant smile, that he has, after all, captured a meaningful way of life. Let's listen to him briefly talk about himself:

What you see is what you get. I'm not trying to conquer the world or win anybody's races. I'm jist trying to hang in there. And I don't want to set the world on fire. I jist want to keep this body warm as long as I can. I like to see everybody doing his own thing, takin' care of business. I ain't got no enemies, they're all dead, jist friends. As long as you treat me like a man, we got to make it. I like Belmar. I like the people here, cept this nigger here [joking with a passing male]. I like them, and they like me, I'm God's gift [joking]. I ain't hungry, and I got a place to lay my Black ass. What else can a old Black fart like me ask for? I ain't got child, chicken, or cat, so I'll do my worryin' after I die. Liquor and women and smokes may kill me, but it damn sure won't be worry. And if you can't get liquor, women, and smokes you mise well be dead already. Life is short and it ain't shit no way. So I'd jist soon take the low road. I can't do no better way. But this is my world [Belmar] and I'm king around here. I'll be king with the rats. You can be rats with the kings. I'm like the president, everybody knows me. I got two Continentals [points to his feet] and my own private jet [pointing to his jitney-operating friend's car and laughing]. I got wine and women and song, and if you scratch me deep enough, you'll find soul. I go to the doctor free, the dentist free, get free whiskey, free pussy, and food stamps, and these old church women tryin' to get me to sign up for heaven. I got somethin' to show the cats in heaven [laughs]. What else is it? If you find out, don't tell me 'cause I might want it, and that would make me worry. All kidding aside, man, I'm doing the best I can with what I got and who I am. And if I do say so myself, that ain't bad at all.

Here, then, is a man who does not have a meaningful family life, but he has a family substitute—the members of his neighborhood. At 57 years of age, he could be lonely and by himself, a recluse on skid row. But no, Golf-stick George has a viable, meaningful life style. If you judge from the way he walks, talks, and lives, he is about the happiest man in the world. He has a welfare income which takes care of his material needs, and he has friends and associates who supplement those needs because he also supplements their needs when he has the resources. He is one example of a resident in Belmar whom we have to get to know well in order to describe and understand the quality of his life and the meaning of his death.

In 1983, Golf-stick George met a woman who was buying her own house. She invited him to share it. He moved out of Belmar into the Hill District to live with her and organized card games there to enhance their income. He was shot and killed seven months later during a dispute in one of his games.

DEACON GRIFFIN

Deacon Griffin is a resident of Belmar whose life style is different ("mainstream") from that of Golf-stick George. Furthermore, an indication of the complexity of personalities in this neighborhood is the fact that they all live within 50 feet of each other.

Deacon Griffin is an ardent churchgoer. He is a member of a Pentecostal church, as is his wife, and that church is his life. He and his wife spend most their time, energy, and money supporting the church (see Williams 1974 for a full discussion). For a resident of Belmar, Deacon Griffin has managed to accumulate quite a bit of wealth. He owns his own home and has just recently built a new garage in the rear of it. He has two cars, a 1965 Cadillac and a 1971 Ford, and his wife has her own car to use. Deacon Griffin is concerned about the upkeep of his property, and he does a thorough job of maintaining it. He retired after working in the steel mill for 35 years. He still walks with a limp from a leg injury he suffered there. He and his wife are supported by his pension and Social Security, as well as their income from raising foster children, which they have done for many years. In fact, one foster son is now an adult, married, and also a member of Deacon Griffin's church.

The Griffins are a quiet family. The only noise ever heard from their home comes during the summer, when they sit on the porch with other church members, quietly conversing while the children run and play in the yard around the house. Deacon Griffin's activities consist of helping his teenage boy deliver newspapers, cleaning his property, and cleaning his automobiles. He tries to be a helpful neighbor and often offers his help to anyone in the neighborhood who seems to need it. His adult son often visits him, and together they work on the cars in a lot alongside of the Griffin house.

The entire Griffin family is well respected in the neighborhood. The foster children that Deacon Griffin raises or cares for are well mannered and are recognized as being different and distinctive from other children in the neighborhood. They spend most of their time traveling back and forth to church and doing chores around the house. Deacon Griffin's foster children presently include John, who is 15 years old, Sarah, who is eight, and Carolyn, who is six. Other foster children who have been raised by the Griffin family are now adults and have left their home. Deacon Griffin's home is large; it consists of three floors and ten rooms. When out-of-town people come to visit Deacon Griffin's church either to preach or participate in a ceremony, they are often invited to stay in his home. For many years, Deacon Griffin has leased his second floor, which he converted into a separate apartment with a private entrance. But, in spite of this, he still has room to accommodate people who come to visit him or the church.

Deacon Griffin seems to have an intensive interest in cars. It is not clear whether this interest is influenced by his adult son or whether it is one of his own. Together, they spend a great deal of time with automobiles. His son has owned about five cars in five years, and he always brings his cars to his father's house where he works on them, cleans them, or just shows them to his father and his father's friends. This son has no children, and he and his wife seem to derive pleasure from buying vehicles; he also owns a motorcycle, and his wife owns her own car. He trades cars just to make a change and for the fascination. He also changes his residence frequently. Lacking children and focusing only on the church for his life, he seems to enjoy moving and buying cars to create meaning in his life. In order to afford these activities, he holds two jobs, and his wife also works. They seem to have accumulated a large amount of savings; they have invested it in a home that is worth approximately $25,000; and when I mentioned the apparent accumulation of wealth, he told me that his wife really "knows how to make money."

Two years ago, Deacon Griffin became disenchanted with the residents in Belmar. He has lived here for 20 years, and he has seen this neighborhood change radically. He felt that he would rather move to the country where he could live the rest of his years "in peace and quiet." But, like most residents who have lived in Belmar for the last five years, he experienced difficulty selling his property. His property was up for sale for six months, but there were no buyers. As a result, he was forced to stay in Belmar in spite of his desire for a quieter, more rural or suburban atmosphere. The excitement in the neighborhood is well understood from the fact that Jody (see description below) lives directly across the street from Deacon Griffin. Fortunately for Deacon Griffin, his next-door neighbors are middle-aged people with no children and are concerned about keeping up their property and being model middle-class citizens.

Deacon Griffin attends church three or four times a week with his wife and children. It is like watching a regular ceremony to see them leave their home on Sunday morning dressed in their church attire, enter their clean and shining car, and drive to the church services. I will not detail their participation in church because I have done this elsewhere (Williams 1974), but they are typical members of the church subculture in the Black ghetto. This brief description of Deacon Griffin again illustrates the complexity and range in the types of residents who live in Belmar.

The Deacon, notwithstanding his proclaimed desire to relocate in a rural or suburban neighborhood (more distant from his church and friends), removed the "For Sale" sign after six months, and he is resigned to "live out his days" in Belmar. His income is adequate for his life style, and he lives comfortably within his capabilities. He has effected a combination of church community life (Williams 1974) and middle-class living. His middle-class orientation is tempered by his religious values so that he lives within his "means." He is not "genuine"; he is "mainstream."

JODY, A STREET-CORNER MAN

Jody is a neighbor and he lives about 35 feet from Deacon Griffin, again indicating the proximity in residential patterns for different kinds of people in Belmar. Jody lives on the second floor over a Pentecostal storefront church.

Jody, like Golf-stick George, is a street-corner man. Jody has lived in this building since 1970, having moved there with his wife and two daughters. When Jody moved to Belmar, his wife worked as a nurse's aide in a Pittsburgh hospital, and Jody worked as a maintenance helper in a new-car agency in Sharpsburg. He moved to his present residence in Belmar after living in nearby Homewood; thus, he frequents the same tavern. Jody has been a participant in the street-corner subculture for almost 15 years, excluding the five years he has lived in Belmar. During these years, Jody's total round of life has depended on his interactions with the people who frequent the tavern where he spends most of his time. On the way to work in the morning, he stops by the tavern to get a drink or to converse with his pals. On his lunch hour, Jody often drives all the way to Belmar (about five miles) to visit this bar again, and returns immediately after work before he goes home. Often, Jody goes home only to sleep. The street-corner tavern is Jody's raison d'être; it is the nucleus of his way of life. Here he finds his social network, his membership in a subculture, and people he can interact with day and night for weeks and months, year after year. Jody's wife also drinks alcohol, but, as expected, she has never been satisfied with her husband's activity, which largely excludes her and her two daughters. She has good reason to be dissatisfied; besides the fact that Jody spends very little time at home, he spends a large part of his income, sometimes all of it, as a resource for his street-corner-tavern subculture. He often enters the tavern with his entire paycheck and leaves with very little, if anything, for the family. This is one reason his wife works, and it accounts for her efforts to catch Jody on payday, usually at the tavern, in order to secure even a modicum of his salary for the family. In the same way, anyone else who wants money from Jody, such as his landlord or his insurance agent, must find him in the tavern before he or his friends spend all the money on drinks.

Jody, like Golf-stick George, is a great human being: a good conversationalist; always pleasant to others, a lover of people, and loved by most of his associates. "He is really a likeable guy," they say. One may spend hours talking to Jody because he, like Golf-stick George, can tell you anybody's business in Belmar; he knows everything that is going on, including the intimate details in the lives of his associates. He knows the latest sports news, whether it be baseball, football, or boxing, and he can generally hold a conversation about almost anything that is communicated in the news media. Furthermore, everyone in the neighborhood seems to know Jody. Anyone can walk in his street-corner tavern and ask, "Where is Jody"? and everyone there will know who you are asking for, even though they may not tell where he is, especially if the visitor is a stranger to the Belmar network.

Jody is a "genuine" member of Belmar society, and like Golf-stick George, enjoys a very intimate group of friends. He has a way of life that he would not trade, but his way of life exacts a high cost from his family. In 1972, Jody's wife decided that she could live just as well without Jody as with him, so she moved out and took her two children with her. Jody continued to live in the six-room apartment and soon sublet other rooms to friends. Since this activity did not have the landlord's permission, it precipitated many arguments between Jody and his landlord. Nevertheless, Jody is so personable that he is able to maneuver out of problems, and he did so with his landlord. The landlord thought that *now* he would pay his rent. Thus, Jody has continued to sublease the rooms in his apartment to people the landlord considers to be undesirable tenants. Most of them are alcoholics who spend most of their time drinking and gambling (when they have the funds) and engage in loud, raucous behavior. In the summertime, when the windows are open and the taverns closed, Jody's apartment often resembles the corner tavern, full of people who are drinking and "making merry." Jody's friends have created out of his apartment what most people at the street-corner tavern consider an extension of the tavern, only two blocks away. If they cannot find Jody or his tenants at the usual place (the street-corner tavern), they will go to the apartment and stay as long as they would at the tavern. In addition, one of Jody's tenants has begun to buy cheap wine by the case and to sell it at the apartment. He has a great deal of traffic on Friday and Saturday nights and Sundays, when the state liquor stores are closed. Since his wife has moved out, Jody's apartment has become what is termed "a speakeasy"—that is, an extension of the street-corner tavern. As a result, Jody's house is frequently the scene of high-intensity human interaction aided by wine. People often stand on the street or sit in their cars calling to somebody in the house. Much conversation ensues between the person in the street and the person leaning out of the window of the apartment. Automobiles stop in front of Jody's building and horns blow, waiting for their passengers to come out. These "jitneys" are merely members of the social network that have scheduled their rider by telephone.

Other sources of activity and excitement also emanate from Jody's apartment. For instance, Red, a 57-year-old tenant, was crippled in World War II and normally walks with a cane. Frequently, Red becomes so intoxicated (usually at one of the street-corner taverns) that he cannot return home by himself. Sometimes stranded only a block from home, he will solicit a pedestrian to summon help from home. In the usual pattern, someone goes to Jody's apartment, asking people there for help. Usually, two men come out and walk up the street. They return shortly, carrying Red back home. When at home, Red often communicates with his visitors through the second-floor window.

Recently, Red had an interesting encounter with Jody's landlord, on the rear one-story roof. The landlord had climbed onto the roof to investigate the possibility of roof damage causing a leak on the first floor. When the landlord reached the area of Red's room (where the rear window leads onto the roof), he discovered a case of wine and some food items, apparently put out on the roof to stay cold. The landlord complained to Red about the food and wine and was told that Jody's refrigerator had broken, so he had put them out on the roof to save them. In the course of their conversation, the landlord discovered that Red was articulate and intelligent and that his speech had an upper-class air. Red's command of the English language surprised the landlord in view of his alcoholic habits.

During another incident, Red and some of his companions were in Jody's apartment drinking when one companion went to the window, looked out, and saw someone on the street whom he did not particularly like. He threw his glass at the person, who turned out to be Bobo. Bobo was upset; he had not seen who had thrown the glass, because by the time he looked up the person had ducked back into the window. Bobo went upstairs and complained to Red about the incident. Red, in his articulate manner, explained that he was not responsible and that he had not been aware that the glass was going to be thrown, but he told Bobo whom he thought had committed the act. The person lived on the first floor rear below Jody. Red also related the incident to Jody when Jody returned home later that afternoon. Both Bobo and Jody approached the alleged culprit, Jim, who by this time was intoxicated and resented Bobo's accusation and Red's audacity in revealing his identity. Jim, highly indignant over the whole incident, went home, got his 20 gauge shotgun, came back to the front of the building, and fired once at the second-floor window where Jody and Red lived, blasting a five-inch hole in the window frame. He then lowered the shotgun and shot through the door where Bobo lived. Bobo, who had gone back inside by this time, heard the blast, and realizing what was occurring, jumped out of his kitchen window, in the process tearing off the window screen. Bobo then called the police and the landlord to the scene. Of course, the police, notified that someone was shooting a shotgun, brought several police cars.

These kinds of noise occurrences (although not shootings) frequently take place around Jody's apartment. Police cars and ambulances are regularly seen in this area. In addition, children who congregate near the schoolhouse frequently ring the fire alarm, to bring the fire engines on a false alarm. In contrast with the boisterousness and activity of this area is Deacon Griffin and his quiet neighbors, who are forced to endure it all.

Adding to the characteristic noise from Jody's apartment is the tremendous amount of rubbish which accumulates because of all his visitors. In spite of his three five-gallon garbage drums, there is a constant overflow into an adjacent city lot. Consequently, this city lot (approximately 60 feet by 40 feet) is full of debris, including old furniture which is mainly from Jody's apartment.

Compounding these activities is a situation that began nine months ago. A member of the same street-corner network as Red and Jody, a woman with six children, was evicted for not paying her rent. All her belongings were piled into the street, and because Red and Jody knew her well (in fact, Jody felt obligated to her for past sexual favors), Jody moved her into his apartment as another tenant. Although all her children could not stay with Jody for lack of room, three of them settled in Jody's apartment. The other three children went to her mother's house to live until she could get a larger place of her own. Now within Jody's apartment, the site of constant activity, live three boys, who are three, five, and eleven years old. Thus, they are forced to witness the weekend conviviality in Jody's apartment. However, this living situation illustrates the reciprocity occurring within these social networks. Jody had no obligation to give this woman a place to stay, but he felt an obligation toward her as a fellow member of his street-corner-tavern network. She has been there nine months and shows no inclination of finding a place of her own. She seems comfortable staying with Jody in spite of the "genuine" crowd.

VIOLENT JIM

Jim, the alleged glass thrower who lives on the first floor of the same apartment building as Jody, is also a major character in the neighborhood. A heavy drinker, he spends time in Jody's apartment, satisfying his habit. Jim has a political job. He works for the state as a state highway employee, and he generally takes off four or five days a month because he goes on an alcoholic binge. When Jim wrecked his car, almost totaling it and damaging someone else's car, he escaped by taking a quick flight to Los Angeles. He was thus able to avoid any liability for the damage to the other person's car. This escape pattern is frequent for Jim. Whenever he is being sought by the authorities for something he has done, he disappears until the "heat" is off. For instance, he disappeared after he fired the shotgun blasts at the apartment building. He was not in the vicinity when the police arrived or during the next few days. After the "heat" was off, though, Jim returned to the neighborhood but was never prosecuted for his deed. Jim is described by Bobo as a dangerous man. Bobo alleges that Jim has killed before and can be expected to kill again. Bobo explains that Jim is a nice person when he is not drinking, and I have also found that to be true: He is an intelligent conversationalist; he walks well and dresses well, yet when Jim is on an alcoholic binge, Bob claims that he is likely to go crazy at the least provocation. In spite of knowing all this, Bobo is his "buddy," his "close friend," a relationship encouraged by fear and proximity.

To the uninitiated, these are disquieting events in the lives of Jody, Red, Bobo, and Jim. But to people living on the poverty level, in a ghetto, these activities become meaningful kinds of human relationships. They provide excitement, substance, and content to one's life style. This life style, however, like the life style of all men, sooner or later brings one to the doors of death. For example, I received a report that Jody lay close to death in a Pittsburgh hospital in August 1975. Jody's brother had passed away after having surgery on his liver. It had become diseased because of an overconsumption of alcohol, and Jody's brother had been told, as was Jody, that death was imminent if he did not cease drinking alcohol. Depite the warning, Jody's brother continued to drink heavily before and after the operation, and now Jody appears to be an imminent victim of the same life force. About six months before his hospitalization, the upper portion of Jody's trachea was removed because of a malignant growth created (or at least aggravated) by strong alcoholic beverages and cigarette smoke. After the operation, an opening was made into Jody's throat so that he could breathe and expel mucus from the lower portion of his bronchial tubes and trachea. He could make vocal sounds only by passing air over his vocal chords while covering the opening mechanically with his Kleenex-covered hand. Soon after the operation, Jody began cobalt treatments on the neck and throat area, but he began to drink again. The crucial point is that Jody, like many street-corner men, has few alternatives to drinking because it is not only a habit, but also a way of life. His friends, acquaintances, associates, and his setting for social commingling are located in a Belmar corner bar. For Jody to go there every day, to spend most of the evening (six nights a week until closing), and to abstain from drinking is practically an impossibility. He would have to change his entire way of life to stop drinking, and he is not able to do that. As he explains,

> They want me to lie down and die before I'm dead. If I quit going on the avenue and stay home all the time, I might as well be dead. If I can't see anybody and can't talk to anybody and I have to live like a hermit, I'm already dead. I don't mind cutting down on the drinking, but you know how it is. You're sitting around, somebody's going to offer you a drink, and after drinking as long as I have, if you never take one, people will think you're dead anyway, just waiting to be pushed over. So if I have to die, I might as well die while I'm living. No use in me dying while I'm already dead. So I'm going to live until I die and when I'm dead at least people can say that I lived while I could.

Jody continuously denied that he drank as much as he used to before his operation. After a few drinks, he seemed to forget how much he was drinking, and the pain from the cobalt treatments as well as the aftereffects of the operation itself (not to mention the embarrassment of having an open hole in his throat) were enough inducement for him to tinker with his perception of reality.

It is these early deaths and short-lived childhoods that make one wonder about the wasteland in Belmar and poor Black ghettos throughout the country. Most children here do not live many years as children because they are often caring for other, younger children (when they are only nine or ten years old themselves), or their own (when they are in their early teens). It is difficult to be a child when one has children of one's own. If childhood is valuable and if its longevity is meaningful in and of itself, then one must question the quality of this life stage of the people in Belmar.

THE CAT LADY

Deacon Griffin's rear alley terminates on the street where Jody, Jim, and Bobo live. Directly across from the alley's dead end live Susy and Neil Cobb. Susy, 64 years old, is the mother of Neil, who is 41. They have lived on this street for 19 years in four different residences, all of them within a 40-foot radius of each other. They have moved repeatedly to occupy what they consider the better apartments. Their first apartment was only two rooms. The problem, as Susy explains, was that the bathroom, located in the basement, was cold and damp. They moved into another two-room apartment, and eventually, this apartment became too small for them because of the dogs and cats which Susy bred and would never relinquish. The animal family finally crowded them out of the two rooms. In contrast to their two previous apartments' rear-alley entrances, their third apartment had five rooms on the second floor with an entrance in the front and in the rear. Susy was elated; this apartment contained more rooms than she had ever had, and she used that extra space to continue breeding cats and dogs. By the time she left this apartment, she had approximately eight dogs and 25 cats. The landlord explained that she left the apartment with an animal odor that he has not been able to remove in two years, even though it has been emptied, repainted, and cleaned.

Susy and Neil moved out of this five-room apartment because Neil, after having been on welfare for 15 years, finally landed a job as a maintenance man, and with his increased income could afford his own apartment. Neil and Susy considered buying a house, but they did not have enough money for a down payment, so they decided to move into the building next door. They divided the two available apartments between them, Neil taking the second-floor, four-room apartment, Susy with all her cats and dogs taking the first-floor, four-room apartment. This enabled Susy and Neil to remain close together and yet have their own private quarters.

Neil is Susy's only child, and he has stayed with Susy all his life. Both are "spurious." Neil has no female companions, no dates, and no intentions of getting married. He recently bought an automobile and applies his attention and interest to it and to his church, a church of the Seventh Day Adventists. During Neil's 19-year residency in this neighborhood, he has remained somewhat aloof. He plays basketball in Mellon Park, reads comic books, discusses sports with a few of the males in the neighborhood, and naps throughout the day and night. At one time, Neil had a library of comic books which he added to every week and traded with various people in the area. His reading material then consisted of comic books and *Sports Illustrated,* to which he subscribed. Seeming to have very few other interests, he spends a great deal of time in bed with his comic books or his radio. His mother seems to be rather satisfied with his style of living, though she complains frequently because they have so little living space that they constantly get on one another's nerves. Susy seems to be relatively content that Neil will remain with her for the remainder of her life, and she does not want to do anything that will antagonize such a prospect. Susy herself has not had a male companion since Neil's father abandoned her over 35 years ago. She is a dominant and aggressive woman who is stubborn, convinced that she is right in most of her opinions. She is five feet, one inch tall, weighs approximately 170 pounds, walks with a haughty swagger, and stands with her back bent, not due as much to age as to poor posture. She has always dominated her own household, and now that Neil has his own apartment, she dominates his household as well. She administers all the money, Neil's income as well as her own, which consists of relief checks from the Department of Public Assistance. They have a joint checking account and each of them can write checks, but Susy controls the check writing and often writes checks for Neil rather than allowing him to write them himself, rationalizing that he confuses the account.

Susy spends most of her time with her animals. She now has 37 cats and eight dogs. Many times she must separate the dogs in order to stop their fighting. In her rear room she has made a place exclusively for some of the dogs, and she keeps the others in the front room facing the street. This arrangement causes a problem during the summer when she tries to take the dogs from the front room into the back yard. She cannot take them through the other dogs' room because they create an animal riot and violently attack one another. She solves this problem by taking the dogs out of the rear room, putting them into the common corridor until she gets the dogs from the front room into the yard and then returning the dogs in the corridor to this rear room. Totally absorbed in her cats and dogs, Susy relates to them as if they were human, and she is very reluctant to part with any of them in spite of the fact that the Board of Health, if they knew of her activities, would order her to cease and desist.

Furthermore, Susy can identify each cat and dog by name when no one else possibly could distinguish them from one another. I will never forget the day that I walked into her apartment, went to the kitchen, and to my dismay, found the entire kitchen area (only 10 by 12 feet) covered with cats. Cats were on the floor, on the sink, on the stove, on the chairs, on the kitchen table; they were literally carpeting the entire area. Nevertheless, I did not overtly react; I was somewhat elated that Susy would allow me to see such a sight. She began to call them by name, ordering them individually out of her way and relating to them as though they were members of her family. I suspect that when Susy moves out of her present apartment, it will also have an abiding animal odor.

Occasionally, Susy has made casual friendships with other women in the neighborhood. These women seem very much like her—dominant and aggressive— and in some instances, they have lesbian relationships. Susy has consistently made an effort to be friendly with younger women in the neighborhood, but I have never seen her attempt to create such a relationship with other males. The only male besides her son to whom she ever relates is her landlord, and her congeniality is demonstrated only during infrequent occasions when she has reason to contact him.

Susy is also a saver. She attempts to save almost everything. Her apartment and yard are full of junk that she refuses to throw away, and she spends some of her time marauding the junk of others, especially during the spring cleanup period when the neighbors put out their castaways to be picked up by the city. She rambles through these piles of debris, trying to salvage a piece of furniture or an appliance that she can take home with the assumption that one day she will repair it. As a consequence, wherever there are no animals in her apartment, there are piles of collected junk. I have even seen her run up to someone who was moving something in or out of his home and ask, "Are you going to throw that away?" intending to secure it for herself, though she has very little space to store any additional items.

Moreover, Susy is a chronic complainer. She complains about the children in the neighborhood and how the neighbors treat their animals, setting herself up as the ideal animal owner by comparison. Nothing excites her more than finding a distressed cat on a rooftop, in a tree, or on top of a pole. She considers herself a friend of all animals in the neighborhood and frequently discusses the treatment of such an animal with a neighbor. In fact, there is no better way to engage Susy in a conversation than by discussing your pet. She also complains about her health, her son and his activities, her neighbors and how they trespass in her yard and damage the fence around it, and, in general, the activities in the Belmar area.

On the other hand, Neil spends a great deal of time on his job. He is an ideal employee and is well liked by his employer; he often tries to do jobs that most of his fellow employees consider above and beyond the call of duty. At home, he watches sports on T.V. or reads sports magazines or the comic books he continues to buy. In the last year and a half, he has become an ardent member of his religious group, and he is also involved in religious activities. One or two of his friends from his group come to se him, but otherwise he is a loner. He seems rather embarrassed when the subject of a female companion is discussed. Although his life seems narrow in its range of interests and activities, to Neil it is a very good life.

Neil, like his mother, complains about the activities in the neighborhood, but I am convinced he is not as concerned about them; he merely uses them as a basis for conversation.

Neil and Susy will probably live at their present address until one or the other dies. They seem to be stable and happy here, and I expect them to be residents of Belmar for a long, long time. Both are "spurious," but both have escaped into themselves and their few treasured possessions.

Looking back at some of the people in this chapter, we see that Jody's family was at a corner tavern. Was that because he was an alcoholic or was alcoholism the result? On North Lang Avenue, he was recognized and well known. He was liked and cajoled. Many people throughout the area knew him. He was a great conversationalist, a kind human, and a person who loved other people. But his take-home pay was often about $40 a week. (He purchased his used cars and obtained periodic crisis loans from his employer that were deducted in payments in perpetuity). He never earned enough money to support his life style, so he persuaded others to contribute (women, fellow alcoholics, and even his landlord, who could not bear the potential neighborhood antagonism or his personal guilt of "persecuting such a nice guy"). So Jody is representative of white America's image of an oppressed Black in Belmar. His visions of power, prestige, and position are translated into a style that the values of the majority condemn, in the same society that creates those visions. This is the American dilemma.

Golf-stick George is a "man of leisure," not a "bum." He strides as if he owns the world and he does (at least, his expressive one). He thinks he should talk to kings and walk with presidents, with the street kings of Belmar and the presidents of various neighborhood organizations. His style is the only style that gives him access to his perceptions of the American dream.

The Cat Lady is fearful of the Belmar "world." She leaves her house only to purchase necessities. For 40 years, she has trained her son to be fearful and to put his trust in cats and dogs. To them, Belmar is a "jungle" of people who commit all the evils documented by television and newspaper reporting. They believe the stereotypes of poor Blacks in America, and, like their white counterparts, they withdraw themselves from a meaningful social context. Thus, "genuine" and "spurious" live side by side here, both victims of and responses to the American way.

The nature of ghetto subculture and society is described by means of the Belmar residents in this chapter. I would like to demythologize poverty in this society, but I give descriptions here which can be used as vivid evidence to perpetuate the myths. Yet the nature of the language, the culture-bound perspectives of behavior, and the attitudes and values attached to the particular life styles allow little escape. I cannot change values, attitudes, and culture. However, I can live among and accept our poor and recognize through the mirror of their poverty what this society does to all of us.

What was termed as "an American dilemma" (Myrdal 1944) is really a human dilemma. The values, attitudes, and cultures that create poverty in Belmar and throughout the world are destroying the Earth. We must change those values, eliminate poverty, cease the destruction of the biosphere, and accept all humans, and all of life as crucial components of a healthy Earth. This is the Ecological Revolution.

5 / Landlords and Tenants

When the "genuine" Black asks, "Can I fuck it, eat it, or spend it?" in order to express the bounds of utility for all worldly goods, he is demonstrating the nature and character of limited access to institutional resources that provide a breadth of appreciation and utilization of sociocultural rewards in the wider society. But he is also peeping under the facade of American ideals and reacting to the raw face of power that is unmasked in his ghetto context.

The language and values in our society do not tolerate or appreciate the expressive behavior and style of the "genuine" Black. There is a built-in bias against him. Yet, in spite of the overwhelming and persistent prejudice, his life is full and meaningful, and if you wear the appropriate eyeglasses, his way of life is as good as any. His predicaments and dilemmas, like those of all humans, are part of the substance of his existence. And a meaningful life must have substance. The reader must recognize that the written page distorts the living process, especially when handicapped by a prejudicial language and his own contemptuous eye.

So much of the description below is capable of provoking various reactions. Yet these are some of the ways that the people described make their lives in America, and through my eyeglasses, most other Americans live about the same.

Many of the behavioral dynamics among the residents of Belmar are housed in the relationship between "mainstream" landlord and "genuine" tenant. The following discussion of these relationships is based on information from reliable informants and observations. Such relationships, as we will see, contain a wealth of "genuine" behavior in style and content, and they highlight the conflicts and dilemmas created in this neighborhood by pervasive American values.

ROSE AND CHARLES

Charles Tower is 20 years old and "genuine." He has been married to Rose for two years, and they have two daughters. One is 31 months old; the other is 8 months old. Both Rose and Charles are lifelong residents of Belmar. They have a furnished kitchenette, which consists of one large room approximately 15 by 20 feet in area, with a four-foot-high counter separating the room from the cooking and eating facilities. This furnished kitchenette is located approximately two blocks from Rose's parents' home, where she was born, and three blocks from Charlie's parents' home. Charlie's father has spent most of his working life as an employee of the city's department of refuse. When Charlie decided to drop out of Westinghouse High School, his father secured him a job with the refuse department. Charlie's pride and his unwillingness to spend eight hours a day at difficult and unpleasant labor (which also required six to eight hours of rest at night) caused him to quit his job at the refuse department. Charlie's present way of life is more to his liking. He works periodically at a carwash, which is close enough for him to walk to work, and he is required to be at work only on those days when the carwash has ample customers. Charlie's wife, Rose, receives a check from the Department of Public Welfare and food stamps to supplement his income. His part-time work schedule and his wife's income give Charlie the opportunity to spend much of his time standing on the corners in Belmar and walking the streets of Homewood. '

Rose is a dutiful mother and spends most of her time with her children. She, too, is "genuine." At home, she reads or sits outside on the stoop as her children play on the sidewalk. She often walks with her younger child sitting in her stroller while the older child holds onto it in a way that leads her to believe she is actually pushing it. Rose visits her several sisters in the Homewood area and spends a great deal of time at her mother's house. Rose has trained her older daughter to take care of the younger, and she can often leave the baby with the other one for short periods of time. I have seen Rose go into the bathroom with a comic book in her hand and stay there for 45 minutes, sitting and reading. She is a very poor housekeeper. At 18 years of age, she is like many young wives in the area: She has no conception of what it is to keep what is considered a clean household in "mainstream" society. Her bed is seldom made because she and the children normally use it all through the day and night. She has no specific routine for periodic cleaning. She does it "when she feels like it." Her kitchen area, which is very small as described, usually is cluttered and, as a consequence, filled with roaches. Roaches are everywhere—in her cooking utensils, her clothing, and all of her household equipment and furniture— but the Tower family consider roaches a normal part of the household.

On one occasion when I was in the house, the landlord visited and asked if he could use their apartment to transport a mattress from another part of the building. Charlie agreed, and the landlord and his helper proceeded through Charlie's apartment to the rear corridor where the mattress was located. As the landlord passed through Charlie's apartment, he glanced quickly and subtly at the appearance of the apartment and its furnishings. As he walked back to Charlie's kitchen, he noticed in that tiny area approximately 19 large brown bags of garbage on the floor piled on top of one another, waiting to be taken outside to the main garbage drum. Apparently, this scene upset the landlord because he immediately stopped his helper from entering the corridor where the mattress was located. Instead, he sent him to take the garbage bags out to the drum. The helper grabbed two of the bags filled with garbage and started out the front door where Charlie was sitting and enjoying the breeze. As he passed, Charlie asked him what he was doing. The assistant explained that he had been told to empty the rubbish into the rubbish drum in the rear of the building. Charlie became enraged. He ordered the assistant to put back his garbage. He began to "rant and rave," saying that no one had permission to take anything out of his house, that the garbage belonged to him, and he would empty it. The landlord tried to explain to Charlie in a tactfully subdued tone that he was merely offering a hand in the matter. Charlie again raved that he did not need any assistance; when he was ready to empty his garbage, he would do so. The landlord dropped the subject, headed toward the area where the mattress was located, and he and his assistant removed it from the building by passing through Charlie's apartment. After they had left the apartment, Charlie began to justify his actions. He exclaimed that "that son of a bitch" [meaning the landlord] had a hell of a lot of nerve coming into [his] house and taking something without [his] permission." Charlie continued, "I pay rent here, and as long as I pay rent here nobody comes into my house and takes anything out of it. These bastards think because they have a little bit of money they can do anything they want to people. But I'm not goin' to take that shit."

In spite of the fact that the landlord was earnestly appalled at the small kitchen area half-filled with stored garbage and was merely attempting to do what seemed to him almost a necessity, Charlie was being an assertive American. Since he had the attitude that no one has the right to take anything out of "my house without my permission," he could not appreciate (as most Americans do not) that the environment he had created out of his own whims could destroy his children and his children's children.

Five months later, during the month of May, Charlie began to work less and less frequently at the carwash. The nice weather had begun; the sun was shining warm spring rays. Moreover, most people, at least according to Charlie, were washing their own cars, and business at the carwash had dropped dramatically. This did not seem to bother him; after all, he had no utility bills to pay, since utilities were included in his rent, and, as I subsequently discovered, he was not paying his rent. His wife was able to use the income from her welfare check to manage the household and take care of the children. During this period, the landlord frequently confronted Charlie about his overdue rent, and Charlie would promise to pay it next week, the week after next, next Monday, or next Saturday. Of course, none of these promises was kept. The landlord, surely recognizing that Charlie was giving him "the runaround," began to reject the excuses, and Charlie's next tactic was to absent himself from the apartment. Whenever the landlord came, Rose would explain that Charlie was responsible for paying the rent. This had been exemplified even when previous rent payments had been paid with Rose's money because Charlie, as the symbolic head of the household, would always hand the rent money to the landlord. Thus, Rose's excuse was consistent with the landlord's previous experience. This went on for several weeks, and it meant that Charlie had to be very tactful, subtle, and shrewd to move about the household only when the landlord was not in the vicinity. This was rather difficult since the landlord lives in the area, but Charlie managed to do it for several weeks, until the landlord gave Rose a final warning. Rose, in her nonchalant manner, considered this merely one of the many empty threats from the landlord and paid no heed to it. Two days later, while both Charlie and Rose were out with the children, the landlord installed a padlock on the front door, the only access to the apartment. When he discovered the locked door, Charlie asked another tenant if he could enter through the door to their common bathroom, which had a rear entry into his own apartment. Charlie discovered, however, that his rear door was locked from the inside, and he could not enter his apartment even from that door. Consistent with his usual pattern of behavior, Charlie became enraged and indignant at being locked out of his apartment, apparently disregarding the fact that he owed the landlord approximately two-and-a-half-month's rent for an apartment on which the rent was due weekly. Charlie went to a phone booth and called his landlord. He expressed his indignation over the phone without reserve. After ranting and raving for approximately three minutes and probably realizing that his tactics were not succeeding, Charlie again began to promise the landlord that he would soon make certain payments. The landlord, no longer satisfied with the commitments that Charlie made, requested that they talk in person in one hour, and they set a meeting place. Charlie returned from the meeting pretending to have been victorious, and in the process of explaining his victories, described an arrangement he had been forced to make with the landlord: Charlie would work on certain other properties in the area belonging to the landlord in order to liquidate his account. Charlie agreed to the arrangement, and the landlord unlocked Charlie's front door, but left the hardware on the door in order to lock the door again if Charlie reneged on his promise to work. The next few days saw Charlie fulfilling his promise to work for the landlord on his other properties. His jobs for the landlord included moving furniture, painting apartments, and doing odd jobs like installing mail slots in doors.

As expected, this labor, being consistent, organized, and without pay as far as Charlie was concerned, soon began to aggravate and frustrate him. It meant that he could no longer sit out in front of his apartment and interact with passersby. It meant that he could spend fewer hours on the avenue, swaggering from bar to bar, talking to those who hang out in the area and in the doorways of such areas. So, after Charlie had worked long enough to pay the landlord most of the arrears, he discontinued his arrangement and began to pay the landlord from his wife's income. Through the entire process, it became evident that the landlord was rather anxious to keep Charlie as his tenant and endured quite a bit of harassment in order to retain him. After all, the landlord did not have to improve the apartment they occupied, which had no windows that could be vented, no private bath, only one exit, and a minimum amount of space for four people.

As an epilogue to these events, the economic strain persisted in the lives of the Tower family until they separated after three years of marriage. Rose took the children, and Charlie took to the streets of Belmar as they sought their individual destinies.

Perhaps neither will change very much but will live each of their lives much the same as observed here. Most of the time, they will not be aware of or concerned with what "mainstream" Americans think of their life style. They will move among a social network of friends, employers, governmental agents, and kin. They will live in a ghetto where their behavior is expected and tolerated. But their children may be "spurious" in reaction to that life. If their children acquire sufficient resources, they can be "mainstream." Yet in this urban wasteland, it is difficult for the superficial observer to appreciate the teeming life here. So Charlie and Rose will continue to represent the dark and ugly side of America, diverting attention from the society's basic human problems.

DORIS AND FLOYD BOYD

Doris and Floyd Boyd had lived in Belmar approximately a year and a half before their relationship with their landlord began to take on an intensive pattern. Doris and

Floyd were common-law spouses, and Doris, who was "genuine," had two children; only the younger was fathered by Floyd. The younger child was a 25-month-old girl. The older child was a four-and-a-half-year old boy. Doris and Floyd both appeared to favor the younger child, while the elder seemed to be consistently neglected, as evidenced by his dress and the constant lack of attention given to him around the house. Furthermore, on several occasions, the younger child was taken south on extended vacations with her "father's people," whereas the older one and the mother remained at home. The older child appeared to get into various predicaments around the house to get attention and was often reprimanded and scolded.

Doris and Floyd resided in a six-room, two-and-a-half story frame house. They had a living room, dining room, and kitchen on the first floor, two bedrooms on the second floor, and one large finished room in the attic. The attic was used only for storage, and the dining room was primarily used as a corridor since it was the front entrance both to the kitchen and to the second and third floors. Being a rather small room, it did not appear unusual to use it merely as a corridor.

Doris received a check from the Department of Public Welfare for herself and her two children, and Floyd worked as an insurance salesman for a large international insurance company. They were able to arrange for these two incomes because Doris used her maiden name on the check and Floyd used only his name on the company's employee records. According to the record, Doris was not receiving any support from Floyd, and as I subsequently learned, that was, indeed, the case. With two separate incomes, the Boyds appeared financially secure, and for a year and a half they were able to pay their bills without much harassment from creditors. They also managed to give several weekend parties for friends, and they discovered to their dismay that after such parties, the same people who had been entertained in their home would later return when no one was there and rob them. It is common in this neighborhood for people to have their household goods taken by people who have been guests in their homes and have had an opportunity to familiarize themselves with the valuables located there. In most cases, the burglars are invited to a party or accompany another guest to the victim's home.

After Doris and Floyd had lived in the house for approximately a year and a half, Floyd, whose left arm was deformed and somewhat shriveled and smaller than his right arm, suddenly began to behave "genuine." He bought himself a new car, a diamond ring, and a new wardrobe. He began to dress fashionably, and he had his hair "processed" at a barber shop noted for creating hairdos for entertainers and "pimps." He initiated relationships with various women other than his wife. The purpose of these relationships in most cases was to secure money, as most of the women held jobs or received an income from the Department of Public Welfare. Floyd had decided that he was attractive enough, glib enough, and could "rap" well enough to become a "pimp." He decided to "hustle" as well as work for his income. After a few months of hustling, Floyd became disinterested in his job with the insurance company, and he was fired. It was during his job as an insurance salesman that Floyd discovered his potential as a pimp. As a salesman, he gained access to homes inside and outside the area. In the process of entering people's homes, talking to the women, and discovering and using his persuasive ability as a salesman, he realized that not only could he sell insurance, but he could also sell himself. As a result, he decided to sell himself rather than the products of someone else.

These new activities not only interfered with Floyd's employment, but they also interfered with his home life. Floyd began to stay out all night, sometimes for several nights in a row. He and Doris began to argue over money because it required all Floyd's finances to support the life style he had grown accustomed to. As a consequence, Doris had to bear more of the household expenses. Subsequently, she found that she had to contribute to Floyd's style of life if she was going to maintain their relationship at all. It was at this time that Doris and Floyd began to have problems with their landlord. They did not pay the rent, and they began to tell the landlord various stories about why the rent was late. They arranged to have the landlord come several times a month to collect the rent piecemeal. During this time, Doris managed to convince the landlord that the rent was Floyd's responsibility. Whenever the landlord came to the house and Floyd was not there and she did not have any money, she would merely say that Floyd had not left any rent money. Floyd's debt became progressively larger. He paid less and less rent, and at first, the landlord did not seem to be overly concerned because he realized that Floyd had managed to pay his rent for the past year and a half; he assumed that he was temporarily having a difficult time and would soon catch up on the rent. However, this did not occur. Payments became less and less frequent and finally ceased altogether. The landlord initially contacted Floyd at work after discovering that it was almost impossible to contact him at home because Floyd now seldom stayed there, and even when he did, he would have Doris tell the landlord that he was not at home. These contacts with Floyd at his place of employment were successful for about three weeks until he left his job. Then, it was necessary for the landlord to contact Floyd at his various "loafing" places, and for a while, this method was successful. He would drive by the restaurants and bars which Floyd frequented, and if he noticed his car parked outside, he could make contact with him inside. Eventually, Floyd used all his income to maintain his life style, even requiring his wife to contribute to it. Doris contributed to his income because she wanted his companionship, as scarce as it was, and attempted in every way to get along with him. Nevertheless, the situation at the Boyd's became worse: Floyd remained away from home more often, and Doris discovered she was less capable of taking care of all the expenses with her income. Finally, the landlord asked Doris to move because it was too difficult to contact Floyd, who successfully managed to avoid him. Doris was thus put in a desperate situation, having to move and to pay her utility and food bills.

Doris, counseled by her friends and neighbors, followed the procedure which was normal for people living in Belmar who could not manage to pay their rent. She called the Allegheny County Health Department and the City of Pittsburgh Building Inspection Department and filed complaints against the landlord for code violations in her home. These agencies dispatched inspectors who, as usual, sympathized with the tenant and managed to cite enough violations to qualify Doris for rent withholding. This meant that Doris was no longer required to pay her landlord rent. Instead, she was supposed to deposit the rent at a city bank where it was to be held in escrow for the landlord until the violations were eliminated. This is a technique used by tenants, often in collusion with inspectors and social welfare personnel, to survive when in financial straits at the expense of the landlords. The building occupied by Floyd and Doris had been inspected by the City Building Inspection Department and the Allegheny County Health Department before they moved in. The landlord had been cited before by the former tenant, had had money held in escrow by that tenant, had made all necessary repairs at that time, and had received the escrow money after inspections by the city's inspection department and the county health department had ensured that all repairs had been made. Now, only two years later, the landlord was being sujected to the same process by another tenant. Thus, in this situation, the landlord felt persecuted by the city's building inspection and county health people, as well as by Doris and Floyd. He was receiving no rent payments, the Boyds were four months in arrears, and he was given 30 days to eliminate the violations for which he had been cited, even though some of them were structurally impossible to correct. Two weeks after the landlord was notified of these code violations, during the winter months, the Boyds' gas line was mysteriously disconnected, and they were left without heat. After the gas had been turned off, the landlord appeared and requested that the water be turned off also so that the pipes would not freeze. Without water or gas, Doris immediately contacted the Allegheny County Health Department, which issued an emergency citation against the landlord. The landlord was summoned to Housing Court, where he explained that a gas leak had been discovered in Doris' line. A plumber had disconnected the line and had been negligent in not repairing the line quickly, despite the landlord's request. The judge in Housing Court ruled that although the plumber had been negligent, the responsibility of repair belonged to the landlord, and there was some doubt as to the existence of the leak; perhaps the line had been disconnected purposely in order to avenge the landlord's indigantion. Thus, the landlord was fined $500 plus court costs. To summarize, the landlord was issued various code violations to rectify damage which he believed the Boyds were responsible for, especially since all violations had been corrected before they moved in. In addition, the Boyds were not paying any rent at all at the time, not even to the bank's escrow account because the health department does not enforce rent collection when it is put in rent withholding. Thus, tenants may pay rent if they please, but in many cases, they do not. Furthermore, during the time rent is supposedly paid into escrow, no tenant can be evicted. Doris and Floyd, therefore, four months behind in rent and paying no rent at present, could not be evicted, whereas the landlord had to somehow find, within 30 days, a way to rectify violations they had created and pay a $500 fine plus the cost of going to court. To aggravate matters even more, the landlord ("mainstream") lived in the neighborhood and saw Doris every day. The landlord was enraged, tensions were extremely high, and both Doris and Floyd feared for their physical safety.

As pointed out, Doris had more problems than those with the landlord: She was having utility bill problems; she was having problems with Floyd; and she was having problems managing her household. Doris packed her clothes, gathered her children, and left for her mother's house. She moved in with her mother, leaving the furniture and many of her household items at her own home. Floyd and Doris were still on speaking terms during this time, and Floyd periodically used the house during Doris' absence. She was concerned about her house being empty most of the time because her husband frequented it only periodically, so she took her dog to the house to watch it during those long periods when no one was at home. The landlord discovered this arrangement when he attempted on several occasions to get into the house to make the repairs ordered by the Allegheny County Health Department and the City Building Inspection Department. He found the dog at the door and no one at home. After several such experiences, the landlord went back more frequently, discovered that no one was living there and that often the dog was left two, three, and four days without food or water or access to the outside. This further aggravated the landlord, for now he was not able to enter the home to make repairs, and the large dog, running around without any care, was depositing waste throughout the house. This situation could continue for months without the landlord being able to do anything about it, so he contacted the two agencies requiring the repairs, but they indicated that they were not in a position to require tenants to be at home for the landlord's convenience. The landlord had a definite problem.

Meanwhile, as the weeks went on, the relationship between Doris and Floyd become more and more strained. Floyd had requested that Doris allow him to take over the house; since she was no longer staying there, he would like to use it for his own purposes, a convenient arrangement because Floyd would have a rent-free household to himself with all utilities (including the telephone) reassigned to his name, as a new account. Starting afresh with his utilities, he could live there as long as he wished, apparently without paying any rent. Doris balked at this request from Floyd, feeling that if she was denied the use and enjoyment of the house, she was not going to allow him to profit from the unique, nonpaying situation she had created. She was also adamantly against Floyd's idea because she felt he had betrayed her by not giving her and the children adequate attention. Floyd became angry because he felt Doris was denying him something (which would not cost her anything) out of spite, without any rationale. He reasoned, why should he not have the house, when it was sitting there empty? In response to her denial, he took his child from Doris, but with her approval, since the child was just another mouth to feed. He left the child with his relatives in the South, and later, he went to the house in Belmar and broke all the household goods. He damaged the furniture so that it could not be used, feeling that if he could not have his way, at least Doris would never have the use of the household goods in the future. However, Doris had decided not to return to the house; she was going to live with her mother. She had already transferred her Department of Welfare checks to her mother's address, and she periodically went back to her own house only to pick up a few items she needed. Even though she did not live there, she decided to keep her house in case of a change, especially since it was not costing her anything.

The landlord was in a state of anxiety. He had 30 days to make the necessary repairs, no access to his building, and problems created by two large dogs (since Doris had also decided to leave her mother's large dog in the building on certain occasions) without care and without anyone cleaning up after them. After two months of such anguish, the landlord finally decided to take some action on his own in spite of the risks involved. He called the City Animal Control Department and reported that the dogs were locked up for a long period of time in his building without care. This information was verified by the neighbors. The landlord met the animal control men when they arrived, and in an ostensible effort to rescue the dogs, the landlord broke through the front door. He and the animal control guards were appalled. The place was filthy with dog excrement and broken furniture scattered throughout. The animal control guards took the large dog that belonged to Doris' mother, placed him in the truck, and drove away. The other dog had been removed. The landlord changed the lock on the front door and barricaded the rear door so that no one else could enter. At last the landlord had access to his own building.

His troubles were not over, however; during this episode, some neighbors had called Doris, probably because she had asked them to keep an eye on her house. Doris arrived after the animal control guards had taken her mother's dog but before the landlord had left the scene. She met him as he was getting into his car after locking the doors to the house. Doris began to shout obscene names at the landlord, swear, and accuse him of incarcerating her mother's dog. People in the neighborhood, many of whom were friends of Doris and Floyd, gathered around Doris to support her. A large group formed, and the traditional animosity between tenants and landlords was in danger of being acted out on the sidewalk. Fortunately, the landlord managed to drive away before being physically attacked.

Now, for the first time in many months, Doris tried to communicate with her landlord and even had her mother make an effort to do so. The mother succeeded, explaining to the landlord that she was very indignant that her dog had been incarcerated but that she understood the landlord's plight as she was aware of the details of the situation. After the mother had contacted the landlord, she discovered that he was willing to talk. After all, he realized that he was liable for breaking into the house and that he still could not evict Doris. Then, Doris contacted the landlord, telling him that she would be moving out of the house in a few days, as soon as she got someone to move her. The landlord jumped at this opportunity. He offered to get someone to move her, or he, himself, would help to move her if she were willing. Doris agreed. Here was an opportunity for her to move without any further expense; the landlord provided a truck and movers at his own expense. Doris arrived on the scene with the movers and the landlord and began to move out the items she thought could be salvaged. She promised to pay the landlord for his moving expenses, but she never did. Floyd had been notified by now that Doris was giving up the building, and he appeared on the scene to take out a few items that he had left there. Floyd was visibly angry that Doris had not allowed him to take over the building and had conceded to return it to the landlord.

Thus, the landlord-tenant episode ended with the landlord's bearing the expenses for moving out Doris and Floyd as well as for the other expenses described. The landlord was relieved to get possession of his building and eventually repaired it and removed all the furniture destroyed by Floyd. In the subsequent months, the landlord again had his building inspected by the City Building Inspection Department and the Allegheny County Health Department, and again his building was approved for leasing. This was a process that would happen over and over again. Yet, now when Doris rides by him in her car, she waves and speaks to him, and when she sees him at various places, she acts as if nothing had ever happened. Of course, the landlord does not feel as magnanimous toward her, but he goes along because he seems to appreciate his vulnerable position as a Belmar landlord. Such drama fills people's lives. They lose themselves in the predicaments of daily life. It is no surprise that they often handle such situations by drinking or taking drugs to escape their problems.

THE COKE FAMILY

Elliot Leibow (1967), Ulf Hannerz (1969), and others have described in detail the life style, behavioral patterns, and distinctive adaptations to life of the so-called "street-corner" men, but the Coke family in Belmar represents a unique aberration of that pattern because they are a "street-corner" family. The father, the mother, and the three daughters and their spouses spend most of their spare time, day and night, in the same Belmar tavern. The Coke family has lived in Belmar for approximately 11 years; during that time, all three daughters have grown to adulthood, married, and continued to live in Belmar, periodically with their parents. The remainder of the time they have lived in their own residence, which have never been farther than four blocks from their parents or from each other.

This gives rise to a peculiar phenomenon which makes this geographic area difficult, if not impossible, to describe as a community because traditional definitions of community do not apply; yet, in the minds of some residents and based upon their patterns of behavior, it is evident that some people in Belmar conceptualize it as a community and interact with one another in a style that would qualify it as a community orientation. The Coke family falls into that category. To them, Belmar represents a distinctive cluster of familiar places and people with whom they interact intensively and continually. It is a huddling place. It is conceptualized as a secure place. It is where each of them wants to be as many of their waking hours as possible and as soon as the exigencies of life allow. Thus, the Coke family members not only spend most of their time in the same Belmar tavern, but they also can be seen periodically coming from and going to that tavern, greeting friends and acquaintances, and discussing the problems of the day as they relate to their world.

Interaction focused on a neighborhood bar has many ramifications, one of which is the customer's relationship with their landlords. Spending most of one's waking hours in a tavern usually means the consumption of a significant amount of one's income in alcoholic beverages. Thus, a large portion of one's income is diverted from household expenses to support one's distinctive life style.

Mr. Coke has a job as a maintenance man in one of the large buildings downtown. Mrs. Coke is employed as a cook in a nursing home. Two of the daughters are employed, one as a barmaid and the other as a paraprofessional in a community agency. The former is married, with no children; the latter has a husband and one child. The third daughter receives a check from the Department of Public Welfare for herself and her five children. Yet, in spite of their income, the members of the Coke family are constantly being evicted from one building or another.

I will describe the events of the last eviction of Mr. and Mrs. Coke. After living in their four-room apartment for four months and paying their rent on time, the Cokes ran into trouble. Mrs. Coke became ill and entered the hospital for an operation, so her income was drastically reduced. During this time, one of the daughters and her spouse moved in with Mr. and Mrs. Coke after being evicted from their apartment. The Cokes had only one bedroom, so the daughter, her husband, and their three-year-old daughter converted the living room into their bedroom. This meant that whoever entered the apartment had to walk into the daughter's bedroom in order to enter any other room. During this same period, the daughter who works as a barmaid stayed for days, even weeks, with her parents because of the violent arguments and physical combat she had with her husband. She slept on the couch, which was placed in what would normally be the dining room. She was pregnant at the time, but she had no children. This arrangement worked rather well, except for the fact that Mr. Coke would often come home so intoxicated that he could not reach his own bedroom in the rear of the apartment and would spend his evenings on the couch where his daughter was supposed to sleep. The daughter, finding her father on the couch, would then sleep in the master bedroom. The Cokes seemed to get along with each other, even though they were confined to an apartment in which the rooms were unusually small: the living room was approximately 10 by 12 feet in area; the dining room (the largest room) was about 12 by 15; the kitchen (the smallest room) was approximately 10 by 10; and the master bedroom was about 15 by 15.

The Coke family had a unique financial arrangement. It was understood that Mr. Coke's income was basically his own, and any distribution of it for household expenses was a recognized household privilege and it occurred as infrequently as possible. Mr. Coke's income was used primarily to bolster his pride, prestige, and recognition at his local corner bar. Mrs. Coke acknowledged and accepted this arrangement and used her income primarily for household expenses and to supplement the quickly expended income of her husband. Of course, Mr. Coke was a popular figure in the corner bar; he commanded the attention of many people because on payday (and sometimes for several days after) he had funds which he allocated for alcoholic consumption. Mrs. Coke also enjoyed this, because whether by design or pattern, she was usually with her husband and partook of the wares he dispensed freely. Likewise, she enjoyed the prestige and recognition that her husband received as a dispenser of alcoholic altruism, and perhaps this was one of the attractions for their daughters, who could often be seen sitting at the same table as their parents, enjoying the camaraderie and mutual intoxication.

Such a long, ingrained pattern is difficult to break, so when Mrs. Coke was hospitalized and out of work for at least four weeks after hospitalization, Mr. Coke and his family found it difficult to change their way of life. As a result, the landlord could not collect his rent. He could be seen weekly at the corner bar on Mr. Coke's payday, trying to persuade Mr. Coke to relinquish some of this money for rent. The usual outcome of such encounters was merely to remind Mr. Coke that he had rental obligations, for Mr. Coke felt it beneath his dignity to pay a bill, especially his rent, in the midst of his comrades. He resented the appearance of the landlord, and the only satisfaction he ever gave him (in my presence) was a promise of payment later that evening or the next morning. This meant, or course, that Mr. Coke's priority was his tavern, and whatever money he managed to keep after the evening would be evaluated in terms of subsequent expenses in keeping up his appearance at the bar for the next few days. As a consequence, he made periodic, partial payments on his rent, but for the most part, he was too intoxicated to communicate in the evening and too sick to "give a damn" in the morning. When Mr. Coke was sober, he would explain to the landlord that his wife would soon be back to work, and then, he would catch up on his rent; the landlord should not worry. The landlord was persistent in trying to contact Mr. Coke, but Mr. Coke was unable to change his drinking habits. Consequently, by the time Mrs. Coke returned to work and began making partial payments on the rent, the balance was so large (at $79 per month) that she had no hope of liquidating it and catching up on other household bills (electricity and gas) at the same time. The situation created an atmosphere of frustration for the landlord, Mrs. Coke, and her husband. Mrs. Coke, a quiet, meek, and shy woman of 52, expressed her frustration in an attitude of general resignation. Mr. Coke expressed his frustration with indignation, anger, and threats of violence. The entire Coke family felt persecuted by their landlord. Mr. and Mrs. Coke took the traditional route of calling the Allegheny County Health Department and the City Building Inspection Department. For some unexplained reason, however, these two agencies did not find enough violations to qualify the Cokes for rent withholding, which would have nullified any eviction process. Therefore, as the landlord began correcting the violations that were cited, he also initiated eviction proceedings against the Cokes. A few days before the Cokes were scheduled for eviction, they moved from their four-room apartment to another one approximately six blocks away. My interviews with their landlord made it clear to me that he was extremely surprised and relieved to get rid of the Cokes with so little effort. He divulged to me his suspicion that the reason for the easy eviction was his reputation in Belmar for being a "violent son of a bitch." A few months later, the Cokes' eldest daughter and her five children were physically evicted from their apartment; all her belongings were placed on her front porch and the sidewalk in front of her house. In the process of this eviction, I noticed that the daughter took most of what she considered valuable (her stereo, her T.V., her portable radio, and many other small appliances) and stored them at her mother's house. The remainder of her household goods she left on her front porch for about 40 days after her eviction. Perhaps it was not that she did not consider these items valuable, but only that she had no other place to store them. After acquiring a new residence, she did move those items. Her new residence was an apartment belonging to one of the tavern regulars whose wife and children had moved out because of separation proceedings; he offered her the use of his apartment, possibly because he was attracted to her as a female 30 years younger than he and felt obligated to her as a fellow cohort at the Belmar bar.

This bar is bustling with human activity. Every day, every hour, and especially on Fridays and Saturdays, the bar is busy inside and outside. Men and women loiter outside, drinking and conversing. Self-styled jitney operators get their customers from inside and outside of the bar. Cars line up along the curb in the proximity of that bar. Several men and women sit like peacocks in bright attire and watch the cars and people go by, as they wave, yell, and converse with passersby. Traffic is normally blocked at that corner as someone gets in or out of a passing car or leans through the window while standing in the street to talk to the driver or a passenger; horns blow loudly. This is the site of frequent arguments; some become violent and result in injuries to their participants; others are a periodic distraction and designed, I believe, only for that. By spending time in this bar where everyone knows everyone else and immediately recognizes when a stranger enters, I came to understand why and how a sense of belonging and a sense of membership can be developed among human beings in this context. I received a greater appreciation of man's complex ability to create a social role for himself wherever he happens to be.

Mr. Coke has no anxieties about promotions, vacations, financing college education, balancing budgets, marrying off the children, selecting appropriate schools, divorce settlements, sex counseling, cleanliness, and what the neighbors think. But he has his anxieties, and if he is to be understood, we must begin to appreciate them.

THE LANDLORD SITUATION

All the landlords I have mentioned are "mainstream" Blacks who live in Belmar. I think it reasonable to consider that these social class hostilities of Black against Black might well be a result of the kind of systems we live in: political, economic, and social. I remember many, many years of living in substandard housing when my family's landlords were predominantly Jewish. Other landlords were Italian, Irish, Greek, Scottish, and members of other nationalities and ethnic groups besides Black. From personal experience, I know that from the mid-1930s to the 1960s, the squalor and inadequate conditions that Blacks endured in Pittsburgh's Black ghettos were no concern to the city or county. Where was the Allegheny County Health Department then? Where was the City Building Inspection Department then? They had codes then, too, but these codes were not enforced in Black ghettos. It was in the 1960s, when whites began to move out and sell their properties, holdings, and investments to upwardly mobile Blacks that code enforcement was introduced to the ghetto. Is it by accident that in the 1960s (after the riots) and in the 1970s (when Blacks owned most of the properties in Black ghettos) that rigid housing and health codes were enforced, primarily against Black owners? Is it by accident that ploys, laws, and rules such as rent withholding did not come into effect in dilapidated and hopelessly decayed areas of Black neighborhoods until Blacks, the old, and the poor (incidentally, including some old and poor white who had nowhere to go and no means of leaving) were in ownership of property there? I do not mean to suggest that our massive economic, political, and social system designed this progressive legislation against Blacks. I do suggest, however, that in our social hierarchy, people who are powerless are continually oppressed in spite of changes, and I think the situation I describe exemplifies such continuities in oppression—the reproduction of social inequality.

Obviously, from my descriptions, landlords are an important source of information, and those who are interested can spend many hours with them, listening to what they conceptualize as consistent patterns among Blacks in Belmar. Of course, those landlords with a rather narrow range of attitudes and those who conceptualize their own specific value system as the only worthwhile one will discuss the behavior of others, who apparently have different values, in derogatory terms. Nevertheless, there are landlords who have a broader perspective of values and who conceptualize others' values and behavior on the basis of intent.

From my observations here in Belmar, it appears that our culture and society have successfully managed to create conflict in Belmar by means of restrictive residence patterns. I think to some extent this has been demonstrated in the discussions of "genuine" tenant and "mainstream" landlord relationships. In those discussions, I described the tenant's attitude toward the landlord. Let us take a closer look at the landlord in order to find the basis for the tenant's attitude. Many "mainstream" landlords would like to believe that they are good Christians. They say they believe in brotherhood, peace, good will, love, charity, God, altruism, and neighborliness. These are their ideals, and they would like to believe they are also their ultimate goals—things they strive for but seldom attain. When we observe their concern for money, status, prestige, recognition, property, and material possessions, we realize their real direction.

For example, I questioned one landlord about his willingness to spend $500 in legal fees to prevent a poor Black tenant from residing in his dwelling without paying rent for six months when he would lose only $480 in rent. Thus, by allowing the tenant to remain in the dwelling, he would save $20. His response was that he could not tolerate such behavior in his business because it would damage his reputation and his business relationships with other tenants in the neighborhood. He believed that others would be encouraged by such actions to try similar procedures. This could lead to a number of maneuverings and strategy concoctions that would eventually destroy his business. He explained that it was sound business practice to spend as much as necessary to keep tenants in their "place" and make them recognize that they could not outmaneuver the landlord.

Yet, in spite of the explanation given by this landlord and others who agreed with him, we have to keep in mind that these landlords are willing to spend large sums over and above the amounts they are attempting to protect in order that those less fortunate than they do not secure financial advantages. They would rather give it to the lawyer than to the poor. Some landlords responded more aggressively: "I'm not going to let my hard-earned money be snatched away from me by people who don't deserve it." "Let them work to get their money like I did or beat some of their own ["genuine"] kind out of money, not me." Another stated, "I got mine the hard way, and I'm not going to let the likes of them take it from me." Thus, we discover middle-class ("mainstream") Blacks who insist that poor ("genuine") Blacks will not gain advantages through their losses. Many are convinced that these "ignorant, poor, dirty, and violent people" deserve their plight. "There is nothing I can do to help them." "They have to learn how to help themselves." Such attitudes are exacerbated when tenants and landlords are forced to live among each other (see Wilson 1978).

There is a belief that it is good business for the landlord to scheme and maneuver to earn as much income as possible from his dwellings, usually at the expense of tenants. But it is wrong for tenants to do the same. Thus, when the tenant aspires to better his lot in any way available to him, that tenant becomes a "trouble maker," an "ungrateful" person who disregards all the "breaks" the landlord has given him and "stabs [the landlord] in the back." I have observed landlords who seem intelligent, good natured, and reasonable become enraged—ready to burn, maim, and kill—when their tenants secure rent-withholding privileges through the Allegheny County Health Department and City of Pittsburgh Bureau of Building Inspection. (The withholding privilege is extended to tenants whose dwellings have been certified unfit for human habitation.) Yet these same landlords find it difficult to understand why some of their tenants become angry when they appear to collect rent.

Landlords are as much antitenant as tenants are antilandlord. This again brings me to the point that in our culture and society, people who have achieved some financial status, prestige, recognition, or success are pitted against those who have not, as well as those who have achieved more than they have, especially when they are Black.

The people of Belmar are like people everywhere—they have their pains and their pleasures, their drama and their boredom. But life here is often full and exciting; poverty only helps set the stage. In addition, this chapter demonstrates the pervasiveness of American values in Belmar. The "genuine" Blacks defy "mainstream" values and their fellow Blacks who manifest them. Struggling Black landlords blame their plight on the "genuine" poor, and their "spurious" bitterness is directed against them. "Mainstream" Black landlords often disavow the "spurious" and the "genuine" Blacks and associate with whites when possible. Yet, they are all the victims of the past, when Belmar was selected as an economic and social dumping ground. Today, it is a desert with most shelters being old and inadequate. But the land is potentially as valuable as it was a century ago, so it is being cleared. It is being accumulated by the local governments one way or another. This process destroys the human ecology and the social network, but it creates attractive sites for investment. When this process goes far enough, the money interests will take control of Belmar once again.

The people of Belmar represent some of the best people in the world. Some (the "genuine") have demonstrated that in spite of restricted access to the institutional resources touted by the ideology of "mainstream" culture and society, they live, enjoy life, and "make it." If for no other reasons than this ability to sustain themselves in a particularly hostile environment, these people are worthy of study. They are proof that even though they have not achieved the ideals of America, they survive. Here we find people who recognize that they will spend their lives in Belmar or places like it. They are aware that they will never have much more money than they have today or many more possessions than they had yesterday.

Some of the problems and predicaments are a result of being poor and Black in America; others exist because of the variety of life styles in Belmar. Whatever the plight we discover here, it is indigenous to American culture and society.

What people do to the Belmars of America they also do to other peoples throughout the world. They exploit people and places for profit. That exploitation has reached its zenith. The Earth cannot tolerate the ravaging of its resources with such abandon. Soon, we must create values that will save Belmar in order to save ourselves. That is the human dilemma.

6 / Activities in Belmar

When someone during the Harlem riots of 1964 begged the street crowds to go home, the cry came back, "Baby, we *are* home!"

In this chapter, I attempt to give the reader some sense of the "action" in the neighborhood. This account is by no means a complete repertoire of activities or a description of the formalized agencies which provide activities for the residents. However, it contains descriptions by the researcher who has lived there, personal impressions of the pace and atmosphere.

The dominant dimensions of Belmar activities are people, space, and interaction. The people here have learned to live with the pervasive attitude that their neighborhood, like most Black ghettos, is a dumping ground for the undesirable. Their living space is limited, and they have defined most of it in terms of meaningful activity. That is, in restricted space, they intensively interact with one another, and that interaction often results in conflict, companionship, and conspiracy. They kill, cut, love, and batter each other while exposed to one another intimately and frequently. To them, this adventure and excitement have substance and meaning in their confined portion of America.

Yet all Blacks in Belmar have not been "ghettoized"; there are others, as Drake described:

> . . . indistinguishable from any other middle-class neighborhoods except by the color of the residents' skin. The power mower in the yard, the steak grill on the rear lawn, a well-stocked library and equally well-stocked bar in the rumpus room—these mark the homes of well-to-do Negroes living in the more desirable portions of the Black Belt. Many of them would flee to suburbia, too, if housing were available to Negroes there.
>
> But the character of the Black Ghetto is not set by the newer "gilded," not-yet-run-down portions of it, but by the older sections where unemployment rates are high and the masses of people work with their hands—where the median level of education is just above graduation from grade school and many of the people are likely to be recent migrants from rural areas. (1965:777)

Man is the only animal that persistently pursues images and conceptions of the future. Joe will "go out on the avenue searchin' for his love tonight" in spite of repeated failures. Bill will laboriously wash and wax his car during the day to attract the women at night, even though (based upon past results) it is not likely that he will succeed. The evening finds the streets of Belmar frequently filled with people who are "searchin'" and wondering, "Will I find my love today?" By morning, most of them have not succeeded, but they will continue to pursue their dreams undaunted as long as "another day has passed and left me."

FIRE IN THE NIGHT

One circumstance that generates a social gathering and a context of intensive social interaction is a fire in the night. The later the occurrence (especially after 11 P.M.), the greater the potential for a social gathering rather than merely a crowd. Depending on the duration of the fire, people may come from several blocks away (some by car) to view the spectacle and to be involved in what they have come to appreciate as a social "happening." Women and teenage girls congregate in nightgowns or pajamas covered by robes of various kinds. They wear their curlers and bedroom slippers, and their faces are not made up. Such attire seems to contribute to a very congenial social atmosphere. The nature of this kind of exposure is a topic of conversation among them, but no one seems to be really upset by how she or he looks. Many of the women discover neighbors whom they have not seen for long periods of time, and they renew their fellowship after exclaiming over the absence of interaction and the seriousness of the fire. Often, men discover acquaintances they have not seen for some time and attempt to renew relationships or establish closer ties. Teenagers find the excitement and informality a rich context in which to joke and tease one another. Children, aware of the license of being in the streets in the early hours of the morning, glow with excitement and communicate such to their peers.

All of this is reinforced by the commotion of the fire itself and the destruction of life and property. The direction in which the wind blows the smoke will determine the movement patterns of the gathering. The escaping water from the hose connections will often shift the positions of certain groups. The large intoxicated woman escaping nude from her burning shelter (on North Lang Avenue) and other such incidents are invariably cause for some humor to be interjected into the tragedy, especially by teenage observers, who encourage laughter often by pretending to suppress it. The arriving family member who has to be forcibly denied entrance to the burning structure; the occupant who risks all to save his suits and his television; the frenzied landlord who arrives in panic and is more concerned about the damage from the firemen than that caused by the fire itself or suffered by his tenants; the stubborn bystander who has to be arrested because he refuses to stand back; the rush by observers to expose themselves to the television cameras; the dogs running about trying to locate their owners after chasing around with other dogs on the vivid scene; the sound of sirens and the flashing of red lights everywhere, upon streets covered with hoses, busy firemen, and resigned police—all of these break the calm of the night and create subjects of discourse for many nights to come.

The eventual abandonment of the disaster scene to those involved and to the quiet of the night reminds one that the streets of Belmar are often the setting for social behavior. Any incident that occurs there is upon the neighborhood stage, and that drama, depending upon its magnitude, will always have its audience. These residents are adept at manipulating such phenomena and structuring them into meaningful social experiences.

NEIGHBORHOOD BARS

A good case can be made for community in the neighborhood bars of Belmar. These may be the last vestiges of community in Belmar other than the small storefront churches. Here, the knowledgeable landlords seek out their tenants, the experienced insurance agents go for their premiums (both on the appropriate paydays), and some of the residents look for their friends. Here, some of the neighborhood residents spend their days (if not employed during the day) and their nights. Here, many of them live, debate the issues of the day, meet their friends and lovers, converse, laugh, cry, make friends and enemies, fight, and sometimes die. Here, there is always someone to listen to your troubles, to try to understand the injustice of your trials and share your victories, large or small, as well as your income. There is always someone here 20 hours a day, six days a week. And for the few hours that the bar is closed, the community merely moves to the favorite "speakeasy."

This is one of the few places in the neighborhood where "partying" seldom stops, and the sight, smell, and flow of that great social lubricant—alcohol—commingles with laughter, music, and song to create a feeling of well-being and membership in the fraternity of man. Here, one finds familiar faces, periodic excitement, love affairs at their best and their worst, and a picture of the world made tolerable even in this ecological niche. The smoke-filled, dimly lit, juke-box-booming room becomes a second home to many whose first may not be adequate.

Refurbished bar on North Lang Avenue

Everyone is welcome here. There is no discrimination, no ostracism, and no isolation. There is even a spirit of camaraderie that those from outside the neighborhood soon discover if they manage to antagonize one of the regular patrons. Here, the unemployed, those on welfare, the sick, the old, and the young whose futures may all seem dismal imbibe, converse, and interact (see *Time Magazine* 1977).

Many residents in Belmar have a schedule that includes regular hours here in the neighborhood bar. Their children, spouses, and other relatives and friends come here to retrieve them if necessary. In many ways, it is similar to the corner grocery store for the teenagers because the bar patrons interact and engage those teenage neighbors who make repeated trips to purchase takeout "six-packs." On Friday and Saturday, the pace and action quicken, and many plan to be present when the bar closes and the "party" goes on for hours behind locked doors away from those who might be more discriminating as to after-hours sales. As the door is unlocked to release patrons one by one, the sounds of music and laughter that fill the outside air make one think that he is missing one of the liveliest Belmar parties.

One of the regular patrons of a Belmar neighborhood bar, 46-year-old Ben, explains:

> My mother always told me I wouldn't amount to nothing because I was too hard-headed [stubborn]. Seems like I chased pretty women most of my life. And when I caught up with 'em, they always caused me more trouble than they was worth. But I was sharp [handsome] and young then, and I thought that way of living—wine, woman, and song—was where it was at.
>
> Women spoiled me. They gave me so much [materials and affection] I didn't have no ambition to look further ahead and see where I would end up. I didn't realize then that you don't get something for nothing and that I had to pay—one way or another. Some of them thought they owned me and tried to hurt other women who I lived with. Some had niggers [men] who tried to hurt me. So it looked good at the time, but it wasn't good for me.
>
> I never got married and had a family. Didn't get a education either, and now I'm a doorman at _____ Hotel and wear a monkey suit all day. So this bar is like my second home. I know all the people that come in here. Most of 'em are my buddies. They're closer to me than my own people [relatives].
>
> Everything happens in here. I've seen babies born in here when their moms didn't get the message fast enough and friends killed in here over a silly argument. You can come in here and get help if you need it, or you can come in here and get hurt if you want it. We can tell what you're looking for—trouble or a good time. And you can get either one.
>
> There is a lot of good about this place. You can watch T.V. when yours is broke or in the pawn shop or ripped-off. And you can watch it with your buddies. If you got an emergency, you can always come here and get the guys to help. Many of 'em are always here, and most of 'em are a good bunch of guys. It's a good feeling just knowing that there's always a place you got to go to where you can talk and laugh away your troubles. On the weekend, this place is packed and the babes [women] be looking good and the guys be spending good. The whole weekend goes like a hour. But like everything else, there's always some bad that goes with the good. A lot of the people that hang out in here are hooked on the stuff [alcohol]. You can sit here and see people who are drinking themselves to death. But I guess they'd rather be dead than sober in this fucked-up world.
>
> Me, myself, I feel guilty sometimes about wasting so much time in here. But I don't know much that's any better. At least I ain't on dope or in jail or in the hospital. Nobody is looking for me [for harmful purposes], and I've got nothing to worry about but myself.

It don't sound like much, but that ain't such a bad life, man. If you can get a little happiness out of this short life, that's about all you can expect. There's not much more no matter how you slice the cake. I think sometime I'm about as well-off as anybody else. We're all going the same place tomorrow no matter what we do today.

A "genuine" Black has a distinctive way of entering a crowded bar, cabaret, banquet, dance, musical extravaganza, and the like. He will be sure he is "dap" (neat) and "clean" (dressed) in bold, attractive attire of the latest ghetto fashion. He will enter in a strut (tall, hands slightly behind, arms straight, fingers clutching coat sleeve or in a slight fist). He will sway from side to side as he walks. He will greet everyone he knows or thinks he knows with a jerky movement of his head, arm, and hand, accompanied by a grin. If he discovers someone he knows well, he will move in that direction with loud greetings of "Hey man, my man, my main man, what you doing here?" He will slap the friend's hand, shake his hand, and otherwise engage in intensive physical interaction. He will then stand tall, display his attire, often by opening his coat and pulling it back with both arms as he puts his hands slightly inside his pants pockets (or some variation of this). This will all be performed in as much view as possible of all potential onlookers, who will determine his status by how many people he greets upon entrance. Depending upon that status, they may hope to get him to stop at their location and anoint them with that contagious prestige accumulated in a ritual of intensive interaction.

CHURCH SERVICES

The "Genuine" Church   The churches on North Lang Avenue in Belmar reflect the diversity of the people and life styles that I have attempted to describe in

A "genuine" church on North Lang Avenue

A "spurious" church on North Lang Avenue

this volume. This diversity creates conflict and requires seasonal rituals and ceremonies of Black solidarity in the neighborhood to keep it at tolerable levels.

To illustrate this diversity, pictures of four different churches are presented here (see Figs. 6.2, 6.3, 6.4, 6.5). They are all on North Lang Avenue. These churches are attended by African Americans, and all four are located within approximately a two-hundred-yard section of the avenue. Yet the churches, their services, and the people that attend them are very different. Freedom Temple ("genuine") is a traditional storefront church. Its members practice a Pentecostal religion (see Williams 1974, 1984). I refer to them as "genuine" because they appear to deny, defy, and defile mainstream values. Their services are loud with percussion musical instruments and emotional outbursts. The members speak in tongues and when possessed roll in the aisles ("holy rollers"). They seem to reject mainstream standards of religious behavior. On their building, they have no religious symbols. On the contrary, they announce their church with a commercial soft drink sign and advertisement. Inside, the church auditorium extends to the front door, and when the weather allows, this door is opened to expose their members and services. They welcome neighbors to congregate at their door and to observe or participate in their services. During the offerings, members come outside and solicit from those who are standing on the street and sidewalk. They behave as if the church and the neighborhood were one, as if they belong to the neighborhood and the neighborhood belongs to them. They welcome the interaction between the two. To them, both are "genuine."

Prayer Tabernacle is "spurious." The members are just as poor as those in Freedom Temple, and their church is directly across the street, a distance of approximately 30 feet. But the values of the members in Prayer Tabernacle are mainstream. They announce their church with appropriate religious symbols on their building. Notwithstanding that their auditorium is similar in size to that of

A Catholic mainstream church on North Lang Avenue

Freedom Temple, they do not extend it to the front door. Their auditorium is separated and insulated from the outside in order that one must come in their church to hear and participate in their services. They do not welcome passersby or neighbors into their services. They would not even have their church here if they could afford one in a "better" neighborhood. Each week before services, one of the members arrives to clear the church area of undesirable people and debris. The members of their church think that Freedom Temple is "disgraceful."

Down the street is Holy Rosary. Once a predominantly white Catholic church, most of the white members no longer attend. They have moved away in body and spirit. But the church remains a "mainstream" church, and most of its members identify themselves as middle class.

Approximately 40 yards from Holy Rosary is the Nazarene Baptist Church. It has always been African American, "mainstream," and middle class. On Sunday, the vehicles, apparel, and behavior attest to this.

Religion is the first, the strongest, and the most pervasive institution among African Americans. To be able to observe "genuine," "spurious," and "mainstream" behavior in these religious contexts assures me that these are meaningful and useful explanatory categories notwithstanding their value-laden defects.

A Baptist mainstream church on North Lang Avenue

HEALING IN THE "GENUINE" CHURCH

Healing in the "genuine" church operates within the intense communalistic atmosphere of church life itself. Furthermore, the church's teachings on the conduct of life in general are arguably conducive to good health, at least in certain respects. These teachings are compounded of Biblical references, interpretations of these within the canons of fundamentalist Christianity, and cultural traditions deriving from the Southern Black ancestry of the church members. Members do not drink alcoholic beverages or smoke in public. They do not attend evening parties or engage in an active night life. They can retire to sleep early on most evenings when there are no church services. Their food-tastes include garden foods in a greater variety and abundance than is typical in the ghetto, and in season, they often grow their own. One member boasts that he can eat cabbage every day for his evening meal (although the mode of cooking, with excessive salt and fat will no doubt influence the nutritional value of this food). The other tendency in eating habits which may be maladaptive is that of occasional overeating. Slim bodily forms are not aimed at as an ideal.

The general state of health or well-being of the church members will, of course, have some influence on the efficacy of the healing practices performed within the church context. This may be the relevant background against which to consider the members' claim that "the body heals itself." Many ailments are minor and run their course in a week or so. Others are due to stress, and the church services provide excellent cathartic releases for such stress. Faith, or belief, in God and His ministers certainly does have an impact on the sick person's handling of ailments. In any case, all results, whether recovery, chronic illness, or death, are finally interpreted as "God's Will" and seen as part of God's overall plan. For church members, death means that as a reward for their saintly living they will go to Heaven. Thus, in this sense, the prognosis is "good," regardless of whether the patient gets better or not. (Whether this in some way may lead to a fatalistic attitude toward illness is another question.)

Older members expect to have "tired old bones," and they plan and discuss their forthcoming funerals while they are still reasonably well. At the same time, they request, and receive, lengthy "prayer lines" during services when the minister asks if anyone needs prayer. Thus, old people both accept the inevitability of their demise and attempt to prolong their lives, within the understood framework of "God's plan."

We give now three case histories of apparent cures that have been effected through prayer, according to the participants themselves. How these accounts are to be evaluated is a separate question. From the standpoint of biomedicine, certain conditions might be more susceptible to cure through faith (or mental concentration) than others. But from the actors' viewpoints, such a distinction is unlikely to be made, since the aim is both to get better, for whatever reason, and to validate and strengthen one's own system of beliefs. The latter desire itself motivates people to claim that they have been cured and to vacate their "sick role."

Case 1   Jodie and several of his siblings were born with herniated navels. The family was too large and too poor to afford the simple corrective surgery needed. The parents had been advised that the "rupture would go away" as the children grew. The parents and many of their friends and associates in Zion also believed that hernias would heal themselves in time. The children were taken to church regularly, and during these church services, the children had many occasions to be taken through the "prayer lines" that are often conducted in the church. These and other prayer events are not designated for any specific ailment but are for the general well-being of the members.

One day after many of these prayer services, Jodie noticed that his hernia was gone and that his navel looked normal. He was delighted because whenever he went swimming or dressed and showered during school physical education activities he had been embarrassed about his protruding navel. Jodie now believed that the prayer had succeeded. Jodie's parents also believed this. They refused to discuss or consider the concomitant "folk wisdom" that the child simply "grew out of it." They were convinced that prayer can help the body to cure itself.

Case 2   The next experience (that I describe) is the healing of an allergy. Flossie, a 27-year-old woman, suffered severe hay fever in the spring and fall and sinusitis, postnasal drip, and frequent bronchial inflammations all of the year. The trauma from these conditions caused Flossie to have frequent colds and bouts of influenza. For six years, she sought relief from doctors and allergy specialists. For one year, she took a weekly battery of allergy shots from an allergy specialist who was located in the Jenkins arcade in downtown Pittsburgh. This was considered a prestigious location for medical specialists, and the costs were staggering to Flossie's budget, whose sole source was from her position as a nurse's aide in a local hospital. For two additional years, she was treated at the University of Pittsburgh student health unit while attending the University. Nothing worked. The prognosis was that she would suffer for life, and only a minor level of relief through drugs was certain.

Flossie had no alternative but prayer. She began to rely on it more and more. Every opportunity for prayer in the church was taken by Flossie, who now felt betrayed by the biomedical world. She had been bold enough to enter that world and persist with treatment in spite of the taunting she received from her parents and fellow members in church. Now, after a biomedical failure, her faith was renewed and was at its strongest. After several healing ceremonies, her allergy became less severe. The hay fever shortened its duration in the spring and the fall. Later, it disappeared entirely in the spring. Finally, it became so mild, even in the fall, as to be hardly noticeable. With the disappearing hay fever, the sinusitis and associated medical problems lessened. Flossie became self-conscious about the allergy medicines she carried at all times. She eventually became concerned about the age of the unused medicine, and her parents encouraged her to begin to discard it. She was reluctant and uneasy, but she was also amazed at her own progress.

This healing process was so gradual that Flossie was surprised by her new state of health. She had taken the small improvements for granted but had not expected them to remain. Finally, when it was obvious that she had been healed, the memory of the past made her reluctant to bask in the full joy of it. Did the healer succeed? Did the body heal itself? Is the process more complex, including, possibly, both? Perhaps the body healed itself with the aid of prayer, altered habits, and time. Flossie thinks it was God and prayer.

Case 3   Josie, a 45-year-old woman, had had a benign stomach tumor (professional diagnosis) for three years. The doctors had advised her to have it removed with surgery. Josie was afraid of surgery because she believed that, once air "gets to your insides," if the surgeon does not completely remove the problem, the problem "gets worse." She was also embarrassed by the protrusion of her stomach that the tumor caused. Josie has stood in many prayer lines without most of the people knowing her specific ailment. But at a special healing service with Elder Champion (see his description below), he announced to the audience that Josie had a stomach tumor.

Elder Champion administered to Josie for 25 minutes at the healing service. He asked her to walk, run, and jump. He told her to bend her body as far forward as she could. He required her to profess her faith, to retrieve his thrown handkerchief, and to allow him to touch and rub the approximate afflicted areas. After these exercises, Elder Champion prayed for Josie for approximately three minutes with the participation of the audience. He then declared that she was healed and told her to go forth and serve the Lord. Josie took her seat and from this time on she served the church in any capacity requested of her.

From my own observation, Josie's abdomen did not decrease in size. But she appeared healthy, and she no longer accepted doctors' care. She and the members of Zion believed that she was healed. Josie behaved as if she were healed. I have had no further evidence that she is not. She remains active and involved in the church.

Elder Champion is a renowned healer in the church. He had his own church in Detroit, Michigan, but he is a traveling evangelist, as well, who journeys to the various churches in the international organization to lead fund-raising events. Elder

Champion is well compensated for his efforts by offerings and a percentage of the funds. He came to Pittsburgh to liquidate the mortgages on the church.

Elder Champion is a short man of five feet and three inches. He weighs approximately one hundred and sixty pounds, and he is very agile. He has black hair that he stretches from the left side to cover his bald crown. He has a mysterious look in his eyes and enjoys toying with people and patients. He loves an audience. They enjoy seeing him perform his healing rituals.

When Elder Champion came to town, the members were very excited by his arrival. They communicated the news throughout the city. Every night of his healing service, there was standing room only. People came from throughout the city to watch and to be healed.

Each evening before the healing ceremonies Elder Champion would conduct a regular church service. During these services, he would raise the funds for the debt service. He had great patience during these exercises; and after everyone had given, he would walk around the church personally collecting money to reach a certain goal for the night. As he walked about exhorting the members and visitors to give, he would tease and joke with them. The audience enjoyed this informal contact with him. Most of Elder Champion's time was devoted to raising funds. So from 9 P.M. until after midnight, there was no healing. Shortly after midnight (a bewitching hour to some and bedtime for some curiosity seekers), Elder Champion would ask the members of the audience about their ailments. Those whom he chose to heal he would call to the front row. A few patients associated with church dignitaries would already be sitting there. After the patients for the evening were all seated, Elder Champion amused the audience by joking and playing with some of the patients as they sat and waited. Such humor delighted everybody because the auditorium was tense with excited anticipation.

As he administered to the sick, he continued the drama. He would ask them to retrieve his handkerchief that he had thrown to the floor. Some would be requested to walk to the rear of the auditorium. Others would be asked to run. Some would be relieved of their crutches and canes. All of them would be engaged in extended conversations about their illnesses and about their faith. All would be touched, anointed with oil, and "prayed for." Most appeared to be healed and most acknowledged the healing by running, jumping, and being possessed by the Holy Spirit. The session would end at approximately 2 A.M., and some of the patients were always forced to go home before this, because of the lateness of the hour. But the drama and the excitement and the faith in the possibility of cure motivated the sick and the curious to return every night.

The excitement of such visits by Elder Champion remained even after he had ended his "healing revival." People talked about him and his behavior and his healing for months afterward.

SUNDAY SERVICE

Sunday is a day of dress and human drama in Belmar. "Genuine" and "spurious" children and adults model their attire, shoes, and hair styles along the streets of

The last white church in Belmar

Belmar, in front of the church buildings, and at the bus stops. Their "Sunday clothes" or "dress clothes" tend to lift their spirits and reinforce their sense of identity. Many walking the sidewalks slow their pace as they pass storerooms and parked cars to get a glimpse of themselves in the windows. Some are vain enough to focus the exterior automobile mirrors upon themselves to get a better look. Few are quick to enter church before the services or to depart after them. They linger to talk, interact, and display themselves in their "best" image.

Inside the church, the parade of clothes continues. Every head seems to turn as people arrive. Sometimes they turn to speak, nod, wave, or otherwise recognize those who are entering. At other times, they look to be sure who attended so that they can report to their friends. But always, they notice the attire. Some dresses are "too short," some are "too long," others have clashing colors. The hats, the hairdos, the shoes, the coats, the jewelry, and the suits are all important in this weekly fashion show.

When the minister calls the audience to the pulpit to pray, one often wonders how many parade forward from all parts of the church auditorium (sometimes even a balcony) specifically to display themselves in their Sunday attire (this may be especially true of the teenagers). The ushers, deacons, trustees, ministers, and "mothers" move about the church auditorium in full exposure to their audiences. And such movement and minimeetings with other church officials document their role and status as well as their stylishness. The seating arrangements reinforce and validate positions. The choir and chorus are decked in colorful robes, and the pastor wears his usually more elaborate and expensive one. The choir sings its songs. The pastor tells the news of the week, often sprinkled with the humor the audience loves. The ushers march and collect the offering. The minister preaches. The choir sings. Some members are overwhelmed emotionally. The pastor calls for nonmembers to join the church. The people are dismissed, and they begin a period of interactions with one another that in some cases extends longer than the services themselves. After such a period, the parade of clothes and shining cars begins anew. The sidewalks and bus stops are filled with people whose brightly colored attire somehow gives a special meaning to Sundays in Belmar.

TEENAGE PARTIES

Every weekend, groups of "genuine" teenage boys comb the Belmar neighborhood in search of "parties." Most who attend such affairs are invited or recruited by word-of-mouth. But there are always those who do not "get the word," and they must roam the neighborhood to search out the "happenings." Such "happenings" are not difficult to find because the crowds that spill out into the street and the amplified music that booms out to everyone within a hundred feet make it easy to identify the "scene." These affairs are usually planned and financed by the females and their families. Often a girl and her friends will plan and publicize a party with financial help from their respective parents. The affairs are not expensive, as only limited amounts of food and beverages (if any) are expected to be provided, depending upon the financial status of the families that sponsor them. They major requirements are record albums and shelter. The girls pool their music supplies and borrow others. Often, the guests bring their own favorite records. The males always bring their own alcoholic beverages and seldom come in anticipation of dining.

An outsider might wonder what attracts 50 to 100 teenagers to such affairs, in which the dimly lit rooms are jammed wall to wall with guests and the air therein seem to be 60 percent smoke. One might also wonder how anyone can dance on such crowded floors with almost zero visibility (especially for those guests wearing sunglasses for style). But this is all part of a glamor that transcends reality, a euphoria that is reinforced by the captivating rhythmic sounds that explode upon one's senses. In such a state, the guests seem to be dancing by instinct or long-entrenched habits of movement that require no conscious thought. Even those who mill about outside seem to be engulfed in the atmosphere which is accentuated by the large group of people to interact with and be a part of.

Inside, the ritual and ceremony surrounding the disk jockey provide the only contrast to the otherwise dark, hypnotic atmosphere. The disk jockey must know his "sounds." He must know the techniques of providing continuous music, often with the use of two turntables. He must be adept at alternating the speeds and amplification from one turntable to the other. He must be sensitive to the moods of the crowd in alternating between slow and swift beats, jazz and blues, rock, rap, and classical upbeats. He must select music from piles of available disks and often respond to the demands of onlookers who seem as fascinated by these procedures as they would be with a live band. It is amazing to watch him control, simultaneously, his audience, disks, turntables, amplifiers, drink, and cigarettes.

These scenes are the subject of discussion for several days and the impetus for the next person or group to plan the following party. They keep the marauders combing the neighborhood every weekend. They give substance and content to these young people's lives, substance and content that may be absent in the institutions of an oppressive society that impinge upon their daily lives.

This social interaction is part of the learning process as well as the reward that supports "genuine" learning. It demonstrates to teenagers that "people who love people are the luckiest people in the world." It helps to provide techniques and strategies for manipulating one of the few resources available to them in Belmar— people. It is the context for courting, for having companions of the opposite sex, and for arranging future rendezvous. It is another bit of evidence of the quality of life here in Belmar, evidence that helps me to sustain the conviction that it is not inferior.

STREET CORNER BOYS

Teenagers, just like flying insects, are attracted to the bright lights of the neighborhood grocery stores. The street-corner boys spend hours after dark congregating and interacting with one another. Such crowds are often so large as to interfere with the access to the grocery stores themselves, and the proprietor must continually ask the boys to stop blocking the entrance. Not only do these teenage males interact with each other, but they delay, engage, tease, taunt, cajole, court, and seduce others who are attempting to enter or depart from the store. These frequent encounters create a lively scene as the members of such gatherings seek to entertain one another and enhance their own social prestige.

Often rendezvous are arranged here, and future meetings at the store or at a different location (many times at or near the local schools) are also arranged. This activity tends to explain why so many teenagers, especially females, find it necessary to go to the store four or five times during an evening.

The interaction here reminds one of that of the street-corner men, and a good case can be made for the enculturation that occurs here for future roles. The conversations are loud. The laughter is boisterous. The ridicule is rampant. Many stories are told which are sprinkled with the untrue. Jokes are shared. Information is communicated. Exploits are recalled. It is a rich example of peer-group identity and an effective learning situation.

Here one can observe much of the style of ghetto behavior. There is continuous touching of one another in conversation and at approach and departure. Laughter is a major ingredient of the communication. There is constant sharing of confections which are purchased within the store by members of the group or by shoppers. Often, bottles of soft drinks, concealed within brown paper bags to create a suspicion of alcoholic beverages, are passed about from person to person as within a wine-drinking group. I am sure the similarity of procedure is not by accident. Members of the group will usually examine the purchases made by another teenager in order to beg or interact. This is a frequent mode of interacting with females, and they have grown to expect it. (Many of them conceal chewing gum and cigarettes, attractive items which they do not want to share, before they depart from the store.)

In the light of day, the area around the store can be compared to a disaster area in terms of the debris that accumulates there. The entire sidewalk is covered with discarded chewing gum that has been pasted down by the pressure of shoes. Empty bottles stand against the store walls still wrapped in the brown paper bags. Confection wrappers of all kinds litter the area, and broken glass is sprinkled about, evidence of the bottle-hurling excitement of the previous night.

Thus, it is that a small commercial enterprise designed for limited trade purposes in Belmar becomes a major social enterprise and demonstrates some of the techniques and procedures that the residents use to manipulate their limited resources into meaningful ways of life.

CHILDREN'S GAMES AND PLAY

. . . If the games of children . . . be examined with an eye to ethnological lessons to be gained from them, one of the first things that strikes us is how many of them are sportive imitations of the serious business of life. (Tylor 1958:72)

. . . Man has been described as the most playful of all animals (Homo Ludens, Huizinga 1955). At any rate, playing and games are among the cultural universals in all mankind. (Murdock 1949, from Dobzhansky 1966:213)

. . . It is curious to see that when growing civilization has cast aside the practical use of some ancient contrivance, it may still survive as a toy. (Tylor 1960:174)

I will describe here some children's games and play from Belmar. These exemplify the distinctive behavior and interaction of this "genuine" subculture (see Hartley et al. 1952).

I have suggested elsewhere (Williams 1974, 1989a, and in this case study) that "poor" Blacks, denied ready access to "mainstream" middle-class status, economic mobility, and a range of institutional resources tend to sustain their group solidarity by combating the social distance inherent in American social and economic mobility. Some of the instruments and mechanisms for such a process are institutionalized patterns of intensive personal interaction as well as denying, defying, and defiling of "mainstream" cultural values (Williams 1974, 1984, 1975). I suggest that this latter phenomenon may not be restricted to oppressed Blacks, but may extend to other subcultures (Williams 1989).

One approach to examining such a thesis is to investigate instruments of socialization among the children to try to determine whether there are patterns of learned interaction in childhood which prepare the children for adult roles in distinctive institutionalized behavior (see Erikson 1970, Lehman and Witty 1927, Piaget 1951, Piers 1972).

Games are a form of play. Play among children is usually a voluntary, and to some extent pleasurable and transcendental, form of behavior which is not consciously utilitarian. The proclivity for play is a biologically inherited characteristic of the class of mammals. It seems to have survival value for primates (see Caillois 1961, Huizinga 1955, McLellan 1970, Norbeck 1974, Riezler 1941, Robbins 1955, Sutton-Smith and Roberts 1963). Human play is culturally expressed and varies, like other human behavior, from society to society and perhaps from social subsystem to social subsystem. The nature of play in each society seems congruent with pervasive values and attitudes in that society (see Roberts et al. 1959). It is one of

Developing majorettes at the recreation field on North Lang Avenue

the assumptions here that this congruency can be found within social subsystems of such societies.

Hide the Belt   This game is the epitome of intensive interaction. It is part of a social syndrome in the poor Black ghetto in which one or more persons become the object of pain, mental or physical, for the excitement and enjoyment of a group.

Verbal games such as the "dozens," "chumping," "razzing," "rippin'," as well as other physical games ("hot hands," "kuncks," and the like), are significant elements in this pattern. This syndrome is evident in adult life when on Friday, Saturday, and Sunday, members of the ghetto neighborhoods converge on the "avenue" to see and be involved in "who's gon' get punched out" ("cut," "done in," "stabbed," "shot," or "killed tonight") as a climax to a session of intensive human interaction. The aggression of Blacks against Blacks in the urban ghetto is part of a pattern of interaction that is fostered in their life styles and is one result of their distinct political and economic statuses within their respective societies.

A group of seven to sixteen children decide to play "hide the belt." They select a base (a porch, stoop, or corner) and someone to hide the belt. Unlike most games I have described here, in this game all the members are anxious to be "it" because being "it" gives one the privilege of hiding the belt (see Gump and Sutton-Smith 1955). One of the children brings out a leather belt from his house, usually one that is thick and substantial, used at home for punishment. Often a preliminary to the games is the emotional discussion surrounding the beatings at home that are usually inflicted by the object on display. In these discussions, the children whose parents own the belt take pride in desribing the punishment they are subject to at home which they are stalwart enough to withstand. One of the most persuasive children (because of size, strength, or other characteristics of prowess or influence) convinces the others to allow him to be "it." While the others turn their faces to the wall, or otherwise hide their eyes, the child hides the belt. After the belt is hidden, he signals to the others, and they hunt for the belt. As the children hunt, the person who is "it" calls out the names of those closest to the hiding place and describes them as "warm." As the children move about the vicinity of the hiding place, they are described as "warm," "warmer," "cold," "colder," "hot," "real hot," and "burning up." These descriptions cause rapid movements. When a child is described as "warm," the other children immediately move near that child to make their own search. As children get "warmer," there is a great deal of hesitation, indecision, and dilemma evident in their movements and their facial expressions. These are moments of intense excitement as they try to decide whether they should continue to look for the belt in the "warmer" or "hot" location and accept the risk of others finding the belt before they do and, thus, being beaten with it or whether they should move back toward the "base," where they can be safely off limits from any beating, when the belt is found. For the object of the game is to be the one who finds the belt and, therefore, the one who beats all the other children with it until they are safely on "base," then, the finder has the privilege of hiding the belt and, thus, being least likely to be beaten in the next session. During the period when some of the children are being described as "hot" and "burning up," only the most courageous children pursue the search. The person who hid the belt and the more timid souls remain in easy accessibility to the "base." These are moments of intense anxiety. There is pushing, scuffling, and scrambling among the most-competitive children. The climax of emotions arrives when one finds the belt and begins to beat the others mercilessly until they are safely on the "base," and sometimes after they have arrived while those secure, near, or on the "base" jump with ecstasy. The person who finds the belt now hides it again, and the game proceeds in this fashion until someone is hurt, disgruntled, or persuaded into physical combat by the children on the group because of a severe beating.

Tin Can Copper   A group of ten to twenty children decide to play tin can copper as soon as it becomes dark. Two or three of the children search for a discarded tin can whose top has not been cut completely but whose contents have been emptied. The searchers usually return with two or three usable tin cans; one is used and the others held in reserve, in case the first one is thrown beyond recovery. If the cans found have already been cut open, their lids are broken off.

With the prescribed can in their possession, the children gather in the middle of a street intersection where a manhole cover is clearly visible, usually by means of a nearby street light. The manhole cover is called the "base." The group decides who is the first to be "it." They usually choose one of the children who is younger, undesirable (in the hiding tryst), physically inept, overindulging (in disputes), or anxious enough to play that he would be willing to make the sacrifice. Otherwise, a more equitable decision is made by tossing coins or a baseball bat. The decision having been made, one of the boys with the strongest arm throws the can as far from the base as possible into one of the streets, and while the designated child chases it, the remainder of the group hide. During these periods of hiding, there is a great amount of intensive interaction. The girls and boys romance each other. The boys discuss among themselves their recent exploits, sexual and otherwise. The girls engage in conversation also, and certain groups plot access to the "base" without being caught. For if one is sighted by the person who is "it," his name is announced loudly as the can is pounded against the manhole cover, "Tin can copper on ____." Usually, if one is the first to be "caught" (at the discretion of the person "it"), he is the next person to be "it." This means that everyone attempts to stay securely out of sight so as not to be the first "caught." As the game proceeds, thorough searches are made for the hiding children, and several of the group are eventually "caught." This leads to one of the highlights of the game. For, as they are "caught," they group themselves on one of the street corners and wait to be rescued by their fellow playmates so that they will be able to return to their hiding rendezvous. This is accomplished by one of the "uncaught" children's clandestinely catching the "base" guard inattentive, racing to the can sitting unguarded on top of the manhole cover, and throwing it again as far as possible, while all those who have been "caught" are allowed to hide again. The "base" guard is, thus, required to guard the can sitting on the manhole cover at the same time that he must cautiously venture out to discover the hiding places of his playmates. He remains "it" until all his playmates have been "caught." This usually means that whoever is designated as "it" will usually remain "it" throughout the evening, until he quits in disgust or with outcries that "they're cheating." A skillful guard, however, sometimes catches all his playmates and is, thus, relieved of his duty.

This, too, is a game of intensive interaction in which the players literally run over one another "getting away to hide." The game is also another example of the mental anguish of one ("it") for the pleasure of the group. Often, the group enjoys the protesting and disgust of the exploited child ("it") more than the running and hiding itself. In this game and others, the children often become so involved in interacting that they forget they are involved in a game. Sometimes, this also causes "it" to quit in disgust.

Cut the Corner   A group of ten to twenty-five children can play the game "Cut the Corner." They select a street intersection with four sidewalk corners. One of these corners, where there is the least risk of an irate resident, is called the "base" or the "corner." Then, by one means or another—decree, tossing a coin, tossing a baseball bat, or coercing the most gullible, anxious to play, or inept member of the group—someone is chosen to be "it" to guard the "base." The game begins with the entire group, except the guard, standing within the parameters of the corner; upon a signal, all those on the "base" scatter into the streets with the guard in chase. If the guard is able to touch any of the scattering group, they are "caught" and must return to the "base" until liberated by another member. The guard remains "it" until he catches (touches by hand, and this often means a good pounding) every member of the scattered group. It is difficult for the guard to "catch" all the members of the group, for one of the objects of the game is for those who have not been "caught" to seek every opportunity to dash across the diagonal of the corner ("cut the corner") without being touched by the guard and, thus, set free all those who have already been "caught." This means that not only must the guard periodically give chase to a daring liberator in order to capture him, but he must also take care not to venture too far and leave his "base" unguarded. A significant pleasure of the game, and others described here, is the ridicule, laughter, and humiliating chiding of the guard, or his frustration when he has "caught" most of the group only to have them liberated by a strategic maneuver of a swift adversary. Those who have been "caught" yell stratagems to their potential liberators as they wait to be freed. Others who are "caught" take this opportunity to interact playfully with one another while awaiting liberation. This game, somewhat similar in principle to "Tin Can Copper," is often ended when the frustrated guard quits in disgust after arriving at the conclusion that he will never succeed in catching the entire group.

Again, in this game, we see the victim-for-pleasure syndrome that is pervasive within the poor Black neighborhood. This syndrome results in children's encouraging "after-school fights" and providing the large audience that enjoys and sustains them. Members of other groups in America enjoy their victims vicariously or in more subtle ways, but the ethos is the same in a ruthlessly competitive society. The poor Black child who is not aggressive will be a permanent victim. He will be exploited in games, beaten after and in school (for the most unreasonable excuses), ridiculed about his physical features or his clothes, and "ripped" daily concerning his mother, sister, grandmother, and father. He must be "bad" to survive. If he is "bad," he will fight back, "rip" back, and will have a temper that will protect him even in play. His teacher may call him unruly, but he is actually well adjusted.

Buck T Buck   A group of 14 to 20 boys have two group leaders select competing teams for "Buck T Buck." After the two teams are chosen, a coin is tossed and called by the leader to determine which team will be the "goat." The team designated as the "goat" forms a line starting at the wall of a building and usually extending out as far as the curbstone. The leader stands with his back against the wall, his hands placed at his abdomen with palms out to grasp the head of the next member in line as that member bends forward with his back horizontal, his hands against the wall or around the waist of the leader, and his legs stretched widely apart. Each succeeding member of the team places his head between the legs of the member in front of him, with his back horizontal and his arms wrapped around the spread legs of the one directly in front of him. This formation creates a line of horizontal backs which the opposing team will ride.

The leader is the first to ride. He stands far back in the street and takes a running jump as high and as far as possible onto the opposing team's backs. He does this in order to leave sufficient space for all of his teammates to sit (otherwise his team forfeits the ride). Each of the team members successively takes his running jump, each getting as close to the front as possible. When all are seated, the leader of the riding team extends from one to five fingers, at his own discretion or at the specific urging of his teammates, in view of the leader of the opposing team. The crouched members of the "goat" team must accurately guess the number of extended fingers of the opposing team's leader. Each time the guess is in error, the riding team disembarks and jumps all over again. The object of the game is to ride the "goat" as long as possible. There is a great excitement created by the collapsing goats under the crushing bodies because each time the "goats" collapse, the riding team gets another opportunity to jump without risking the guess of the fingers. Only when the "goats" hold their riders securely do they get an opportunity to guess "how many fingers are up." When the leader of the riding team extends his fingers, he calls out, "Buck T Buck, how many fingers are up?" The members of the riding team have to watch that the leader of the "goat" team does not pat his feet or signal with his hands how many fingers are being exposed to him. If the "goat" team guesses correctly, the riding team becomes the "goat." The game proceeds in this manner until someone is hurt or disgusted.

The term "riding the goat" is considered a harsh adult initiation ceremony within secret fraternities, according to several informants. This game must be adequate training for that initiation. Training in this kind of endurance for enjoyment, comradeship, and competition is a fitting prelude to the adult lives most of these children are destined to live. The child learns early to live and endure a life of police brutality, prison torture, economic degradation, social humiliation, political powerlessness, institutional inaccessibility, and denial of freedom.

A characteristic of this game is intensive physical contact even to the point of crushing pain. This close physical contact is a consistent feature of games (football, wrestling, boxing, all of which are frequent preludes to a fight) in this neighborhood, as well as an abiding characteristic of poor Black social behavior. This feature extends also to elaborate forms of greeting (hand slapping, elbow touching, "butt bumping," and the Afro handshake) as well as forms of dancing ("slow drag," "grinding," and "doing the pussy"). Such proclivities are mechanisms of socialization which operate to restrict the development of social distance accompanied by its decorum, poise, and formality.

"Fart" Play   A group of boys stand on a corner (or in school or other settings), interacting in laughter and conversation. A lull occurs in the interaction. One boy with a deliberately placid face and motionless body releases a loud burst of flatulent gas from his anus, creating a sound that the others immediately identify and react to by loud laughter, moving away from the source, holding their noses. The laughter is joined in by all and is accompanied by body jerks synchronized with the bursts of laughter, allowing the entire body to move in support of the jovial feeling. After several minutes of reaction to this first "fart," the laughter subsides, and now each boy in the group is determined that he too will attempt to generate an equal response by a louder, more-animated, and more-sustained burst of anal gas. Each act is responded to with similar reactions, although some of the acts get greater reactions than others because now each boy is listening intently for the variation, intonations, and frequency level of the sounds and is prepared and anxious to react. After a period of about 20 minutes, the boys have exhausted most of their resources; then, for effect, they not only engage in flatulence but accompany their releases with the appropriate body positions (for example, head forward, the leg lifted to the side, and so on). This continues until all of the boys have spent themselves. Then, the activity shifts to belching, which takes a similar format. And finally, the play ends with artificial flatulence which is performed by the rubbing friction of the palm of one hand against the underarm area. Such friction creates similar sounds and variations of flatulence.

This play is clearly offensive to the sense of decency in the larger society. It seems to be organized behavior which socializes Black children to enjoy the animal nature of their bodies in spite of the sanctions within "mainstream" America.

Discussion   One of the abiding characteristics of the play and games described here and others played among ghetto Black children (for instance, the "dozens," "ripping off," "signifying," "sounding," and so on) is the systematic exploitation, humiliation, and degradation of one or more of a play group for the pleasure of the other members of that group. Often, this takes the form of consistently selecting certain appropriate members who fall prey easily, but actually every member of the play group can and does periodically provide pleasure for the group by his own suffering. This too suggests to me instruments and mechanisms for combating social distance among the members of these play groups, which will set the stage for similar adult roles in institutionalized behavior (see Bett 1929, Douglass 1931, Riezler 1941, Williams 1989a).

A neighborhood grocery store

The children concentrate upon games that give an opportunity for interaction—often to the point of mental or physical pain—and allow the players to demonstrate how much punishment they can endure. These games and pastimes appear to be adequate socializing instruments for children destined to live much of their lives in priksons, ghettos, and tenements, or otherwise denied access to the economic, social, and institutional resources that are flaunted before them as norms of the wider society.

These Blacks exploit games and play for intensive interaction. The rules and ceremony of the games are secondary to the opportunity for arguing with, laughing with, humiliating, and touching one another. Often the action, interaction, and expressive style become so intense that members periodically forget that a game is being played.

I have tried to describe briefly expressive representations of subcultural behavior in the games and play of children. Their forms may be diffused and pervasive, but the styles are distinctive. I have attempted to explore the possibility of observable relationships between these selective children's games and the distinctive patterns of behavior within the subculture. I emphasize the exploratory nature of this effort.

These children's games illustrate the adaptiveness of man. Black children play in an urban ghetto with limited space and few recreational facilities. Blacks are isolated and denied access to the economic, social, and cultural resources of the wider society. Yet they thrive, and the idiosyncratic elements of the games they play seem to be consistent with a socialization process uniquely designed for the subcultural and structural dynamics of later life.

It is apparent that child training, health, and growth, to which games and pastimes are major contributors, have ramifications in the complexities of culture. This is an important consideration in my desire to compile more raw material for the functional analysis of children's games and pastimes so that their origin, diffusion, persistence, modification, and extinction may be progressively better understood. Furthermore, the impact of cultural change may not be as immediate upon children's games and pastimes as upon other activities. These games may thus serve as indicators of cultural configurations of the past that exist among distinctive activities of more recent times.

CHILDREN IN SCHOOL

As I have mentioned above, the school in Belmar provides much opportunity for observing behavior. I have been a participant-observer on the school grounds as a neighbor and inside the school as a substitute teacher. My exposure here has been supplemented by substitute teaching in other public schools on the periphery of Belmar and in Black neighborhoods throughout the city of Pittsburgh. I will describe here some brief encounters.

The school children of Belmar reflect the variations in the population. Many arise on school mornings on their own initiative. They must provide themselves with a meager breakfast, if any; decide upon grooming procedures, if any; and depart on time, if at all. They must select their clothing for the day from a small collection of soiled, unpressed, and worn clothes. Their parents have already left for work, have never returned from the night before, do not arise that early, or are awake but just never participate in this preparation process. These are households where the level of resources and the concomitant attitudes obstruct or prevent such participation. The standards that motivate preparing children for school are not operative here because of the disjunctures in their normal life styles. These children often arrive at school with uncombed hair and with remnants of bedding on their clothes. They are unwashed and ungroomed. Their clothing is often in disarray. The neglect of such children seems thorough to the "mainstream" eye. They are malnourished and unmotivated in scholastic goals. In their peer-group interaction, they are constantly abused. They are "sounded" upon and "ripped" often until they are forced to respond with violence. They are often the objects of disdain from the school's staff, faculty, and administrators.

There are other households where the parents rise with the children or before to ensure that the children get an appropriate early start. They supervise their children's selection of prepared clothing and monitor their grooming procedures. They prepare their breakfast and give them a final check before they depart for school.

Still other households have eager parents who do not only participate in all these preparations for school but also provide them with school supplies, the containers to carry such supplies, and their personal protection to and from the school building. These parents are acquainted with the school personnel and are familiar faces at all school affairs.

Most children come to school unchaperoned. They are assisted only by the nonchalant and perfunctory supervision of the school guard. The school guards cross them at two intersections where, in most instances, the children could cross themselves without the aid they seldom get. The two school guards assigned here are relaxed about their responsibilities. They are "genuine" Blacks, and they spend most of their time conversing with teachers, staff, administrators, neighbors, and favorite students and their parents. This leaves little time for guarding the crossing children. These guards almost never stand in the intersection with their arms outstretched stopping the vehicles as the children cross. On the contrary, they are on the corner or as far as 30 feet away from it talking and merely indicate to the children when they can cross themselves. Often, the children miss these vague cues and signals and use their own initiatives in crossing. If such initiative results in a threat of danger, the guard then becomes indignant and abuses the children for such "dumbness." Throughout this process, favored "mainstream" students receive favorite treatment. The denial of institutional resources to ghetto Blacks is pervasive, even at the hands of their own people.

Candy, potato chips, chewing gum, and other confections deluge the school buildings and grounds every day as supplements and substitutes for meals. Thus, during the day and after each school day, the school grounds, corridors, and classrooms are cluttered with the litter of these wrappers and containers. It is one more way for these children to demonstrate that this school belongs to them, in spite of the institutional cues and sanctions. It is denial and defiance of "mainstream" standards of behavior by the young Black generation in Belmar.

Most children enjoy attending school notwithstanding the obvious pressures. But this enjoyment is usually not of academic pursuits. It is of the process of interaction with one another. Thus, the school grounds, corridors, lavatories, and classrooms are rich contextual milieus for such interaction. Quiet study is an imposition and an effort for most students. Such study requires that the teacher be well organized and have her daily schedules well planned. This planning aids in suppressing bursts of energy and interaction among the students and may set the atmosphere for large portions of the class time. There is the constant danger from the teacher's viewpoint that an eruption or interaction on the part of some students will be perceived by other students as an opportune moment to reinforce the disturbance. The eruption can then escalate until the classroom is a chaotic scene of intensive interaction perceived by the students as an effective challenge to the teacher's authority and ability. One student may make an animal noise in the quiet context of study; another will laugh at the sound. Encouraged by the rewarding laugh, that student or another will make another sound to obtain a laugh. This time, more students laugh, and others laugh at the laughter and the disruption. The further this process escalates, the more difficult it is to control. One student may touch another and the one being touched screams in indignation, not to express pain but to become the center of attention with a justified alibi. The scream is recognized by the other students for what it is designed to do, and they all cooperate by reacting appropriately. Often, students will stage mock fights that the teacher considers serious but which are designed to create pandemonium. After the teacher mediates the dispute, the students have a laugh about the entire episode. Students have a keen perception of the gullibility of teachers and will exploit it to the fullest.

Students are required to suppress energy most of the school day, and they seek constant opportunities to release it. Thus, students will attempt to engage one another throughout the day. Often, by the time the teacher discovers these engagements, they are well advanced toward disrupting the class. These persistent minor engagements carry the ever-present threat of involving the entire class. This, then, is a stage where such dramas are forever being attempted, and the tension of controlling them can destroy the will and tenacity of teachers incompetent to deal with them. Teachers must be sensitive to all the precipitating clues and capable of disarming them before they detonate. Such teachers are eventually recognized by the students as formidable and are seldom put to the test. Others are called to battle every day until they are defeated and must rely upon appealing to the students or placating them for their cooperation. This often means that certain potentially disruptive students have more power in the classroom than the teacher.

This social context for teaching often means that an ineffectual teacher spends most of his time controlling behavior and little time teaching. But there are techniques for utilizing such proclivities among the students in the execution of teaching activities. In the teaching of various subjects, problems can be written on the blackboard which require several steps in their solutions. A student can be selected to come to the blackboard and solve the problems until he makes an error in the process. Then, he is asked to take his seat, and another student is permitted to come forward and continue the solution. This procedure is continued until the problem is solved. It has been my experience that the students wave their hands enthusiastically to be selected and are very attentive in this kind of learning experience. They have a sense of interacting with one another, and this sense is being translated into learning. Other techniques that I have found useful involve allowing the students to come to the front of the class in groups and act out certain performances related to the lessons being taught. The students that are seated are very attentive to their peers, especially if they are invited to detect mistakes in order to replace them. A certain level of noise is controlled by the admonition that the "game" will cease if that level rises.

I have never seen students more adept and skillful at manipulating the behavioral dynamics of their classrooms. It is one of the tragedies of institutional dominance from the wider society that these skills are not developed in ghetto schools but are suppressed and interpreted as delinquency. Left undeveloped, these skills get more disruptive as the children become older. In junior high school, among students of 13 to 16 years old, these disruptions can reach such a level that they appear as violent rebellions. I have seen students in classrooms, who had become confident that the teacher could not control them, develop disruption into a frenzy of intensive interaction that looked like a violent television or movie scene. Each one attempted to outperform the others in acts that denied, defied, and defiled the classroom setting. The student audience encouraged the behavior and reinforced it whenever possible. In such frenzies, chairs were thrown across the classroom, ostensibly to strike another student but not intended to make contact. Boys participated in animated wrestling, lifting one another and pretending to slam each other to the floor with a ferociousness that equaled a staged television fight. Other boys threw one another against the walls, making loud sounds that gave impressions of crushing one's opponent. With most of the students engaged in this kind of activity in a classroom, normal classroom activities had no meaning for them. Pieces of chalk were used as missiles, as were blackboard erasers. Yardsticks were used as weapons. Boys made threatening sexual gestures at the girls, causing some of them to escape into the corridors for safety. Most of the students realized that this was a staged drama, but they acted as if it were real. Such scenes continued until a person of authority entered the classroom. To a teacher unfamiliar with such behavior, this could be perceived as a riot, and the students, I am sure, intended to communicate such perceptions. To participate in such activity in a classroom in the presence of a teacher was considered a rebellion by those students participating and observing. This was a drama being acted out upon alien soil to react to the institutional framework which that setting represented.

Several teenagers in the neighborhood are high-school dropouts, and some of them attend a federal manpower trainee school located in a different neighborhood. I followed them there to make some observations on the experiences of these select young Blacks. As a teacher in this school and other public schools in the city, I made some observations based upon these experiences as well as on my knowledge of the neighborhood students aforementioned. The descriptions here are another example of how the people of Belmar are perceived and manipulated by those in the wider society.

The manpower trainee is typically the student who has been previously disenchanted by the formal system of learning in our public schools. He has discovered that the learning process and the behavioral system validated and legitimized in this institution are alien to the rewards he has learned to value and to the capabilities that have been reinforced outside the formal educational structure. As a consequence of his disenchantment, he has usually sought means of learning other than the formal educational structure in our society. He has left school and begun to work. He has refused exposure to an irritating formal learning process and has been incarcerated because of that refusal, or he has exhibited such defiant behavior during his former classroom experiences that the instruments of the formal educational system have been successfully used to exclude him. The manpower training program attempts to collect this discarded human debris of our formal educational system and to resocialize it in the values of learning. This time, the rewards offered (money) are more immediate and more meaningful to the student. The context of learning itself is more individualized, less structured, and more personalized. The idiosyncrasies of the various students are tolerated in the classroom, and there are emotionally supportive personnel utilized outside the class. Otherwise, the materials, goals, and values of the formal educational system in our society are about the same. The student is expected to develop his language, mathematical, and scientific skills and is rewarded by symbolic evidence of his mobile status in the educational structure.

The manpower trainee, because of his past adult-like experiences in achieving status outside the formal educational system, is highly conscious of his own symbols of adulthood. He is motivated to display characteristics recognized as those of being a "man" (adult) whenever possible. He is very sensitive to any evidence that he is regarded as less than a "man." His broader experiences have been packed with efforts to demonstrate among those with whom he interacts that he has developed the characteristics that validate and legitimize him as an adult. Unfortunately, our educational system is not very amenable to the nature of these individuals. It is an educational system steeped in the ideology of patron-client, sage-neophyte, parent-child relationships. The language, dress, and behavior of the teacher are usually a reflection of this ideology. Thus, in spite of the efforts to create a different learning atmosphere for this special kind of student, the traditional classroom symbols are pervasive and defeating.

The inadequacies of this program should not overshadow its successes. The program itself is a fitting tribute to the efforts in our society to attempt to reach again those individuals that our educational system has failed. It is another effort to change the learning process in such a way that it takes into account the nature of the individuals involved in that process. Thus, the rewards (wages) and the supportive direction, as well as the teaching procedures, have been altered for this program. The program is one of the many searching experiments to make formal learning in our society more meaningful. The teachers and other personnel involved in these efforts deserve much praise because they are faced with the difficult task of trying to alter the characteristics of an institution of American culture and society. Until we change the values in the larger culture and society, it will be almost impossible to create meaningful change in the instruments and mechanisms of formal education.

This brief introduction to my observations will, I hope, help the reader to understand my interpretations of classroom behavior. My experiences in the classroom have been limited and highly structured (among federal manpower trainees and as a substitute teacher in the public schools). But I operate under the assumption that there is a certain unity and consistent pattern of human behavior wherever one finds it. Thus, my observations under these limited conditions and my conclusions about them may have some value for understanding the classroom as a system of social behavior.

The ideal teacher brings to a classroom stimuli and materials for learning. The teacher is a catalyst for generating energy that is to be directed toward the process of learning. He/she is a symbol of the rewards, satisfaction, and joys of full participation in the learning process. He/she comes to a classroom materially prepared, emotionally keyed, and energetically endowed to instruct his awaiting students. The material he is to present is not the end in itself, but it has been prepared as one item in a total process of persuading others about the joys, satisfactions, and rewards of learning. Thus, the material for any classroom presentation should be designed for presentation in such a manner as to make that presentation appealing and interesting to the students. The students should have an awareness of how such material relates to their own system of meanings, and they should be convinced that such material has a significant impact on the system of meanings of their teacher. Such an approach to a classroom situation gives a teacher a certain element of control over classroom behavior. A group of students confronted with such a potentially rewarding package are apt to await in anticipation of all of the contents therein. A teacher endowed with such a commitment and preparation is likely to demand a certain level of respect from his students. Such preliminary behavioral control is a tremendous asset to any potential problems of classroom discipline.

Classroom discipline is a complex exercise in human behavioral dynamics. In the inner city, among a predominantly poor Black student population, such as that of the manpower trainees, social interaction is one of the prime mechanisms for adaptability. The average student who has reached high school has been socialized in the process of a high level of intensive social interaction as a means for most of the rewards that are accessible to him in his social milieu. The inner city is a conglomeration of human subcultures, some of which thrive on a high level of intensive interaction and cohesive social networks. The student brings to the classroom the product of a socialization process steeped in these behavioral dynamics. He is extremely keen and sensitive to all the cues of potential interaction with his fellow students. His teacher, if he is to control his classroom, must also have that critical awareness of such interactional cues. For example, if a teacher comes to such a classroom bent on a formal classroom atmosphere (partially because of his own feelings of insecurity), he will perhaps generate suspicion among his students that he is unsure of himself or irrelevant to the real world. These are students who place a high premium on the ability to intensively interact and excel in the very process of that interaction. They are likely to test the teacher's self-confidence with their familiar interaction process. One student will give a signal, a cue for the interactional participation of the other students. Depending on how the teacher responds to that signal, other students may or may not continue such signals. This test may lead to the breakdown of the teacher's control of the classroom by means of a spontaneous interaction of all the students with each other in defiance of the teacher's presence, or it may lead to a demonstration of the teacher's self-confidence and his ability to handle such interactional cues. This awareness of the nature of one's students lends itself to the exploitation of such propensities, expertise, and values for interaction for the learning process itself in the classroom context. In other words, the teacher who is aware of and capable of channeling such a tendency for interaction into classroom exercises has begun a process of creating a most-effective learning environment for the nature of the students within that environment. The classroom material can be presented in the form of hypothetical interactional questions. Students can then be asked to analyze such questions. Students can be allowed to examine the material itself vis-à-vis other students in the class; thus, we utilize a process familiar and rewarding to the students themselves. The critical point I make here is that one must be aware of the nature of one's student population.

This awareness includes some determination of the level of growth, development, and personality of the individuals who make up that population. Students in secondary school are adolescents usually in a transitory development stage from childhood to adulthood. In our culture and society, there is no formal rite of passage for such a transition. This results in the individual use of a diverse range of mechanisms and instruments to validate and legitimize this transition. An adolescent is usually very sensitive to an overt, awkward, and unnecessary threat to his self-image. Such a threat is a challenge to his approaching status of adulthood and may seem to him a "put down" toward childhood. Depending upon the level of insecurity or agitation of that student, he may react violently or make a systematic attempt to undermine the classroom demeanor. Students at such a level of developmental growth, then, should receive reinforcement of their tenuous rite of passage, for this, too, is an available force that adds significant energy and thrust to the total learning process.

This process should have another important ingredient. The relevance of all material to the student's life and the student's future must always be established. An intrinsic ingredient in motivation, curiosity, and commitment to materials is a broad relevance to the student's immediate goals and his future rewards. The smallest component of academic materials can and should be placed in the context of the larger picture.

When we look at the larger picture, we inevitably see the themes in our institution of education and in the American culture of which it is a part. We live in a competitive society. We socialize our children from an early age in the values of prestige, status, recognition, and relative position. Our classrooms should utilize these proclivities if they are to be realistic. We must reward with prestige, status, recognition, and relative position the motivation, curiosity, and propensity to learn. This can be done in a variety of ways. The teacher must develop the ability to saturate his classroom with those rewards that are appropriate to the nature of the student he teaches. He must convince his student that the techniques of research open doors to fascinating domains of human experience and discovery. He must persuade his students that products of curiosity have led to much human satisfaction and continue to promise the highest intellectual rewards. Unfortunately, he must do this in spite of the values that dominate our institution of education in American culture and society.

The institution of education determines the teaching setting. The traditional classroom may not be the ideal learning context where intellects are stimulated, respond, and interact. The competitive nature of differential achievement in the traditional classroom setting may not be functional for developing the humility in the scholar eternally seeking knowledge and perhaps even truth. This means we have to decide what formal education in America is designed to accomplish. Are we training and socializing the individual as an instrumental cog for our economic system? Or are we developing a human mind sensitive to discovery and eternally searching for human meaning in human experiences, past, present, and future?

COLLEGE-BOUND STUDENTS

We often refer to the subculture of African American students in an abstract context. But we need to recognize the concrete manifestations of that subculture if we are to be supportive and effective educators of these students who represent the pool from which our middle class will emerge. I will attempt a brief example here.

The children of my "genuine" African American informants in the anthropological studies that I have completed (Williams 1981, 1984) grew up in homes where deadlines are not perceived as they are in middle-class majority homes. In such majority homes the deadlines for the payment of bills are often just an aggravation—a time that one must sit and write the checks for the month. The resources are there in the form of a checking account with an automatic credit card loan for an account that is overdrawn. Shopping for food, clothing, and housewares is organized for convenience and not for a pending crisis.

But for many "genuine" African Americans, deadlines for rent, electric, gas, telephone, installment loans, insurance, and the replenishment of food are often ignored, as are the rituals of scheduled mealtimes. The basis for this inattention is not negligence, irresponsibility, or indifference; on the contrary, it is a psychological survival tactic. Parents who can pay their bills and buy food only on certain days of each month when their incomes arrive would be unduly stressed if they were attentive to deadlines that they could not meet. Such stress and tension over long periods of a lifetime would be emotionally unbearable. So these parents focus their attention not on such deadlines but on the days that their resources (pay day, check day, or the income of others) routinely arrive. On such days the obligations of bills and food shopping are regularly satisfied. Thus the deadlines imposed by creditors seem to be ignored. They are not. They are merely organized into a psychological and functional pattern that is consistent with the life styles and resources of the people involved.

If the children of these "genuine" African Americans matriculate to college after being socialized in their homes for eighteen years, they require special orientation on deadlines. They must be resocialized about them. Otherwise, such deadlines will be unconsciously perceived as general expectations that must be eventually satisfied but not as specific requirements of appointed days and hours. If pressed, these unoriented students will merely repeat what they have heard their parents explain for many years, "I don't have it, but you'll get it as soon as I do." They will expect paper extensions, make-up exams, lab rescheduling, and even postponed graduation requirements. It will not matter if they are told orally and in writing that these will not be forthcoming.

If we are to recruit and retain nontraditional college students, we must understand their subcultures and be prepared with understanding and fortitude to introduce them to a new culture.

Last, the classroom may be viewed from many perspectives. It is a teaching setting; it is an interactional group; it is a competitive enterprise on an academic level; it is a microcosm of our educational institution (and as such reflects and manifests many of the dynamics of the total culture); it is a series of groups (as two or more individuals bring to the situation relationships established outside of the classroom); it is a material setting with distinctive symbols, cues, and stimuli (depending on the arrangement, certain signals and cues are manifested in the classroom decor); it is a human phenomenon. The classroom is a setting for social interaction as well as for academic pursuits. Several individuals of varying personalities, propensities, inclinations, motivations, capabilities, social backgrounds, and human inadequacies take part in a structured interaction, and the teacher must understand the social behavior of his or her students before effective teaching can take place.

Any brief discussion of such a complex behavioral system must exclude significant analysis. But any examination of the classroom context must, of necessity, be directed from various perspectives. This brief discussion has attempted an overview of some significant behavioral dynamics. Perhaps, it is some indication of the complexity of the classroom phenomena. Each and every characteristic of that teaching context has profound impact on the learning process. The material to be presented and the manner of its presentation; the organization of the classroom setting itself; the sensibility, empathy, motivation, and preparation of the teacher; the profound impact of the themes in the institution of education in the wider culture and society; the established social networks of the classroom students; and the individual personalities of each member of the classroom all culminate into a dynamic behavioral system which defies adequate analysis, yet requires profound understanding.

The "genuine" ghetto child does not take dancing or acting lessons. He does not have a piano, clarinet, or violin teacher. He will not spend the summer at camp nor the winter in Florida. He does not sell newspapers or work in his father's store after school. He does not sing in the church choir or act in the school drama group. He is not in the school orchestra, band, or debating team. He has only himself and his peer group. They must create devices for amusement, entertainment, stimulation, new experience, conceptual growth, and play. His playmates are denied the institutional resources that contribute to the socialization of average white middle-class children. But isolated from and denied these resources, he and his peer group do provide for themselves. All they require for engrossing entertainment is themselves.

MARGINAL ENTERPRISE AMONG THE AGED

In a society that emphasizes achievement, competition, success, status, fame, money, wealth, recognition, possessions, property, prestige, and power, the poor

Construction of the new low-rise for the elderly—the old scene

Completed low-rise for the elderly—the new scene

and old are especially left in abandon. They are expected to retire from their occupational productivity on the theoretical wealth, property, and money that they have accumulated over their productive years. Regardless of the incongruity of a human retiring from his lifelong interests at an arbitrary point in his life and of the poor accumulating much of anything, the expectations are the same.

But these expectations have a by-product. Not only are the aged in retirement assumed to be within a distinctive human category, but that category also accrues much behavioral indulgence and relaxation of social control. A category with such altered attitudinal flexibility allows its members to participate in marginal activities that would be inappropriate for younger members of the society. Here, I describe one such activity—the collection of pop bottles.

On any given day, one can see an old man or woman scavenging through the streets and alleys of Belmar. Some are in time-worn trucks collecting iron or rags, others have pushcarts, toy wagons, or collapsible two-wheel shopping carts, and they are collecting soft drink and beer bottles or newspapers. Some sell them for income; others store them for companionship and security. The activity and the people are a part of the character of the neighborhood and, as such, give it a distinctive nature.

There are large numbers of young unemployed men and women in Belmar, but their ethos and attitudes demand that they refrain from marginal and unrespected activities such as collecting soft-drink bottles. The remuneration from such efforts can never be attractive enough to overcome the stigma of the potential embarrassment. As one unemployed young man in Belmar expresses it:

> Man! I wouldn't be caught dead pulling a wagon with pop bottles in it. People would laugh me outa town. I need money, but not that bad, and I damn sure don't need that kind of money. I'd go hungry first.

Well, those old people can get away with it. People don't care what *they* do. They're two steps away from the grave anyway. Nobody pays them any attention. But let me try it. Many a times I needed cigarette money and I was too shame to take my own bottles back [to the grocer for the deposit refund]. Now, you know I ain't about to collect other people's. I even know some little kids that won't be caught taking pop bottles back to the store.

And the old man, John Collier, who practices the business sees it about the same:

You know, when you get old, things ain't what they use to be. I woulda been too proud to do this when I was a young buck, but now the old man do what he can and he don't worry about what people say. Money is money. It don't matter how you make it, as long as it's honest work. At least I ain't stealin'.

John Collier is 74 years old. He is six feet and two inches, even though he is slightly bent with age, and he weighs about 190 pounds. He says that all of his children are grown, and none live in Pittsburgh. Even the foster child he reared from the age of eight after his own children were adults is an adult himself and is making the army a career. John has been married twice, and he lives now with his second wife in a high-rise building for the elderly. He receives a welfare check to supplement his small Social Security check, and he collects empty soft-drink bottles to add to both.

Each day, John leaves home about seven o'clock in the morning. He takes a toy wagon which he found discarded and broken. The wagon has a body about two feet wide and four feet long, and it is supported by replacement wheels that do not match. In his wagon, he carries a large potato sack and several folded supermarket paper bags. He goes in a different direction every day and spends most of his time combing small streets and alleys to collect the discarded bottles. The large bottles bring ten cents each and the small ones five cents. John can recall making other discoveries during his trek. These are the bonuses for a human scavenger. He sometimes finds wallets, jewelry, returnable beer bottles, and other discarded items that can be taken home and repaired. John says he investigates all potential valuables. Sometimes, he brings home an interesting piece that supplements his collection of bottles.

Each day on his journeys, he tries not to get farther away from home than will allow him to return for lunch, and he plans his route for such a return. He likes to enjoy lunch (sometimes only a cup of coffee) with his wife. Otherwise, she would get lonely remaining home all day by herself. Many of the bottles that John collects have to be taken home and washed before they can be sold. The beer distributor who purchases them will not accept those that are not cleaned. But John does not mind this labor. It helps to fill his life. It makes him feel worthwhile, and as he himself expresses:

A man who has to sit home all day with his woman starts to feel like he's not much good for anything. I think a woman appreciates a man more if he goes out every day and brings something home. Even if it's not much, it still looks like he's worth his salt. It makes a man feel like a man if he faces the world every day and tries to outsmart mister hardtime [economic disaster]. And then, in my kind of work, you run across a lot of sights during the day. You see a lot of people, people doing all kinds of things. It makes your day and fills your hours. When you get back home with the woman, you have something to talk about. And then sometimes you pick up something for the old woman that you can clean up or fix up and give it to her and make her feel good. We can't buy much on our little money, so something you pick up—a bracelet or necklace or purse or ring—even if she don't use it, makes her feel good. People don't think much of what I do, but every day I got some place to go and something to do. You'd be surprised at how much that means to me. The children get grown and you don't hear much from them or see much of them, and you have to kind of make your life for yourself. I think I do a pretty good job.

I don't have to worry much about people bothering me because when people see what I do for a living, they figure I don't have anything to take and some even go out of their way to help me. If they know about some bottles some place, they will tell me. Some people even call me to their houses and give me bottles in their kitchens or their cellars. Sometimes they have bottles stacked up there and they are too lazy to take 'em back to the store. Then I got friends up at the beer distributors' where I take my bottles. They know me and I know them, and I stop in there two and three times a week to cash my bottles in. Then there's a lot of people around this neighborhood that see me and know me because I been coming around here a long time.

I carry this sack and these bags to keep the bottles from breakin'. I put the bottles in the bags and then I put the bags in the sack, and that keeps the bottles settled down when I pull the wagon over rough streets and sidewalks. Most days I collect three and four dollars worth of bottles. Sometimes a bit more and sometimes a bit less. And like I say, sometimes I pick up things, but that's not very often.

So John Collier has a marginal occupation and enterprise. But it is one that is despised by most people in the neighborhood. Perhaps they do not realize that John can earn $25 to $30 a week. This is a substantial supplement to his meager income.

Alice Berry is a woman of 67. She weighs approximately 207 pounds and stands five feet and six inches (she is noticeably bent and crippled with arthritis). She has never been married and has no children. She lives alone in a rooming house. Alice also collects and sells soft-drink bottles but not as frequently as John. Many days her arthritis "acts up and get her down."

Alice collects bottles as frequently as she is able because she believes that the exercise "helps" her arthritis. Yet the primary reason she collects is the extra income it allows her with which to support her church. It also "gives me something to do." You can often see Alice moving slowly through the streets and alleys of Belmar with her collapsible two-wheel shopping cart. Her bottles are also protected inside paper bags. You can frequently see her standing partially supporting herself on her cart to rest after a short walk. And sometimes, you can find the neighborhood children taunting her, but she is a religious woman with a large supply of patience. So Alice's life, too, is partly filled by her marginal enterprise, although, unlike John, she has a religious life that occupies much of her time. Her comments were similar to John's when queried about her activities. They are two residents of Belmar who engage in a marginal enterprise, which gives us some clues about the subculture in which they live as well as the unique positions of the aged in that subculture.

Another marginal business practiced by retired men in Belmar is the delivery of a weekly Black newspaper. There is not enough traffic through the neighborhood to establish newsstands at strategic corners as occur in other neighborhoods, so those engaged in the newspaper business here must deliver from door to door. This is also a despised enterprise among those men who are yet in the labor market and is only practiced by children and the retired.

Since the newspaper comes out only once a week, the men can take three or four days to complete their large routes, return where necessary to collect their money, and yet have two or three days to rest from their activities. This pause is apparently very meaningful to these elderly news carriers because I have never seen one delivering a daily newspaper.

You can often see the familiar sight of one of them, bent over from the weight of two bags of papers, with a large stick for the dogs and to balance the weight, and with the steady gait of one determined to complete his route. These men also establish meaningful relationships among their customers and along their routes. The business becomes a significant part of their lives.

FUNERALS

My observations of funerals in Belmar can be divided into two categories—those of the lower class and those of the middle class. (The "spurious" are usually restricted in their behavior here by cost and limited social network, in spite of their aspirations to mimic the middle class.) Funerals among the lower class tend to be rites of intensification and solidarity. Whether or not a person has been sick a long time before death, the demise usually demands a large sum of money that is not frequently available among the members of the lower class. Thus, death among these people means an immediate scramble for funds to provide for an appropriate funeral. A funeral is the one ceremony that must be done in style; as a consequence, most kinship members are willing to contribute to the funeral, since the deceased in most cases did not have enough burial insurance or savings to provide for it. This means immediate telephone calls, often to Detroit, Chicago, New York, Atlanta, Richmond, or Montgomery, to notify the entire kinship network of the death and to communicate the need for required contributions. This financial contribution is in itself a demonstration of family solidarity in a crisis. The next phenomenon of sharing is to provide for "putting up the kinfolks" as they converge on the city and the neighborhood where the funeral and burial are to take place. Relatives get together and decide who will take whom so that as the kin begin to arrive, they have assigned places to stay among the kinship network. Petty squabbles and large feuds are put aside for the funeral ceremony and the rituals thereafter. The kinship network begins to cooperate as they would like to see the family cooperate upon their own deaths. As the relatives arrive with their respective contributions, family meetings take place to decide upon the kind of arrangements that will be made for the deceased. Those who contribute have "something to say" about those arrangements. And in most cases, it seems to be the responsibility of the older women to make the decisions about such matters. The men are able to make suggestions, and in the case of a highly respected male, those suggestions may have a great deal of influence, but most of the time it is the older women who make the final decisions: What kind of suit will the deceased wear, and is his own suit adequate? If not, is there a relative who can give him a suit? For, in most cases, any unnecessary expenses are avoided, and the purchase of a suit in a situation like this would be an unnecessary expense. Will the deceased wear his glasses? Who's going to drive their cars? Who's going to ride in whose car? These are all decisions that have to be made by the older women. In most cases, the choice of a funeral director is not an important decision. In Belmar, as in most poor Black neighborhoods, there is a funeral director who has a reputation for burying the poor Black, and it is usually that director who is called upon after the demise of a "loved one." The older women ensure that all the associations that the member of the family belonged to are notified of the death. In many such cases, such associations will contribute flowers, pallbearers, and often small monetary donations. Representatives from most of these associations will also attend the funeral.

If the deceased has a large and intensively interacting kinship network, very little use will be made of the funeral director's home. This is perceived by the family as showering the deceased with love, but in effect, it means that the funeral will be less costly. The body can be laid out in the home of a family member, and all the relatives and "well-wishers" can come and pay their respects and view the body in the home. Likewise, if there is a large kinship network, one of the members of that network is in all probability a member of a church. If that person is a stalwart member, he can probably get the funeral held in his church, if the deceased was not a member of a church himself and automatically eligible for a church funeral. This means that the funeral services will not have to be held in the funeral home, and again, the cost will be less. If the deceased does not have a large kinship network and is not a member of a church himself, the funeral can be held in a funeral home. In such cases, it is usually a small affair without a large attendance. In any case, the members of the immediate family and the extended family who are available will take part in the funeral and the ceremonies thereafter.

Another consistent pattern upon death is the contributing of food to the immediate family of the deceased. Such food consists of all sorts of cooked meats and

One of few remaining businesses on North Lang Avenue

fowl, fish and vegetables, liquor and beer, soft drinks, and, when in season, watermelons and cantaloups. Such contributions are made by kin and friends alike. Neighbors, distant relatives, and members of associations of the deceased contribute food and drink for the traditional ceremony that takes place after every funeral. The rationale for such contributions is that the members of the immediate family of the deceased should not have to prepare food the evening after the funeral. Most funerals occur at one o'clock and most ceremonies end by four. Friends and relatives can then return home, usually to the house where the deceased lived, and begin their feast and festival (see Williams 1974 for the description of an actual funeral).

The feast begins as the members of the immediate family, the extended family, relatives, and friends arrive at the home of the deceased. If the deceased had no stable household or permanent residence, then one of the immediate family will provide a household for the feast. The older women who are not members of the immediate family begin to prepare the feast; often, these women have remained at the household setting the table and organizing the food in such a way that it can be served efficiently when the people arrive. These older women are excused from attending the funeral because such duties and obligations have to be fulfilled. Everybody understands. The immediate family is served and, then, the extended family; after all the relatives are provided, the closest friends and neighbors and members of associations and churches are fed until everyone in the house has food. This often means that there are "hangers-on" who drift in, even though they may have known the deceased only very casually or not at all. But at moments like these, very few people take the time to investigate a person's actual familiarity with the deceased, and if he happens to be there while there is still food being served, he will be served. During this time (and continuing the rest of the evening and sometimes on into the early hours of morning), there is usually a special room or two set aside for the consumption of liquor, and the appropriate people are continually being notified where the room is located. Usually, the older women, the church members, and those people who are affiliated with churches are tactfully kept out of the vicinity of that particular room. It is usually located on a different floor of the house, so the drinkers have to move away from the general body of people and go to the appropriate place. During the early hours of the afternoon, very few people are aware of the location of the liquor. Although everyone knows that liquor is being served somewhere, they wait patiently to be notified that they have the right to enter the sanctuary where the liquor is. At first, only a favorite few of the immediate relatives and kinship network are permitted to drink, and of these, only the ones who are known to drink. This includes some of the younger women, and often one or two of the older women will slip in and out. But as the evening grows old, most of the original liquor is consumed, and then, it is necessary to take up contributions among all those people who are interested in drinking in order to provide more liquor. This broadens the range of those who are now entitled to drink because, of course, everyone who contributes is included. And as the evening grows into the early hours of the morning, there are very few people who are not drinking.

As the evening ends, the older women begin to clean up the kitchen and the dining facilities and prepare to leave, knowing that their job has been well done.

They are thanked warmly by the members of the immediate family and often are encouraged to take some of the food that has not been consumed as a token of thankfulness. By the early hours of morning, only the drinkers are left, and frequently, out of respect for the immediate family, the party is taken to another household of one of the kinsmen. As one can imagine, during the late hours of the evening, the celebration takes on partylike characteristics, where people are reacquainted or meet new people; often, new relationships are established which last for a long, long time.

A middle-class funeral in Belmar is similar to most middle-class activities. It is designed to establish, validate, and reinforce class status. Among the Black middle class, rites of passage have established procedures which have not been altered in the transition from lower to middle class. But in spite of such procedures, the primary consideration among the middle-class funerals is status consideration. Thus, if the deceased is a member of the middle class, even though all the kin are notified, it is often hoped that those relatives who are not members of the middle class will not come to the neighborhood where the funeral procession is to take place. If such kin do attend, they are in most cases relegated to minor roles in making the decisions about funeral arrangements. One will discover that those who are making such decisions are the older women who have established themselves as staunch members of the middle class. Funeral arrangements are made according to proper taste and decor. Thus, the funeral director who usually serves the lower class is seldom selected as the director for the middle class. Members of the middle class usually select a funeral director who is a member of their social group and well known for his middle- or upper-class status in the community.

A middle-class funeral can be discerned not only by the director who is selected, but also by the type of funeral involved. One purchases a metallic casket. The deceased is buried in the proper cemetery and must have a headstone. One takes great pains to have the proper people attend the funeral and the ceremonies after. The funeral is an elegant one. There are many cars involved, and the cars are expensive; there have even been funerals where there are nothing but Cadillacs or Cadillacs, Imperials, and Lincolns. Such funerals are a sight to see, an occasion of great moment, and something to talk about for months afterwards. In the ceremonies after such funerals, not only are the "right" people invited, but large numbers of people are invited. In most cases, this means that private halls must be rented to provide for feeding the guests; otherwise, community associations or churches provide large halls. In any case, it is typical to see large gatherings of 200 people being served after a middle-class funeral in the Black community. If a middle-class funeral is held at a household, it is usually in an elegant household. One of the members of the family who has the "best" residence is the locus for such a ceremony. The last funeral I attended was after the death of an elderly man who had several married sons and daughers. The funeral feast was not held in his own household, which was by all standards a middle-class household, but in his daughter's large, new home that could seat 50 people in her gameroom, 25 in her garage, and 40 in her rear yard, not counting the living room and dining room space. At such a funeral, one's status determines one's greeting. Those people considered to be lower on the social ladder get a very slight greeting or no greeting at all. Those at the top of the social ladder receive elaborate greetings and are escorted throughout the quarters where people are congregating, to make sure everybody knows that this person of high status has taken the trouble to attend this function. I have witnessed middle-class funerals where members of the immediate family "who have not made it" are ostracized at the funeral ceremonies because they will pollute the social status of the other members of the family who have "made it." So, funerals are no different from most middle-class activities. It is a ritual and a ceremony to validate, reinforce, and perpetuate the social status of the people involved.

Among the middle class, the bodies are very seldom "laid out" at home. They are normally "laid out" in large parlors in the funeral director's home. The immediate family designates specific times for visitation, and they or their representatives are there to greet the guests that come during those hours. Again, this ceremony at the funeral home appears to be primarily designed to expose to one's friends and associates the evidence of one's social status, to greet and support the members of one's class, as well as to comfort the "loved ones" of the deceased. I have noticed on several occasions among middle-class gatherings at funeral homes before the funeral during visitation periods that specific people are designated to go to the home of those of the immediate family after visitation hours to have more intimate interaction. But these people are selected very carefully and number only a very few; again, such invitations reinforce and validate status.

So we are able to see once more how Belmar residents use the vicissitudes of life to reinforce social identity, notwithstanding the predicaments of too much social distance within too little geographical space.

LAUGHTER

In Belmar, uninhibited laughter functions as a social lubricant and interactional catalyst. As indicated above, intensive interaction is a critical component of distinctive "genuine" behavior. Such intensity requires mechanisms and techniques to maintain itself. Laughter is such a mechanism in Belmar. There are several varieties of laughter that can be observed in this neighborhood. All of them have the common characteristic of being uninhibited, uncontrolled, and total, in terms of "putting everything one has" or involving a complete emotional release in the process of laughing. I have seen groups of females engage in this kind of laughter: In the process, they raise their hands above their heads, and while still laughing, they fall into one another, embracing each other and supporting one another with the hands and arms on one another's shoulders or around each other's waist, giving the impression that the emotional outburst is so complete that as it comes to an end, they require actual physical support. Another form of laughter is accompanied by waving of the hands and the arms, as in a good-bye gesture. This usually occurs between two people or groups of people, where one of the parties, by waving his arm and hand, is communicating to the others, "Stop, you're making me laugh too much." A third form of laughter is accompanied by a staggering motion, as if one is intoxicated. The limbs and the body go completely limp, and one staggers around in an area very close to where the action is taking place. This kind of laughter is indicative of the person "being completely broken up" by the statement or the gesture which is the source of the laughter. After staggering around, momentarily reacting to the humor, the person comes back to the group and takes his normal posture. Yet another form of laughter is when the individual shakes all over his body. The person in the situation seems to be purposely shaking his head and shoulders and arms and stomach and lower trunk in a synchronized motion with the laughter itself. There is a form in which persons standing in a group abruptly fall back from the group ten or fifteen feet as they laugh, and as the laughter subsides, they again converge into a group. This can be repeated several times as the laughter continues. Another form of laughter is that in which there are only one or two quick jerks, even though the person continues to laugh.

The important consideration is that all these forms of laughter are used as techniques facilitating intensive social interaction. People meeting after not having seen one another for five or ten years will begin and continue their conversation with loud laughter, which immediately dissolves social barriers built up as an intrinsic part of such a long absence. Children of all ages utilize laughter as a means of stimulating other children and adults. Often large groups of children laugh at an adult in order to stimulate the adult's anger at their activity. Groups of children can always create a playlike atmosphere by selecting out one person in the group and encouraging all the other members of the group to laugh at this person. Often, for a period of time, the person will likewise laugh at himself, unless the process continues too long and the group touches upon some area of sensitivity in that individual. I have seen cars stop in the middle of the street, filled with occupants, laughing heartily, at an intersection or the middle of the street, the driver incapacitated by his own laughter for several minutes until encouraged to move by the horns of other drivers attempting to move. It is very common to see two or three people walking together, engaging in a discussion of an event which highly stimulates periodically breaking out into laughter as they walk, and slapping each other's hands in a physical climax, an expression of agreement, repeating this action over and over again for an entire city block. It is common to see people in Belmar greet each other with a laugh, often without saying a word, implicitly realizing what each other is laughing at or about, and being assured that such a laughter will eliminate any formality and social distance in their greeting. You often hear the expression in Belmar, "I laughed until I cried," legitimating and validating the fact that laughter in Belmar is a recognized emotional release that frequently is so traumatic that it makes one cry. I once witnessed a male, 50 years old, walking up behind a female of 30 and tugging at her purse, which she held under her arm. The female turned around excitedly to protect her purse because her first impression was that her purse was being snatched. She looked at the male, and he looked at her. They evidently recognized each other, and without any formal communication whatsoever, both broke into an intense laughter which continued for several minutes. This was a form of adult play, the critical technique here being uninhibited laughter.

Even mundane activities are organized and manipulated into unique instruments of interaction. For example, two cars (containing two occupants each) were going down a Belmar street one Sunday evening when the occupants of one recognized the other. The driver drove directly behind the other and blew his horn in rapid succession. The driver of the other recognized the signal, pulled to the side of the street, stopped and lowered his window. The other driver drove along the side of the stopped vehicle (blocking all traffic), the passenger lowered her window, and the occupants began to shout to one another in friendly conversation. After several minutes, the blowing horns from the obstructed traffic encouraged the two communicating vehicles to move on. This time the vehicle which began in the rear took the lead. Both turned at the next intersection and went to the intersection ahead. Upon reaching it, the following driver began to blow in rapid succession, the lead car pulled to the side, windows were lowered, and the passenger in the lead car hollered out, "What do you want now?" as the following car overtook it without stopping. He was merely causing them to stop in a competitive game to take the lead again. They drove on now in a sort of competitive challenge. Meanwhile, at the last horn-honking session, a woman came outside onto her porch to see if it was her boyfriend signaling her, and another woman raised her third floor window to see if it was her "jitney" responding to her call. When you consider that blowing one's car horn in certain middle-class and upper-class neighborhoods is definitely not used in this manner, I think we gain some insight into the nature of manipulating mundane actions into mechanisms of communication that occur in this Black ghetto.

We have had a glimpse of the activities that socialize Belmar children, as well as those activities that sustain these prisoners of American urban deserts. The resourcefulness makes good reading and often "good times" for those who live here, but the ethic that tolerates this environment for these people leaves much to be desired in this affluent democratic society. A similar ethic tolerates widespread abuses in worldwide environments in order that a few may live in illusions of luxury. Thus, little Belmar is the "mirror of man." We see in this Belmar context how culture has dealt with unbearable existential complexities to create tolerable human ambiguities.

7 / World View of Belmar

. . . In my observation, Black culture is generally humanistic in orientation, and expresses a profound knowledge of the human condition. In particular, the approach to life's vicissitudes reflects this understanding. The Black person's suspicions of others, whether right or wrong, are more often based on knowledge of human nature than of ignorance. (Aschenbrenner 1975:143)

. . . To look at the symbolic dimensions of social action—art, religion, ideology, science, law, morality, common sense—is not to turn away from the existential dilemmas of life for some empyrean realm of deemotionalized forms; it is to plunge into the midst of them. The essential vocation of interpretive anthropology is not to answer our deepest questions, but to make available to us answers that others, guarding other sheep in other valleys, have given, and thus include them in the consultable record of what man has said. (Geertz 1973:30)

There is an ideological tension in Belmar. It is between the damaging consequences of ghetto dumping and economic deprivation on the one hand and the creative energy, distinctive cultural identity, vitality, and methods of "making it" with dignity on the other. The one is instrumental, controlled by forces in the larger society. The other is expressive, controlled by the "genuine" Belmar resident. The two cannot be separated because "genuine" Blacks constitute a subculture in a large American culture. The two dimensions meet in Belmar and in these pages. If it were within my control, I would resolve the tension to create a better fit, but the real world, if exposed here, would not tolerate that distortion.

Therefore, I describe Blacks in Belmar whose struggle for survival is cast in debilitating terms from the instrumental perspective. The meager economic resources here make their strategems and achievements seem miniscule, even to some of them. Yet, they live each day at a time for the rewarding expressive life they create in spite of their oppression. That life gives them hope that "time is longer than rope" and that their chance will come in the "sweet ole by and by."

If we are to understand the people of Belmar, we must examine their ideology. Here is the best evidence of the conversion of stymied instrumental action into expressive behavior. Behavior is intimately related to ideology. It is interesting and necessary to know how some of these residents feel and think about the world they live in. This chapter contains some of the distinctive features of symbolic expression within Belmar. Values, world view, and symbols are revealed in language as we observe verbal and written expression in Belmar. My emphasis here is "mainstream" American values—money, achievement, education, power, and progress—and the impact of these values upon Belmar residents. My approach is to record short narratives and make parenthetical observations about their meaning where necessary in the text. The narratives have been selected from a variety of life styles and social settings to emphasize the range of views in this neighborhood. Yet this range exhibits a unified perception of the evil world, a white oppressive society and impossible "mainstream" expectations. This chapter reaches for the philosophical foundations of the Black experience in Belmar.

Major themes in the feelings and aspirations of Belmar residents contribute to whatever unity exists among these diverse people. I am convinced that although the "spurious" espouse some of these world views, the "genuine" live by the codes as well; and the "mainstream" Black, although removed, is close enough to understand. This consensus gives meaning to the concept of Black identity which is primarily expressive itself. Some recurring themes are:

1. Our neighborhood is a dumping ground for the undesirable (in industry, warehouses, garages, bars, the transient, the poor, the unemployed, the least-qualified teachers and other public service employees, the least-qualified health care personnel, the worst schools and public services, the worst zoning and law enforcement, and the most-deficient commercial enterprises).
2. Our life styles and "race" are expressive dumping grounds for what is undesirable and inferior in a successful white society (see enumeration on p. 26).
3. We must have our own philosophical dreams and orientations to cope in this white society that restricts our opportunities.
4. We must attempt to combat such a system and its values in order to live in it and with ourselves.
5. What we are and what we do is a result of life in an oppressive white society.

As one community leader ("spurious") expresses:

I have sat in many a meeting with all whites who control our destiny, and I could feel that how they talked about Blacks when together in a group was different from what they all felt inside. And this is when they were trying to be kind. They all knew what they were feeling inside, but they had to talk so that it sounded fair. So they played with the words and bounced the ideas back and forth until it sounded fair and intelligent but at the same time meant what they all felt in the beginning: Don't give up any of our advantages over them [Blacks]. And I had to sit there and listen as they screwed us one more time with just the right words so they didn't feel guilty and I would believe that they were trying to the right thing. But I was afraid to say anything because that would just help them to get together against Blackness. I just waited and hoped. It was like being down river from a dam and just a little mistake would collapse the wall, so you were afraid to talk but you sat there and listened as the wall was dismantled piece by piece and they explained the reasons and how unfortunate that it was that some people's lives had to be flooded in fairness.

In other words, when one knows the cues and the codes of the oppressor and of the value system that keeps one in "one's place," one has little power against it, and ironically, one's efforts threaten to reinforce it all.

A community worker ("spurious") who is a former drug addict works with drug addicts in the neighborhood and tells why "his people" and he himself take drugs.

You wanna know why I get high [on hard drugs]? Well, I'll tell you, man! That's the only time this goddamn world makes sense. Then the world's fucked up and I'm fucked up with it and it all jibes. Man! It's like those Asian religious freaks. It's how you get one with the world, with nature, with humanity, and all that shit. Those ese peoples [East Asians] got something. The self, the I, the me is a distortion of my reality. So when I'm sober nothing makes sense. I don't have nothing! If I work hard all my life like my old man [at a menial job] I don't have nothing. If I don't work at all I don't have nothing. If I steal like the rich and powerful I don't have nothing [no access to large resources]. If I get caught, it don't mean nothing because I ain't got nothing anyway. In jail or out of jail, I'm not free and I got the same fight on my hands for survival. What am I living for if not to get high? Come day, go morrow, I got four things I can count on—being poor, Black, high, and dead. The only thing that changes all this is my high.

My high is my dream. Other people got other dreams—cars, money, being famous, gettin' education, being white [middle-class], getting a good job, and all that shit. But it's all a dream because like my high, when you get it, it's over, and wham! and you're right back where you started, needin' another dream. I can't dream their dreams. So I dream mine, and when the shit goes down [in the end], it's all the same. Sometimes I wish I could dream their dreams because I get tired of dreaming mine. It would be a change and not a change because it's the same old merry-go-round. Sometimes I wish there was no dreams and we didn't have to make sense out of all this shit. Then I could live like my dog, day to day, till death do me part.

So, you see, my man, my high makes me free. It's the only way I can chase the American dream. It's the only way I can put up with all this nonsense called "life." Look at it this way. Anybody who can play this game of living in this screwed-up world and do it cold sober is sick, is a monster made by his maker, is fucked up as bad as the world they live in.

Another member of this same group expresses:

Getting high is not an escape from the real world but adjustment to an impossible one. This society asks of us [poor Blacks] ridiculous feats, then ignores our human dimensions and measures us by our successful output. So I accept the crazy challenge in my style. I'm as tall as any with my high. We all have our own kind of high. Some get high on their rhetoric, their rage, their rags [stylish clothing], their wig [varied hairstyles], their women, their church, their music, their wine, their rap [persuasive conversation], their rip [material exploits], and their scene [any combination of the above]. But we all got our high.

Take away our highs and you would have a revolution in this country, because we would then know what the man has done to our song. So the man lets us have our high. He could stop the drug traffic in 30 days, but no, he just pleases the public with those big raids on the little boys. If he raided the big boys, he would have to raid hisself. And that would blow his high.

Perhaps getting "high" is the reason for the portable radio carried by some residents wherever they go. The radio permits transcendence from reality, boredom, dullness, sameness, quiet, calm, loneliness, and truth. It is one of few possessions in an acquisitive society and is a denial of poverty, isolation, ostracism; it is a simulation of action, a sense of belonging to a scheme of things, a symbol of sophistication, an announcement of cordiality, a code for communication, a sign of a predisposition to interact, a conversation piece, a technological contact with an elusive humanity. In this sense, the radio is like a favorite pipe or cigar after dinner, a summer home, a boat, a country club, golf, or tennis. "Me, I jist got my sounds," said one resident.

I wouldn't know how to act without my box [radio]. I got to have my sounds. It's like my man is playin' jist for me, especially when he plays my songs. People respect you when you know your sounds [the latest popular music]. You're drug [considered inferior] if you ain't up to your music, baby. You can take your box anywhere you go and you can forget all the hassles at least for a little while. You jist get into your box with them sounds.

I asked a community worker ("genuine") if he had a philosophy of life after we had discussed the differences between Black and white people. He responded with enthusiasm:

Yeah! I got one. Tomorrow never comes and once upon a time never comes again. We are people who need people and though that gets us in trouble a lot, we're not phony like white people. White people need more money and things and success. People get in their way if they can't use 'em to get ahead. So they smile at you and don't mean it. Ask you how you're doing and don't really give a damn. Watch people suffering in the world and could care less.

He continued to describe how material success and the thrust for achievement tended to dehumanize people. He was convinced that the middle-class perspective was a threat to all mankind.

You see, what they don't understand is that we ain't like them. We don't think like they do. They can go in a room and shut a door and don't come out all day—just reading and writing and thinking about nothing [abstractions]. They come out ready for a cocktail. I would come out crazy. But you put them in a group of people where there's action with no booze and no weed and they're like fish out of water. Put me in there and I can do my thing. You see, I got a feel for people and places that make me a genius, but I can't sell my goodies. So here I am with all this talent that makes me great with the guys and the ladies, but out there [in the marketplace of "mainstream" America] I get no respect.

Yeah, I want my son to be a doctor or whatever else he can be, but I ain't gon lose no sleep over it and he probably won't neither. If he do, he do. If he don't, he don't. It's up to him. I'll help him all I can, and that ain't much. But if he wants to make it, he will and I'll help him. But it ain't no use in kiddin' ourselves, the chances ain't that good. Still, he's my son whatever he do.

How does the resident of Belmar distinguish between the poor Black and the poor white? Golf-Stick George explains:

It's the way he walks and talks his talk. It's the way he wears his rags and if he's got his rap together. If he's got all his shit [all of the above] together, he may be poor but you can tell he's a brother [Black].

The "way he [the "brother"] wears his rags" may mean that his shirt tail hangs out below his jacket, the backs of his shoes are crushed by his feet so that his feet will "slide" into them, shoelaces are untied and dangling over his feet, and his coat, sweater, or shirt sleeves are ties around his waist, a towel lies around his head or neck, and his undershirt hangs out of a rear pocket. This attire seems to visibly defy the characteristics that define him as poor. On the other hand, wearing his "rags" may mean wearing the latest fashions to a major social event. The teenagers say that there may be no difference if:

the cat can do what we do. Can he do it? Then right on [he is just like one of us]. Does he know how? Then, right on. Can he do this [dances in the street some new dance steps]?

"Grandma" is "flesh and blood" and a symbol in Belmar. As a college student who resides here explains:

Grandma with her plug of snuff in her lower lip, her cutout shoes on her feet, and her long make-do apron wrapped around her waist, is concerned about her own world—family, church, neighbors, and relatives in the South. She is a symbol of being Black in America. She believes that time is longer than rope and after awhile and by and by your chance will come. Trouble don't last always. She understands that boys have to sow some wild oats and girls might have to carry the seeds. In the depths of her soul, she knows that her children and grandchildren do not have the opportunities of others, and she loves them for what they are in spite of what they might have been. She can laugh at their shortcomings in such subtle ways that they are encouraged to do better without being humiliated. She can praise their little successes that most would never see.

A church deacon says of her:

She can look out the window and see a thousand miles. She can see things and hear things [that others cannot]. She can read signs and read people. You can't fool them old people. They knew you were lying before you started talking. Something [wisdom] stuck on them as they went through life and at the end they had so much of it that you couldn't help but see it and feel it.

The minister explains:

She communicates a love that defies decoding and she transmits a strength, especially to her daughters, that equips them to one day carry the weight of the world. She is the personification of suffering, the mirror of unjust humankind, the spirit that defies being conquered, the outstanding symbol of the soul of Black folks, the salt of God's earth, who, though disillusioned, lives greatly.

In these pages, I have tried to describe that which may be beyond description in its fullest dimensions. Being Black in Belmar is an experience in living that one feels as well as exhibits. Thus, there are components of this experience that only the poet can communicate. I have consulted, not with the poet, but with a sensitive young college student who explains for herself the feeling.

It is the continuing endurance of hell that began in the slave ships that crossed the Atlantic. It is being poor and yet being able to laugh. It is having the worst jobs and still going to work early so you can drink coffee with the boys. It is payday and suddenly you are as big as the world, although if you knew how to keep a budget, none of the money would belong to you. It is the smell of Grandma's greens and remembering how she use to fuss about the carrying-on. It is reading about slavery and wondering if you will ever be free. It is trusting in God in spite of the world he makes you live in. It is knowing deep down in your Black soul that the white man all over the world is going to get payback one of these days. It is a Belmar ghetto street on a damp, dark, and rainy night where an intoxicated brother assures you that all is well in the world.

Belmar's undiscovered author, a frustrated and bitter postal employee ("spurious"), gives a glimpse in his writings of mankind through the lenses of the poor, Black, and "spurious":

Suddenly, it all changed. He did not care about people. They all seemed grubby, self-seeking, inadequate, materialistic, insincere, superficial, pompous, steeped in intellectual garbage, and ugly in one way or another. Their imminent demise seemed of no great concern.

He no longer cared about the world, and all its problems—energy, injustice, poverty, racial and religious strife, political conflicts, pollutions of all kinds (i.e., drug, population, junk, and sex), and holocaust. He was resigned to the idea that people deserved people and the pain and suffering of human interaction; that nature in its time [soon] would wipe that animal smudge out of the universe—man with all his toys, delusions of grandeur, and inabilities to manage himself and his societies. He asked himself, "All the ugly people, where do they all come from?"

He thought about children who grow up at a heavy cost to parents and then gravely disappoint them; about jobs that seldom satisfy; the new horizons that even if you manage to reach them soon fade in luster or disillusionment. He murmured, "Life is not worth the effort and nature will remove the 'fardels' if man does not beat it to the draw."

He continued to think, "Who deserves to be loved? Do I deserve the burden of loving the undeserving?" He had come almost the last mile in spiritual endurance when he could look back at a "successful" life and see the debris of failure strewn everywhere in the lifelong path he had taken. He looked at the road ahead and was no longer curious about what lay around the bend or over the next hill—the portion of the path he could not see. He was ashamed of being human. He turned to his "boss," looked at him intently, and finally spoke to him. "You are like this society we live in, you have so many ailments that the trauma of really trying to cure you of any of them would kill you. And since it is only a matter of time until one of them destroys you, we can save you the unnecessary painful experience of cure."

The author continues with his statement:

These crazy white m.f.'s destroy everything they touch. I would still be in Africa hunting, fishing, and fucking; sleeping in the sunshine and bathing in the rain. But they stole me and brought me here. I made them rich and powerful and they kept stealing from everybody everywhere. Now they're so rich and powerful that they have stole it all down here on earth, and they are looking for other planets to steal from. If they don't find them soon, they will kill us all in their mad rage to steal from each other things that there is no point in stealing.

Religion   In the "genuine" church, there has come to be a greater accommodation between church beliefs and biomedical treatment.

Healing ceremonies have changed over the past 20 years. In an urban environment under pervasive impact of Western medicine and some dramatic revolutions in the drug industry that supports and sustains that medicine, the church healers have also adapted. There are no longer special healing services. Healing is a subtle part of regular church services in which all prayer is considered as a call to heal any who are sick. The healing specialist has lost his prominence to the fund-raising specialist as more sophisticated urban members depend more on a medical profession that has miracle drugs and a changing attitude about the nature of positive feelings of well-being in therapeutic treatment. The drama that was created by the healing specialist has been replaced by the drama of the dynamic speaker and fund raiser, nowadays an important source of crowds and funds.

Landy (1974) has described in much detail the anthropological treatment of the curer role, the use of role concepts in anthropology, the adaptive roles of traditional curers, and the analysis of these roles as a tool for describing change. He has called for field studies of role adaptation or the curer confronting the Western medical system. The "genuine" church is one site of such change. The curer has been replaced in prominence, and those who are prominent have acquired a generalized curer role. Most of the church healing specialists were dead or retired when these changes were complete. That role is also generously shared today with the practitioners of modern medicine. After all the changes, and notwithstanding them, the life styles and the faith of the members continue to ensure that the prognoses of most of their ailments continue to be good.

Most church members belong to the poorer strata of the wider society, and their religious subculture is perhaps the most important means they have of coping with this fact. Being "in the world but not of it" is a means whereby defiance of the *status quo* can be expressed.

Sickness and death are pervasive themes in the church. Two of the important purposes of the church are to deliver its members to the other world when they die and to heal them when they are ill. Healing the sick is clear evidence of the power of faith and of the power of God who is worshipped. (Death, on the other hand, might seem to negate this power. However, it can always be attributed to hidden sin or simply to God's will.) Healing illustrates that the miracles performed by Christ can also be done by his followers if executed in his name. It demonstrates, too, that the healer is an instrument of the supernatural and that he is to be feared and obeyed. Then, there is the drama, excitement, and entertainment of the healing ritual itself. This is especially true when a celebrated healer from another city is engaged for a major financial campaign.

Church members believe that the human body made by God is the greatest organism in the world as long as the Spirit of God is inside it and Satan is not allowed to enter. They are convinced that all healers know the magnificence of the human body and use that knowledge to heal, giving the credit to God. It is Satan who enters the body and causes it to malfunction. To heal any sickness, you need only to remove Satan as an evil spirit from the body, and it will function well again. Only God can remove the evil spirit, and the patient must have sufficient faith in God in order for God to operate. (It can be seen that these beliefs do raise a number of theological questions, but such matters are not of concern to church members, who are interested rather in religion in action.)

The healer is God's representative. He or she has been called by God to interpret the Bible to the members as well as to satisfy their other needs. The touch of such a ranking person facilitates the healing process. However, anyone who is able to talk to God can heal. The touch of the ranking person includes contact with anything that he or she has touched or "blessed"—a handkerchief, oil, cloth, a garment, radio, television set. The healer treats the person, not the disease. He or she may have no knowledge of the symptoms or the disruptions of bodily function. The person is treated as a social, mental, spiritual, and physical unity, to which the healer ministers with the power of God.

For the healer, all the different aspects of the human being make one holistic unity. Access to knowledge of the physical ailment (disease) is not necessary since the healer does have access to the mental and spiritual planes that are thought to control physical health. If you are well on these planes, your body cannot be sick. The patient can also take charge of his own health if he has a strong relationship with God. He can pray for himself. But if he is not able to take charge in that way, he must hand his health over to others. There was a hostility toward such "others" who are not church healers. The were seen as charlatans. This attitude extends to medical doctors. They charge you fees for what God and your body themselves combine to heal. The folk attitude was that it was very dangerous to trust your health to such persons because they were seldom interested in your health. When you submit to a health practitioner who does not use God to heal you, it is "like a dog lying on his back with all fours up, beggin for mercy from someone who just wants your money." Members say, "Don't go to doctors, go to Jesus." God and your body will "take care of you, if you treat them right." The members believe that medical doctors "get mad at you if you don't let them take charge of your health. They know that God (and your own body) will heal you, and then they can take the credit and the money."

The church healer administers to health socially, mentally, spiritually, and physically. First, he practices the healing ceremony in a social context, where members of the group comfort you by touching you, speaking words of encouragement to you, and praying for you. Second, he alters your mental state, distracting you from thinking about yourself and your health problems. Third, he "lifts your spirits" by encouraging you to become possessed of the "spirit of Jesus." And last, he soothes your body by rubbing it, oiling it, and touching the affected area (if appropriate). The patient is part of a group ceremony and is "lifted out of himself or herself." The success of the treatment is a test of his or her own faith in God because the healer insists that this can be the only missing portion of the healing formula. The patient wants to validate his membership in the group. He wants to validate the power of his minister or missionary. He wants to please the group by being the instrument of a "miracle" in healing. And, of course, he wants to be healed.

Belmar does not have an official spokesman to articulate the spiritual feelings and aspirations of its people. But the local ministers often fill such voids. As one of them demonstrates as he speaks before a neighborhood audience to celebrate Black Solidarity Week:

"Amazing grace, how sweet the sound that saved a wretch like me. I once was lost but now am found, was blind but now I see."

I, like most of you, have a great heritage—slavery, poverty, and oppression. Many of my boyhood friends are dead, in jail, or drug addicts. But for the grace of God, there goes I. So notwithstanding the inadequacies in our society, the very fact that I stand here tonight makes this the greatest society in the world. But we must do better.

I have been overlooked, pushed aside, ignored, and looked down upon. I have been lonely, isolated, persecuted, and humiliated. I have been beaten, insulted, laughed at, and frightened. But I have also been helped. Oh, have I been helped. One of the greatest disappointments in my life has been the fact that some of the Black people who were so important to my survival did not live to see how important their efforts were for me. The ethos, attitudes, and commitment to help one another is what Black solidarity is all about.

. . . So we are the great-grandchildren of several generations of blood, sweat, and tears. You must be worthy of this heritage. You must live the life they sang about in their songs in order that your children and your grandchildren will be able to "Lift Every Voice and Sing." Don't ever let it be said about us, "Look what they've done to my song, mom. Look what they've done to my song."

Never forget the power of Black solidarity. Early in this century and late in the nineteenth century, it gave impetus to the labor movement. In the sixties, it infected white youth and they used our techniques to make ugly in, dirty cool, poor preferred, and war unacceptable. It set the stage for the women's movement, the concern for the aged, ethnic identity, and even gay liberation. Students in Paris and Peace People in Northern Ireland are singing "We Shall Overcome Some Day." Yes, Black became beautiful in the sixties, but we have started to relax and we cannot afford that kind of leisure.

We must keep a constant vigil against the ceaseless propaganda that Black is inferior. Black cannot be defined. It is too rich with connotations and complexities. But Black to me is the bowels of Africa, the cradle of all mankind. Black to me is that pregnant slave woman in the cotton fields of Mississippi who delivers there and keeps on picking till sundown. It is the pain, humility, and suffering of almost 400 years of slavery that could not destroy our song. It is the courage and rhetoric of Frederick Douglass. It is the pomp, ceremony, and dreams of Marcus Garvey. It is the countless violent deaths of innocent ebony men and children at the hands of white bigots in the land of the free. It is the hurt, indignation, and persecution in the life and songs of Paul Robeson. It is the power, strength, and defiance of Jack Johnson, the punch of Joe Louis, the class of Sugar Ray, and the images of Muhammad Ali. It is the baseball of Jackie Robinson, the scholarship of Franklin Frazier, the diplomacy of Ralph Bunche, and the dream of Martin Luther King. Black is the "colored" soldiers who fought and died for their faith in the United States even when they could not use the restrooms, sit in the front of the bus, or sit at the lunch counters. It is Jesse Owens, the son of an Alabama sharecropper, and his four gold medals being insulted in Berlin in 1936. It is the articulate Black Power of Malcolm and the peerless voice of Marian. It is "freedom" that "comes the hard way, by ceaseless groping, toil, struggle, even by fiery trial and agony."

The educated minister is not the only source of such articulation; the lay member who lives in Belmar but attends a Pentecostal church in the Hill District tells why he loves his church:

You got to live for somethin'. You can't just act a fool all your life. I know when I close my eyes the saints will talk over me and tell what I's done in this church. Then I know my life's counted for somethin'. I's helped a lot of saints. I's helped this church grow when there was stumbling blocks everywhere, and when we old folks die we'll leave the young people somethin' to carry on with.

The people in the world don't know the secret. They look all their life, but they don't find it and they don't know why. But we've found that secret (fellowship, brotherhood, and community). It's like they got a coverin' over their eyes and can't get it off, and the secret is right here in front of them but they can't see it. So they look for it in dope and wine and bad women and stealing and fighting, and even killin'. But when it's all said and done, they's worse off than they was before they started lookin'. This life ain't no plaything. It'll mess you up if you're not careful. There's all kinds of snares out there, and if one don't catch you, the other one will. Most things that look good is bad for you. You got to put the devil behind you or he'll lead you straight to hell.

People is tryin' to jump over the moon when they could have joy inside and peace in their minds if they just got their thinkin' right. I don't claim to be smart, but if people who supposed to be get in the fixes they do, then I don't want to be smart. And it may not be much to worldly folks, but it's all I need. It's just where a few people come together with a pure heart that you find Jesus. (Williams 1974:155)

Thus, the Belmar residents delineate the problems and proffer solutions. They refuse to allow the world to defeat them. They lock horns with life. Though disillusioned, they try to live greatly. Religion, the institutional resource least denied them, has been and continues to be a major cohesive force in their lives.

THE WORLD OF WORK

The world of the Belmar resident is somewhat removed from "mainstream" America. The Belmar resident plays, fights, laughs, cries, and works within the context of the events of his own world.

George, a 23-year resident of Belmar, is described as lazy by his three sisters, four brothers, and wife. His siblings recalled that he "took after" an uncle who was killed by a train because he was too slow removing himself from the railroad tracks. An older brother (and foreman) fired him from a job because he "didn't work." "He would always be somewhere hiding or sleeping," the foreman reasoned, "and I can't have nobody around me who won't work." But George recalls the events this way:

My brother [the foreman] can't stand still. He has to be going all the time, and if you're not like him, you can't work with him.

I've been on construction jobs where they want you to pick up 200 pound bags of cement and run with them. I told the boss I needed a man to help me. He said, "The other men are doing it, why can't you?" I told him I had to work all my life, not just today. He told me to get my money [fired me]. I've been on jobs where you had to go down into dangerous holes and I refused to go. Sometimes the boss would give me something else to do. The white man don't care nothing about your life and health; all he wants is to make a buck out a your blood, sweat, and tears.

But the other men ruin a job. They work like fools and then the boss expects everybody to do it. They don't understand that they have to work all their lives just to live.

I worked in the steel mill for 15 years. It was so hot in there I asked the Lord what I had done to deserve this. I had to clean the furnace around the doors. If you stay in that mill long enough, that heat cooks all your insides just like a turkey in the oven. The company doctor knows it, but they go along with the company because they get a big buck. Some men work in there all their lives. When they retire they're already dead. All they have to do is lay down, they just don't know it. The company doctors know it but they won't tell you.

When I came out of the steel mill, it was the best thing I ever did. But all my wife could think about was the big paycheck. A woman will kill you for your money and then try to cry over you at your funeral. She's almost as bad as the white man. All I got is my health. I ain't gon never have no money because it takes all you make to live. So why should I kill myself to make a few dollars? Some of the boys in the steel mill didn't want to retire even when it was time. The doctors would tell them, "Don't you want to live a few years?" The doctors knew they didn't have much time. They were already dead and they didn't have enough sense to come out.

CHILDREN

Belmar is also a neighborhood of children, and as with children everywhere, their behaviors, their distinctive modes of interaction, and their very communication are characteristics of the values dominating their community (see children's Games and Play, p. 97). The children learn early that intensive physical interaction is expected of them; likewise, they learn to meet that expectancy with vivid language. On one occasion, for example, I noticed that one little girl in a group of ten other girls and boys was sobbing and crying, and I asked the group what had happened to her. A seven-year-old girl answered, "Somebody kicked her butt." One of the males, nine years old, heard her statement and tried to compensate for it, because he realized that even though her language was appropriate for the group, it was not appropriate for addressing an adult. Moving in front of the little girl almost before she had finished speaking, he responded quickly, "Somebody hit her." But the little girl's statement impressed me, and I asked the group again what had happened. Each time, she said, "Somebody kicked her butt." Apparently less sensitive than some of the older children to the context of this conversation involving an adult, she repeated several times, "Somebody kicked her butt." As I watched her expression, I noticed that not only was she glib with her statement, but she also enjoyed making it. She seemed to perceive that acts such as the one she was describing were common and valued among her peers.

A favorite pastime of the children is "ripping": They criticize one another's possessions, often to elicit group laughter. As one boy of eight told another boy (nine years old) who wore no undershirt, "At least I got an undershirt." The nine-year-old boy responded, "At least I ain't got no holes in my shirt." He continued, "I'll knock those Pro-Keds off your feet and make them plain tennis shoes." He was referring to a special brand of tennis shoes that the eight-year-old boy was wearing and which is valued as a high-priced shoe in this neighborhood.

This "ripping" interaction is an expression of social solidarity, as well as a communication technique. As I have explained elsewhere (Williams 1974:168), by the process of social leveling, poor Blacks in ghettos are able to minimize their social distance. Thus, "ripping" is one procedure for controlling a potential social distance among the residents of Belmar. For instance, a group of Black teenagers from Belmar were walking across a predominantly white college campus. One of the boys was slow in catching up to the group, lagging about 40 feet behind. One of the teenagers in the group hollered to him, "Come on, fishhead nigger," and the group broke into laughter. The boy hollered two more times. Apparently, he liked the ring of his expression, and it was reinforced by the group. The point here is that even in the presence of whites, even in predominantly white environments, poor Blacks will use the defiant and defiling techniques of "ripping" in order to validate social solidarity and maintain group identity. It is also significant that the phrase embodies a reference to a very poor category of food, yet a food and a characterization derogatory to Blacks.

Another variation of "ripping" is name calling. At approximately 6:30 P.M. on a winter day I noticed a boy, 11 years old, playing with a man, aged 22. The boy was running and trying to get away from the man, and the man was making a series of quick moves and catching the boy. Every time he caught the boy, he chided him with comments like, "You can't even run, monkey." The term *monkey* reinforced the fact that the boy was being defeated. He was being "out done" and the expression *monkey* left no doubt in the boy's mind that he was being chided. Each time the man caught the boy, he wrapped his arm around his neck, repeated the statement, and then walked away and allowed the boy to try to get away once again. After this pattern was repeated several times, the boy recognized that he could not outrun the man and apparently gave up the game. After giving up, he walked approximately 40 feet away and in defeat called to the man. "You faggot," he said in play. The man responded to the comment as a playful gesture by saying, "That's all right. I'd rather be that than something else."

In another name-calling scene, a boy, nine years old, was walking up the street with his companions, boys and girls who ranged in age from eight to thirteen. He passed a 45-year-old man standing in a doorway. One of the boys, about nine years old, decided to include the man in their intensive interaction. "Hey, mister, you know those faggots over there?" he called and pointed to a house where a family of homosexuals resided. (I use this term to mean that two males were living together as sexual companions and maintained this residence as a household. As a result, most of their friends and visitors were also homosexual.) This family and their friends were usually very friendly and opened their door to the street when they played music, danced, or entertained, and they welcomed teenagers and younger children to this place as a hangout, especially during the summer, and the household became known as a center for homosexuals as well as for group interaction. After pointing to the house, the boy pointed to one of his boy companions, approximately seven years old, and said to the older man, "He's one of them. He fucks boys in the butt." This young boy was "ripping" one of his buddies by linking him with this household. One of the girls accompanying the group, who was approximately 12 years old, was surprised at the boy's brazenness in the older man's presence. She raised her voice, saying "Oooooh!" in amazement, and covered her mouth in embarrassment.

Evidently, "ripping" is a vital part of interaction in Belmar. And in the process of "ripping," anything goes: sex, the "dozens," name calling, criticism of clothes, physical appearance, and the like. This behavior is difficult to understand without first understanding the importance of the interactional process among Blacks in Belmar. But if one understands and appreciates what the process means among Blacks in Belmar, one has a significant clue to the meaning of most behavior that one observes here. That is, the obvious is usually superficial. The name calling, the "ripping," and the criticism are secondary to the fact that one is interacting intensively with another.

The example below shows the intensity of interaction among a group of teenage girls (aged 12 to 14) who are sharing a quart of wine:

> Twelve-year-old girl: I can't let a boy get over on me because I don't have any hair, just a little bit.
> Fourteen-year-old girl: That doesn't matter, girl, most of them can't find the hole anyway. You put it in, and if he has hair he'll think it's your hair. You'll be in the dark anyway.

Thirteen-year-old girl: I got a little bit (exposes repeatedly and rubs).

Fourteen-year-old girl: I got some too (exposes).

Thirteen-year-old girl: (laughs) Mine is straight (repeats several times); yours is all curled up.

Fourteen-year-old girl: When I wash it, it's long and straight. (To twelve-year-old): Let me coach you, honey; see, when he is grinding, there is a hard bone down there and it is cushioned with hair.

Twelve-year-old girl, interrupting: But I don't have any hair.

Fourteen-year-old girl: That's all right.

Thirteen-year-old girl: (breaks in conversation) How do you know when he's come off in you?

Fourteen-year-old girl: You can feel; it's warm.

Thirteen-year-old girl: I had some last night.

Fourteen-year-old girl: I know; you wouldn't give me a chance.

Thirteen-year-old girl: If I am pregnant, I want you to come to the hospital with me, hear? I been missing two weeks.

Fourteen-year-old girl: Now, girl, if you're pregnant, you have a long talk with him. Tell him you know he's got a lot of girls but as long as you're the ace girl.

Thirteen-year-old girl: That's what my mother told me, as long as I am the ace.

Fourteen-year-old girl: Tell him you want him to marry you to give the baby a father. Ask him about the baby's name.

Thirteen-year-old girl: Do you think he loves me?

Fourteen-year-old girl: Yeah girl (continues to drink).

(Another girl enters and tries to throw up "to keep from getting sick." She is also fourteen.)

Fourteen-year-old girl: He was talking about Sharon, but I think he just said that so I would tell you.

Thirteen-year-old (to twelve-year-old): I hate your sister Cookie.

(The twelve-year-old gets offended and leaves for the upstairs amidst pleas of the others for her not to take it the wrong way. The eleven-year-old is sent for two cigarettes; they all puff on them.)

Fourteen-year-old (to thirteen-year-old): We gon mess with some girls this summer.

Thirteen-year-old girl: Yeah, if I see you in any fight I'm gon jump in.

Fourteen-year-old (to thirteen-year-old): I love you. I hate to say it because it sounds funny, but I love you. You're just like a sister to me and I want my raise (mother) to like you, and if I have any money, I don't care how much it is, you can get half of it. You can wear anything I got.

Thirteen-year-old girl: And if I have two cents you can get it.

Fourteen-year-old girl: We ought to cut ourselves and let our blood touch. You know, girl, I hate Ellen. I had on these socks, they're dirty now, and I was running through the halls so no one would see them, and she said, "Look, look, she has on anklets."

(The twelve-year-old comes downstairs mad and reprimands them about talking about her sister. They all try to convince her that they were not. The twelve-year-old starts to cry. They plead with her not to cry. The fourteen-year-old starts to cry in sympathy with the twelve-year-old. The thirteen-year-old pleads with both not to cry. After a crying session, they all begin to laugh and "pop and bop" with the records, playing with a bad needle.)

The teenage girls talk about babies, abortions, and infant deaths. The scene has a Third-World seriousness.

WOMEN

African-American women are double at-risk. They are considered inferior to whites and to males. As I have written elsewhere (Williams In Press b) they, and all women, are perceived as inferior to males as a result of their important animal functions. Females have the additional animal functions of menstruation, gestation, lactation, and labor. Furthermore, who knows the animal character of men better than women? As a mother, she carries him for nine months, ejects him during labor, and nurses him until he must be weaned; as a partner, she copulates with him, has her eggs fertilized by him, cares for him as he ages, and, finally, buries him. So, in this process of DDDAK, women are a major threat to the images of men who think they are made in the image of God. The only means men have for demonstrating their artificial superiority to women is by symbol and force. He subordinates her with expressive symbols of inferiority. He is reinforced in these expressive efforts by her additional animal characteristics. I repeat for emphasis, she menstruates, breeds, is impregnated, lactates, gestates, and rears her brood. By her presence, she constantly reminds him of his vaginal origin, seduction, sedation, and animal kinship. A woman conspiring with a snake represents one of our most vivid symbols of evil.

African-American women, as are men, are considered inferior to whites because of their history and phenotype as well as the human concentric circle perception (see Figure 1.3) of humankind. African-American women have been expected to nurture their men, children, kinship network, and race without sufficient support and sustenance. Throughout their history in America, they have been exploited by all. They still are. As a result, most Black children are even more at-risk—poor, Black, immature, and undernourished (emotionally as well as nutritionally). These children begin and end life deprived of the freedom of the pursuit of happiness and blamed for their shackles in a society where the myth of freedom and equal opportunity reigns.

Some forms of exploitation of African-American women are more subtle than others. Some of it is insidious. Along with the Black middle class who cherish white "mainstream" values, neighborhoods, and possessions (including white spouses and sex partners) African-American women are targets of token affirmative action. They are recruited, employed, and made highly visible in a strategy of token upward mobility. Such a strategy encourages them into an invidious competition with African-American males, most of whom are denied such opportunities. In an increasingly female-conscious society these women are more and more reluctant to nourish, support, and identify with oppressed African-American males who are perceived as inferior in the social and economic circles where upwardly mobile Black women endeavor to succeed.

Without that traditional nourishment, support, and identification, already at-risk, Black males are like male lions without a pride. They form their own isolated predatory groups. They take their cues from such women and become more bitter, destructive, and exploitive. These un- and underemployed males and the vast majority of Black women who are not upwardly mobile become psychological victims of this social movement. They begin to believe that all African Americans of the opposite sex are their enemies and engaged in warfare or exploitive "games" with them. This process destroys the Black community and especially Black children. African-American women are becoming weary of the struggle that includes the tow of Black males. Many are being convinced that they can succeed without the drag. These attitudes along with the abandonment by the Black middle class are rapidly converting the "genuine" and "spurious" into the Black underclass.

African-American women, as has the Black church, have brought the African-American community from slavery to emancipation, from reconstruction to the twenty-first century. They have not received the credit, the rewards, or the testimony. Many are deciding to end the struggle and to strike out for themselves, just as has the Black middle class.

The society supports all of this. Many of the members are unconscious of such support. Many whites have been nourished by African-American women for four centuries. They are familiar with the pleasant advantages of being in the presence and in the arms of nurturing "inferior" women. They have always preferred this presence to that of Black males who they perceive as potentially "angry men beating Mau Mau drums," sexually powerful, and seeking power. White members of the society select "appropriate" Black women, provide them mentorship and solace in the struggles of "success." Some of these African-American women reinforce the attitudes and values that Black males are inferior and are their wrongful competitors, and with white ears and power, they destroy their Black male co-workers.

We must eliminate the concept of "inferior" people and "inferior" life forms. Anything else is a Band-Aid on a raging disease. For in the present arrangement of values, most women seek empowerment while maintaining a system of social inequality. Thus, they eschew coalition with the other oppressed groups—African Americans, Native Americans, Hispanics, the poor, the disabled, and the deformed. The results of such an approach are already visible in the token advancement of African-American women. The only effective empowerment of women is the destruction of all social inequality including that of gender.

So, as are all women, the Black women in Belmar are considered inferior, but in addition, they are Black, and oppressed for it, abused, and probably poor. Yet they work, as domestics or in another service industry. They rear the children, make the homes, and support the churches. Poverty, drug addiction, crime, mental and physical abuse, teenage pregnancy, unemployment, and illiteracy surround them. But they have the support of one another, their mothers, grandmothers, aunts, cousins, siblings, friends, and fictive kin. They perform well under the circumstances. They "run" Belmar, the churches, the schools, the community organizations, and the homes. Black men have the leadership titles, but the women perform most of the tasks. African-American women are the unsung heroines in Belmar and in neighborhoods like it all over America. African-American men often exploit them for their labor, shelter, money, sexual favors, and tolerance. Many of these women sacrifice their personal ambitions for their children and their men.

The plight of Black women in Belmar highlights the need for the viability of the women's movement in America. But here too the social system has effectively undermined that movement with the prolife–prochoice debacle (compounded by the divisive race, class, religious and feminist politics). Of course, every woman should have control of her body. But everybody should have too much respect for life to carelessly create it for immediate destruction. It is a question of values, and the demise of DDDAK will address that question. Until then, women, and especially African-American women, have their place in Belmar and in the human dilemma.

SYMBOLS

Another critical component of group behavior is attitudes and values expressed in symbols (see Williams 1973b). Among the people in Belmar, we would expect to find consistent attitudes and values concerning physical appearance. Such attitudes and values should be distinctive if this neighborhood is distinctive; they should differ to some extent from the middle-class orientation of the thin, unhealthy-looking female as the ideal in display-window mannequins all over the country. How do the people of Belmar see physical beauty among females? As expected, most women in Belmar are not thin and unhealthy in appearance. They appear well endowed with the capability of bearing children without trauma, in contrast to the ideal middle-class perception of females, which would defy child-bearing ability. Even men in Belmar possess a fleshy build. The term *heavy* has a favorable connotation. It can mean intellectually capable, sophisticated in the styles and mannerisms of Belmar living, or, generally, all right. By listening to a variety of conversations among young men in Belmar, one discovers that men perceive desirable females as those who are not thin, but fleshy and who, as a result, are able to keep a man warm on a cold winter's night. As one person expressed, "I like something I can grab hold of. I like to feel what I got." "A rubber hip mamma" is a desirable female, and the term has favorable sexual connotations. "She can shake that stuff." "She's got a whole lot of ass," and that seems important. "She's a big mamma," never a fat one. This is in contrast to describing undesirable women as "nothing but skin and bones"; "there is nothing to her"; "you couldn't find her in bed"; "you would go to bed with her and her bones would jab you all night." Referring to a substantial female, another informant said, "I could lay in that stuff all night."

This indicates that Belmar is more than a neighborhood; it is a locus of distinctive attitudes and values that enable interaction there to be humanly satisfying.

We can expect to find a similar distinctive value orientation for other phenomena within this Black neighborhood. One of those areas is skin color. In this era of "Black is beautiful," we learn of the attitude toward and value of skin color by daily descriptive accounts of it. In Belmar, when a person is labeled half-white, it is derogatory. Other derogatory phrases are "yellow," "red nigger," as well as "shit color." This contrasts with the common reference to Black females: "the blacker the berry, the sweeter the juice." A person with near-Caucasion characteristics may earn the name "white boy," although it must be emphasized that such people are often able to live with such names by exhibiting Black behavior in their daily contacts. In such situations, the onus of "white boy" is lost, and it becomes merely another naming phenomenon in Belmar. Skin color that does not deviate too far from the "Black is beautiful," is described as a "fine brown frame" or "an olive complexion" or "a pretty brown."

Such attitudes also apply to hair texture. Hair with a coarse texture is referred to as "nappy," "kinky," "bad stuff," "terrible," and "hair you can't do anything with." Such references are similar to the obscene names in that they are not derogatory. They may be a way of interacting, merely a part of the process. In fact, there are some definitely positive references to coarse hair, and this is especially true of Muslims. Coarse hair is described as "alive." When one rubs one's hands over it, one can feel the texture. It has definite body, in contrast to Caucasian hair, which is described as "dead hair." Evidence used to support this thesis is that combing Black hair in the dark gives off sparks from the static electricity. These sparks reflect the life in this kind of hair, in contrast to the absence of sparks while combing Caucasian hair or straight hair.

These are all indications that there are distinctive attitudes and values among the people in Belmar, attitudes and values that enable them to live a meaningful life in spite of their lack of resources and their limited access to the institutions in the larger society.

We have samples of statements that reflect the world view in Belmar. These views derive from a particular ecological niche, and that ecology defines to some extent what the people see. One white manuscript reader explained to me that "many of their values are great, but get in the way of economic success. Many of them seem to blame the whites for their poverty, instead of their own values." This reader blames their values for their economic plight rather than an economic system that keeps most of its members poor. She would change their values and keep their environment intact. She would give them the sludge of this rich country along with the values of "mainstream" America. She would make them all despair, live in quiet desperation, be "spurious," have a "lean and hungry spirit," and eventually revolt. Perhaps she is correct. Give them nothing but their chains and they might change their world as well as their view of it.

Perhaps we are reminded here that life is more than meets the eye. Beyond the ebony skin, the broad, flat, and often large nose, the Black English dialect, the urban desert, the economic deprivation, the looting, crime, police brutality, even under the fiery trial and agony, there is a vital human spirit, a dynamic conception of human life, a perceptive understanding of the fate of Blacks in America, and a perpetual human resource that awaits the appropriate day and hour to ultimately overcome.

Notwithstanding poverty, poor housing, inadequate schools, the urban waste-land, and American racism, the people in Belmar have hopes and dreams, failure and disappointments, ideals and disillusionments. Will the politics of power in America keep Belmar and places like it much the same in spite of social theories, ethnographic descriptions, and political programs? There is an accepted view among scientists that the people living in the Sahara Desert and places like it help to create and even to expand their environment by their adaptive strategies in these distinctive ecological niches. But few tackle the problem of why they are there and what forces operate to keep them there—an invisible crisis that will destroy us all, unless we see it for what it is—the human dilemma.

8 / Human Inferiority Feelings: The "Spurious" and the "Mainstream"

Man would necessarily have succumbed before the assault of the powers of nature if he had not employed them to his advantage. . . . Climatic conditions compel him to protect himself from the cold by clothes, which he takes from animals better protected than he is. His organism requires artificial housing and artificial preparation of food. His life is only assured by means of division of labor and by sufficient propagation. His organs and his mind toil continually for conquest and security. To all this have to be added his greater knowledge of life's dangers and his awareness of death. Who can seriously doubt that the human individual treated by nature in such a stepmother fashion has been provided with the blessing of a strong feeling of inferiority that urges him towards a plus situation, towards security and conquest? This tremendous, enforced rebellion against a tenacious feeling of inferiority as the foundation of human development is awakened afresh and repeated in every infant and little child.

Alfred Adler
(in Becker 1962:35)

. . . Tocqueville, after all, posed the prospect of an America without classes—an "equality of condition"—yet one where people still remained restless unto death, forever seeking to find some manner of living in which they felt authentic, worthy of being respected, dignified. Equality of conditions, he wrote, does not dampen the evils of individualism; to the contrary, he thought in America equality would lead to an increase in individual anxiety and self-doubt. A modern social commentator, Robert Nisbet, has said that in this, Tocqueville created a picture of status insecurity outside the boundaries of class analysis. (Sennett and Cobb 1973:257)

My own feelings of inferiority (described below) are not unusual, as I have suggested in these pages. As Frazier (1968:178) has stated, most African Americans feel inferior:

. . . Not all middle-class Negroes consciously desire . . . to be white in order to escape from their feeling of inferiority. . . . But when one studies the attitude of this class in regard to the physical traits or the social characteristics of Negroes, it becomes clear that the Black bourgeoisie do not really wish to be identified with Negroes.

And as his student, Nathan Hare, has expanded:

. . . Black Anglo-Saxons are chiefly distinguishable in that, in their struggle to throw off the smoldering blanket of social inferiority, they disown their own history and mores in order to assume those of the biological descendents of the white Anglo-Saxons. They relate to, and long to be part of, the elusive and hostile white world, whose norms are taken as models of behavior. White society is to most of them a looking-glass for taking stock of their personal conduct. . . . They must keep on grooming to make what they think white society imagines itself to be, accord with what they themselves would like to be: like whites. (Hare 1970:33)

However, the artificial distinctions of race sometimes obscure the fact that whites feel inferior too. Humans feel inferior, and those feelings and the actions that they take to compensate for them or to deny and erase them constitute much of the social life of mankind.

The African-American middle class must understand the American social system. It is not designed to share power with Blacks, only to provide the illusion of power to sustain the African-American quest for power. Any exercise of power must be directed toward other Blacks, and even then, such an exercise cannot succeed if the recipient Black has a powerful white patron.

> . . . The middle-class Blacks assuming positions in the wider society will be increasingly called upon to keep the lid on things by whites and at the same time will be under pressure from below to identify with the continuing Black struggle. . . .
>
> The colonial analogy becomes misleading when it is used to suggest the possibility of meaningful Black independence within the context of American Society. As the size of the Black middle-class increases, the cohesiveness of common racial identity may be lessened and a long term sustained effort to achieve independence made even more difficult. At the same time strengthening the Black community's economic and political power increases its bargaining position vis-à-vis the white society. (Tabb 1971:442)

As is often whispered, some psychologists and psychiatrists pursue their careers because of their own emotional dilemmas. For anthropologists, it seems to be a deep sense of personal inferiority that drives some of them to study "inferior" people. That inferiority complex accounts for many of the personal conflicts within academic anthropology departments.

Anthropologists, like all other humans, are products of their cultures. In America, the pressures for upward mobility are severe, and those without exceptional athletic, business, or entertainment acumen and opportunity may choose academia for such mobility.

As I have suggested above, all humans have feelings of inadequacy, but anthropologists seem to exhibit strong ones. Who else would choose careers that obligate them to live for years among "inferior" peoples of the world? For anthropologists, the statement by Thackery is most pertinent:

> Birket-Smith said: "There is no rank or class among the Eskimos, who must therefore renounce that satisfaction, which Thackery calls the true pleasure of life, of associating with one's inferiors." The same may be said of other primitive societies (Sahlins 1960:85)

These feelings of inadequacy help to explain why anthropologists who work in academia and have what they consider "the best jobs in the world" create so much stress and anxiety for others and themselves in their workplace. The story of two anthropologists that follows attempts to show the human side of these professionals who, like most humans, feel compelled to prove their superiority.

Children are not born feeling inferior. They learn that they are not beautiful, strong, tall, intelligent, articulate, graceful, agile, talented, rich, clean, righteous, principled, virtuous, W.A.S.P., white, or perfect. In a competitive and materialistic society, they are continually taught these lessons. Regardless of their achievements, they will be surrounded by people and things that remind them that there is "more."

As two examples of middle-class achievements that suggest how notions of inferiority develop, I describe here some of my own life experiences and those of another anthropologist.

MY PURSUIT OF THE MIDDLE CLASS

I was born in Mercy Hospital and reared in the Hill District of Pittsburgh. When I was born, my parents lived in a basement at Mercer Street and Webster Avenue (see Lorant 1975:350, *The Sun Shines in the City* and 1975:344, *The Hill in the 30's*). During my childhood, we were evicted many times, but I spent most of my early life in a three-story frame apartment complex at Reed and Soho Streets (2303 Reed Street, see Lorant 1975:349, *Upper Soho*) and in a decaying house at Cassatt and Crescent Streets (#4 Cassatt Street, see Lorant 1975:343, 345, *The Habitat of Humans, Shanties in the Hill District*).

My parents reared their six children (one died at age four) by means of welfare and menial jobs. Neither of my parents completed high school, and only one of my siblings did so. Only I attended college. So I am a stranger to the middle class and an alien in the academic village.

The house we occupied at #4 Cassatt Street was condemned by the city in 1951, and we moved to other Black ghettos. Later, with a professional degree and occupation I moved to middle-class neighborhoods. But after I abandoned my native habitat, I discovered that I belonged nowhere. Middle-class values (in movies, books, and mentors) had enticed me out of the ghetto, but they never integrated me into the places where I arrived. With this alien character, I have a proclivity to study those who surround me. This is the tradition of anthropology.

I will describe my life in the third person (using "Donald," as my parents, siblings, and early acquaintances called me) to facilitate the recollection as objectively as possible.

Donald's father came to Pittsburgh from Alabama after the death of Donald's grandfather.[1] The older children of the family (Donald's aunts and uncles) arranged for their entire family (mother, three girls, and three boys) to travel to Pittsburgh. Donald's father often recounted his family's hardships in coming to Pittsburgh when there was neither welfare nor Social Security. The family often slept in one room with the children sleeping in shifts because beds were in short supply. When one of them was fortunate enough to obtain employment, he or she would help support the entire family. This process continued until each member "got on his feet."

Donald's mother and her family were from Virginia. She went to Pittsburgh after her mother's death to live with her oldest sister, who earlier had left home,

---

[1] A version of this life history was presented in *Umoja* (1978:169)

married, and settled there. She was the third sister to go to Pittsburgh; the others were married homemakers while Donald's mother still attended school. Becoming bored with school and the limited provisions of her oldest sister, she soon found a job in a laundry.

While she was working, attending church, and dating, Donald's mother met her eventual husband. Donald's father had held various menial jobs; he was unemployed when he met his eventual wife, however. Still, he was frugal with his money, and his oldest sister, Hannah Williams-Hunter, whose husband was employed, provided his meals, shelter, and "spending change." Donald's mother once described him as "a good dresser who could fool you to death." Persuading her that he had money, a job, and "came from a good family," he joined her church and cajoled her into marriage.

Only after marriage did she discover their plight—no job, no money, and no home. Her sister, Carrie Barnes-Hill, had warned her not to get married, suspecting that the future husband was a "ne'er do well." She insisted that if her sister got married against her will she could no longer live with her. Nevertheless, the young couple started upon their rugged path of life together. The husband's sister continued to help, and he worked periodically. But the nearly constant lack of security for herself and the children was a psychological trauma that Donald's mother would never forget. She was frequently ill and worried most of the time.

Donald's mother explained that her "bad nerves" were a result of incidents such as moving into vacant houses before leasing them and moving out before being discovered by the landlord (a homeless family). Many times, Donald's paternal aunt, Hannah, became the family doctor when no other physician would come to the house. She also fed them when the cupboards at Donald's house were bare. In fact, for many years, his father ate his meals at her house to keep from using the meager resources at his own home.

Donald's oldest maternal aunt, Carrie, divorced her husband and moved to another city; another older sister of his mother's moved to Pittsburgh and married a man with a secure job. This sister never had any children of her own, so she helped Donald's mother. She continued to help Donald and his siblings ever after most of them reached adulthood.

Donald's oldest brother had died at the age of four, so Donald was reared as the eldest for most of his life. His mother believed that poor obstetrical care in the delivery room had injured the brother so that he never fully recovered. His congenital injury was complicated by the lack of adequate health care due to the family's low income.

Donald begins his own story with the statements "I was born in the Hill. My parents lived in a two-room basement apartment." He continues, informing us that his father had a bad heart due to a case of rheumatic fever and that the heart condition kept Donald's father unemployed for many years. His family moved several times during Donald's early childhood, and Donald recalls his father's many survival techniques during those bleak days. When most of the neighbors' electricity was shut off for nonpayment of the bill, his father secured power for the family "by climbing the tellie pole and putting a jumper on the electric wire." In this way they had a refrigerator when such luxuries in the neighborhood were rare. Occasionally, the children received large expensive toys such as a new fire engine which could seat two children up front and one in the rear. These purchases were made on credit. Once, when confronted with one account in arrears which was not likely to be paid, his father denied the purchase. When asked to sign the paper, he wrote an "X" for his signature; the frustrated creditors dismissed him. These "survival" tactics continued through Donald's childhood, and he recalls, "How proud we kids were when we went out riding in one of the very few cars around here." Such tactics often required that valuable property, such as automobiles, be legally owned by relatives. It also required that the father learn a trade (paperhanging) so that he could work on those rare occasions when he felt well enough. Frequently, all members of the family were gainfully employed, the children with newspaper and shoeshine routes.

Donald recalls spending much of his childhood with his neighborhood peers. He learned early from them that one's place in the world was ranked according to size and aggressiveness. The larger boys would twist his arms behind his back and force him to call them "Daddy" to amuse the groups and display their rank. Even at this tender age (approximately eight years old), these ghetto boys had learned to value the elusive "Daddy" that several of them lived without. The older girls would often beat him for the same reason—to display rank. One had to be bold and aggressive, albeit somewhat accommodative, to avoid too much bruising. Aloofness and individuality were not tolerated. In fact, Donald explained that his younger brother was accepted by the group before Donald because he conformed and cooperated more than Donald.

By the time Donald was seven years old, the neighborhood girls had already introduced him to sexual petting, and he learned to enjoy the pleasure of these tactile experiences before he was able to have intercourse. He had his first girlfriend at the age of seven and walked her home from school and visited her after school. The girl's mother would often allow him to enter the house to avoid the nuisance of their communicating from opposite sides of the first-floor window. Another girlfriend of Donald's would keep him and his male companion waiting for hours outside just to catch a glimpse of her at her second-floor window or in the corridor. Her parents were not so tolerant, but it was worth every waiting moment just for the rare pleasure of seeing her. "It was just fun to be near her house," Donald remembered.

Donald received no allowance, nor did he have any conception of what it meant. He earned most of his spending money by running errands, selling scrap metal and rags, and establishing a network of adults in the neighborhood who provided him with money for various reasons. This network became so well organized that many of the homes he visited (scheduling visits so as not to be a "pest") were a source of money with or without any related chores (because of the good will he had established with the residents). Many of these sources were homes of relatives or his parents' friends with whom he made a special effort to become acquainted. In general, at a very early age Donald was spending much of his time in the neighborhood streets—hustling, playing, and courting. He explained that if he or his brothers remained in the house during mild weather, his mother suspected that "something was wrong."

These were days when Donald did not know what a library or a museum was. He would not learn about them until years later during the school field trips. He was never taken downtown, and his parents subscribed to no newspapers or magazines. There was no television, and children were not permitted to use the radio. These were his formative years during which he developed alternative values.

Throughout Donald's recollections weaves a thread of violence—among his peers, his teachers, and in the streets. One of his early experiences with violence in the streets was when he was about five years old and witnessed a woman being beaten near his house. According to Donald, "She kept crying and he kept hitting her and hollering at her. She looked white and seemed so pretty and helpless. I was high yellow or shit-color and I knew how many times I got beat just for that so I felt sorry for her. She was out of place in that neighborhood just like I was out of place everywhere." In addition, certain neighborhood parents "went for bad," welcoming any excuse for an altercation to display their prowess for aggression. Disputes among their children were frequent sources of these excuses.

One of the family's heroes during these early years of Donald's life was his maternal uncle, Thurman Barnes ("Big Man"). "He was a good-looking man, a gambler and a braggart. The women liked him and gave him money while the men liked to hear him talk. It didn't matter that he was separated from his wife and two children, without a job, frequently in jail, and had had several children out of wedlock. Still, he would maintain: "They ain't no kids of mine."

When Donald was eight years old, his family moved again. He enjoyed recalling the small details of this house where he spent many years. He remembered the several months of labor that his father, his brothers, and he had put into a five-room brick house before it was fit for human habitation. Even with these efforts, it was still a modest house with two bedrooms on the second floor and a frame kitchen set off from the house. Without a basement under it or a room over it, the kitchen was the coldest room during the winter. The only heat came from the range. Often, the water was left running to keep it from freezing and bursting the pipes. Initially, the house was heated by a large coal burner in the dining room and a living-room fireplace that also burned coal. Later, the fireplace was abandoned for a small gas-space heater, and the coal burner was moved to the basement with a large opening in the dining-room floor directly above it. The arrangement allowed better use of the precious space and made the only bath, located in the basement, more tolerable.

The house sat on the side of a precipitous hill that overlooked the Allegheny River, Bigelow Boulevard, and the Pennsylvania Railroad Station. Donald discovered many riches here in this poor, predominantly Black neighborhood. The geographical location was a treasure for boyhood play and imagination. Thirty feet away, at the edge of the hillside, he could clearly see the boats guiding their freight up and down the river. He could watch the trains moving in and out of the station. He could watch the vehicles racing up and down the boulevard. Donald saw his first seaplanes in action along the river; a river terminal was used for excursion flights. He could fly his kites up and over the hillside, free from the usual obstacles of the urban streets. Donald spent many hours playing in the streams that ran over the hillside. Part of the hillside was covered with trees and brush, so he and his peers had their own urban forest. They would roam or camp there for hours, often with food, only a hundred yards from home.

Donald remembers with great pleasure the "bull rope" swings that the larger boys would mount. On another portion of this hillside these swings extended from the upper reaches of a telephone pole. The boys would swing in Tarzan fashion from one side of the hill, around the pole, and out over the precipice, to the other side of the hill. The ride was dangerous but thrilling. The younger boys had few opportunities to swing while the larger boys were on the rope, but it was a pleasure just to watch the excitement. Then, at the end of the day, the big boys would abandon the swing, and Donald and his peers could ride until dark. When there was no school, they would rise early in the morning and race to the swing to occupy it for several hours before the older boys arrived.

Donald seems especially appreciative of living in this small ecological niche. From large cardboard boxes he and the boys would make sleds to ride the loosely packed dirt down the steep hillsides. They had rock wars with the boys who lived much higher on the hillside, boys with whom they did not interact in other ways. They sat upon favorite stoops and porches and through interaction established cohesive peer groups that endured until they moved away or became adults. These stoops were usually located on a corner so that they could see neighborhood interaction in four directions. They observed, talked, told stories, sang, joked, and humiliated one another. They teased the girls, the neighborhood drunk, and the local imbecile. The drunk had been gassed in World War I, and he walked on his heels. They called him "Staglee," and he answered to the name. They would call to him, "Why do you walk on your heels?" and he would answer, "To save my sole." He would often threaten them when they were disrespectful, and they enjoyed the threat of danger. The imbecile was about 19 years old, and his energy never seemed to wane; he chased the boys for hours. Their fear of him made the play more exciting.

During the winter, they made tracks for running and sliding on the sidewalk, battled with the snow, and sledded down their steep street. When the weather was warmer, they played football and baseball in the streets. Their form of baseball was one in which they bounced the ball off a wall into the playing field instead of hitting the ball with a bat. They went swimming in the recreation center pool and often took the time to play in the center's ball field or the schoolyards as well.

During these years, school was an extension of the street. One was forced to abide by certain rules which seemed to have little meaning. For example, one was encouraged to be "bad" by peer-group pressure. Often, this merely meant that one behaved in school as disruptively as one did outside of school. Thus, teachers put the "agitator" in a corner or under the desk. Sometimes, they would beat his knuckles with a ruler, or lead him by his ear lobe to the principal's office where he spent the rest of the school day waiting for a paddling, all the while displaying his bravado to his peers. As one peer expressed:

> My teachers were white and they seemed so clean that they made me feel dirty. . . . And when I was bad that's when their true colors would show. Starting in the first grade you could sense that when their own children were bad they didn't treat them like they treated you when you were bad. . . . They could look at you like you were an animal and if they had to touch you it was with the tips of their fingers or a mean kind of grab. . . . they never really touched you like they did the one or two white kids in the class. . . . They

never got close to you, hugged you, or put their arms around you so you could feel a part of the school. . . . They talked at me, taught at me; they were teaching in the room and I could catch it or not. . . . The school belonged to them and I could stay in the building as long as I watched myself, stayed in my place. Once in that building, you were out of the ghetto and you better act like it. The school was not part of the ghetto which was part of me.

In the ghetto, Donald not only had to contend with the ethos of teachers and their mainstream institutional control and restrictions, but he also had to fight or avoid altercations resulting in physical injuries or humiliation. The pecking order in his school was determined not by grade averages but by aggression, as was status in the neighborhood. Aggression as a major source of excitement and entertainment was almost impossible to avoid. Even when there were no fights, the threat still hung over one like the fabled sword of Damocles on its slender thread: "I'm gon' beat your butt after school"; or "I better not see you outside"; or "You gon' get your butt kicked." Then, there were the bullies who, upon passing a smaller guy in the hall, would grab him by the collar and demand money or sweets or just humiliate him. According to Donald, "There was one guy, Winston, who was into bodybuilding and weights, and he was a 'punch-you' addict. . . . He was always punching the little guys in the arm or shoulder to show you his strength."

Learning in school was incidental and peripheral to the main business of life. That business was to interact, to tease, to court the girls, and to fight. In the sixth and seventh grades, the girls would be attacked with romantic play episodes if the teacher left the classroom. This behavior, combined with frenzied attacks among the boys themselves, continued until the teacher returned. The favorite game in the gym classes was the violent use of basketballs to hit and "put out" one another. The teacher enjoyed this as much as the boys.

Violence in school merged with violence in the home. Donald described how a man shot a woman," . . . five times right there near me." At age nine, Donald witnessed a neighborhood woman severely "cutting" another woman with a knife after an argument. The woman victim in the knifing incident had been arguing with a teenage girl. At the height of the argument, the girl's mother ran out with a knife, and both she and her daughter attacked the victim. The mother was famous in the neighborhood for her knife-wielding exploits and was even rumored to have killed someone.

On one occasion the knife-wielding woman rushed into Donald's house to vehemently protest the aggression of Donald's younger brother against her grandson. During the intrusion, Donald watched the incident as he sat near his mother, who was taken by complete surprise as she stood ironing her weekly wash. In fact, she was so surprised she seemed to be in a state of shock. The woman, her famous knife in hand, yelled and screamed at Donald's mother who hardly knew what was happening. Her voice was so loud that Donald's father rushed downstairs and surprised the woman, who thought he was away. He ordered her out of his house with such rage that the woman never bothered to speak to him—she quickly left. Donald's father was upset that his mother had not used the iron to defend herself. He dressed immediately and went to the local office of the justice of the peace to file charges.

Donald recalled the freedom he had as an adolescent and especially as a teenager. He and his brother (one year and two months younger) came and went almost as they pleased with very little restriction from their parents. Their parents were only concerned that the boys did not cause them trouble. There was little if any pressure (but some encouragement) to get "good grades" in school, to work, to come home for dinner, to go to bed, or any of the other parental coercions typical in mainstream life styles. Their parents' energies were comsumed by the task of providing clothes, food, and shelter. So Donald's summer-evening activities lasted until morning long after his peers had been called home and the group had dwindled to a quiet twosome. Then, Donald and his brother would return home for sleep.

Nevertheless, his parents reminded him that education was important for "good jobs" and professions. But academic excellence was one's own choice, and college was a word with little substance in his household. In addition, a few schoolteachers and Donald's newspaper "boss" often reminded him of the value of education. Yet such ideas were remote when reinforcement was lacking in the context of his life style.

As Donald and his peers became teenagers, their attention turned more and more to heterosexual relationships. Their games and their play often focused upon exclusive time with females. He remembered his unrestricted experiments with sex in the summer evenings. Neighborhood families in which both parents worked provided convenient shelters for adolescent sexual experiments. Homes in which parents were seldom present, day or night, became "dens of iniquity." Donald's brother had an unpleasant experience when his girlfriend, who was 11 years old, was impregnated at such a house. He was 13 years old; an older boy was responsible, but Donald's brother felt obligated to accept the fatherhood. The baby died.

Donald and his friends played several variations of hide and seek, but for most, the real game was "hide and pet." Although sexual intercourse seldom occurred, many youngsters were exposed to the "real thing" on some occasion. All of Donald's sexual education took place in these play encounters. He knew some of the girls who were impregnated during these times and remembered their maternal experiences. He recalled the youthful marriages precipitated by such experiences. Often, the males would resist marriage in spite of their paternal status; but the status itself usually had a profound impact upon their future interests. School became even more confining, and one was anxious to fulfill one's role as a man. The adult world of menial work, money, street life, and heterosexual companionship beckoned them. Thus, the cycle continued—poverty, undereducation, and institutional deprivation. Value stretch was adaptive and simultaneously restrictive.

Donald had the ability to relate well with adults and the adult world. Because of this, it seemed to him that he had never been a child. Somehow, as long as he could remember, he had participated and functioned well in the adult world. He recalled that at the age of 11 it was his responsibility to travel the several miles from the Hill to the North Side by public transportation (the incline and the streetcar) to collect his mother's portion of his father's pay, so she would be able to go shopping before his father returned home on payday. Donald was sent downtown almost weekly to pay utility bills and insurance premiums for his parents and his mother's sister. It was also his responsibility to retrieve his aunt's check from the mailbox every week, cash it, and pay her various debts. When Donald's parents would leave the city or the state on kinship "call to duty," they would leave Donald in charge of his siblings. He recalled that as early as 11 years he would help his father drive the car on the Pennsylvania Turnpike while sitting on a pillow to see the road. At the time, these duties seemed ordinary to Donald because he was able and expected to perform. As he recalls these periods, however, he is impressed with how much of his childhood time was spent fulfilling adult responsibilities.

During this same period, Donald began to sell mail-order products from door to door in his neighborhood. He started with Cloverine Salve; after several successful orders, he began to sell other items. He subsequently sold a variety of Black periodicals and earned profit and prizes. He never forgot his first prize—a Monopoly game. Gradually, he learned that he was endowed with a unique ability to sell. In fact, the quantity of a product seemed to be no problem; only his desire to sell mattered. Donald believed that "If I wanted to sell it and I tried, I could sell it."

Donald's periodical enterprise, brought him into persistent contact with life in the street. He spent many hours in the old Fullerton and Wylie nightlife area. He traveled Webster, Wylie Centre, Herron, and Bedford Avenues week after week. He frequented the barbershops, beauty shops, bars, speakeasies, "gambling joints," pool rooms, private clubs, restaurants, shoeshine parlors, jitney stations, hat-cleaning shops, fish markets, and private homes. Because of these activities, he spent more time mingling with adults than with his peers. He enjoyed the sales activities, and he continued to be very successful. Again and again, he proved to himself that he could sell as many periodicals as he wished. Donald accumulated a considerable amount of money as a result of these activities, but he had little time to spend it. There were many late evenings when he had sold several hundred periodicals but refused to quit and return home until he had sold the last item. The weight of the periodicals had been replaced by the bulk of coin and his entire body was tired from walking and carrying the merchandise, but he pushed on until the end. Week after week this process continued to be a personal challenge that brought him the admiration of his parents, his paper "boss" and other adults, as well as the envy of competitive paperboys.

These activities allowed Donald to mingle with a variety of people in the Hill. He sold to the educated, the uneducated, the intoxicated, hustlers, gamblers, barmaids, bartenders, pimps, prostitutes, secretaries (in insurance companies and other offices), jitney drivers, barbers, beauticians, and theater attendants. He was rebuffed by the belligerent, the aggressive, the exasperated, and the defeated. Many a beleaguered and bellicose tavern owner or bartender tried unsuccessfully to keep him out of the bar and away from the patrons. Other proprietors and customers, whether they condemned or praised him, knew him and accepted him as a part of the scene. Some proprietors and bartenders accepted defeat after being continually outwitted by his tenacity. Some even became friends and customers after witnessing a boy who would use a series of strategic maneuvers to reach potential customers. These maneuvers would usually entail his getting in the door and to the rear of the bar before being discovered. Then, even if he were discovered, most of the patrons would already have been exposed to his wares; few proprietors were aggressive enough to stop a patron from making a purchase if he so desired. On some occasions, though, an exasperated bartender would insist that the patron follow Donald outside to make the purchase.

These regular appearances on the "avenue" and in customers' homes created close ties between Donald and some of his patrons. Some women almost adopted him, and he would always revel in the sound of their shouts that this was their "boy." One woman customer had to be "straightened out" by Donald's maternal aunt, Mattie Ruth Barnes-Franklin, because the customer had romantic designs upon him, notwithstanding the fact that he was 14 years old and she was 40. Thus, he was a regular part of the people parade that marched from tavern to tavern, corner to corner, street to street, and encounter to encounter, wondering most of the time, "Will I find my love today?" He was one of the players in a human drama, most of whom had long been abandoned in the larger economic scheme of things. They played out their lives together in the "spit," sex, liquor, drugs, violence, and games of chance; even "foreigners" (whites seeking entertainment) would come and pay to see these acts but deny them any value when they returned home. Donald was often fascinated by the pomp, ritual, and ceremony of his customers on their public stages—the "high yellow" with their "good hair" and their private clubs, the "high society" and their favorite grill, the Friday night "big spenders" who were "broke" on Sunday, the flesh merchants, and the dream peddlers. The nucleus of this drama was Fullerton and Wylie Streets which were later eliminated by urban redevelopment. After all, it was only a wasteland, a slum, an area of blight too close to the nucleus of the city's economic center—downtown Pittsburgh. So Donald's world was destroyed along with his house; he took his savings and contributed to a down payment on a house in East End (Lincoln District) for his parents and his siblings. He was an unwitting part of an economic process that created urban deserts, forced people to invest in them, coerced residents to live in them, blamed African Americans for their existence, and then destroyed these homelands when it became profitable to do so.

Furthermore, as mentioned previously, Donald had extensive periodical sales routes in residential areas as well as along the commercial avenues. His job took him into the homes and social networks of his many residential customers where he learned how they lived. Because many of them required credit even for such inexpensive items as newspapers, he also learned about their problems. Over a four-year period he became a familiar face; many customers became fond of him and demonstrated their affection with Christmas bonuses.

Many credit customers' payments were collected at their local bars, gambling haunts, or barbershop hangouts. To other customers, he loaned money for cigarettes, the numbers (lottery), milk, or beer, to be collected with their newspaper payments. Thus, Donald was more than a paperboy; he was absorbed into the poor Black corporate process, and as he recalled the experiences, one could believe that he liked it.

However, Donald stresses that his experience was not an isolated one. There were many boys like himself who participated in such life styles. Shoeshine boys with their homemade boxes traveled the same "avenue" routes and competed for the limited money there. Other newspaper boys often raced him to a particular bar to hawk the same wares. Some boys combed the area to beg or roll the drunks or rob other young peddlers. Donald marveled that in all his years of roaming dark streets, alleys, corridors, and tenements, he was never robbed or molested. He consistently carried large amounts of coins and dollar bills without incident. For him, the dangers of the ghetto were never realized.

Donald's success as a newsboy brought him to the attention of Mrs. Robert L. Vann, President of the *Pittsburgh Courier,* which he sold among other periodicals (see *Pittsburgh Courier* 1947, 1954). Mrs. Vann made contacts with university officials and social agencies in Pittsburgh to secure him a scholarship to the university. He graduated with an A.B. degree. Donald's newspaper route supervisor and mentor, Lloyd D. Tobias (Toby), made contacts in the periodical business world to secure him a wholesale periodical distribution franchise. Donald expanded that franchise into a larger enterprise until he felt that the business had no further growth potential. Then, he sold the business and returned to the university to continue his graduate studies.

DONALD IN ADULTHOOD[1]

As an older Ph.D. graduate student returning to the university at the age of 33 after operating a wholesale periodical business for 15 years, I was especially stressed by the new life style and my fellow students. Some of the students had earned master's degrees in anthropology, and I had no training in the discipline, for my B.A. (earned at age 22) was in economics. My fellow students and some of the faculty were younger than I, and all of them were white. I was Black.

One of the devices that I used to cope with this new way of life and the tensions that accompanied it was to keep a notebook and a diary of my experiences. This account is based on those documents.

The department of my graduate study was controlled by men who had made their mark in the profession and in general academic circles. They had the power to "make or break" young scholars in the profession and, of course, the power to determine whether graduate students would continue. I soon began to realize that these men were very conservative and that I should avoid any controversial discussions with them that would reveal too much about myself. My fellow graduate students had warned me that I could create immediate hostility by revealing that I was sympathetic to Catholicism, Marxism, student rebellion, or antiestablishment change. This was especially true for me because I was the first and only Black in the graduate program of the department and one of the older graduate students that they had accepted. I was advised to be very respectful and to accentuate my role as a student since I was older than most of the others. Later, I learned about the unfortunate fate of those who were not sensitive to these admonitions. I was warned that the power elite in my department attempted to mask that power by appearing very protective of the female faculty and staff in the department. The message was clear. If I wanted to graduate from that department, I must learn how to "stay in my place."

[1]A portion of the material below appeared in *The Griot* (Williams, 1990).

The chair of the department was also a victim of the "power elite." He was chair in name only and was allowed to "push the bureaucratic papers," but he was deprived of most of the authority of the position by the close working relationship that the power elite had with members of the higher administration. As a result of this dilemma, the chair was constantly attempting to clarify and fortify his position and role by creating rules and regulations. One set of those regulations caused me to act.

I had matriculated into the department under regulations stipulating that after the completion of a series of core courses, I would be advanced to the doctoral candidacy stage. Later, some of the "elite" professors who refused to teach such courses decided that they would establish a set of preliminary examinations that covered all of the important areas of the discipline. Each graduate student was required to pass these examinations instead of the core courses. I complained that such a regulation should not be retroactive and include students such as I who had come to the department under the core course regulation and who, indeed, had completed some of those requirements. My discussions with the faculty and the chair brought no relief, so I made an appointment to discuss the problem with the provost of the university. The provost promised me that he would investigate the matter and inform me of the proposed remedy. I never heard from him again. I was called into the chair's office, reprimanded for having seen the provost, and given the choice of following the new regulations or leaving the department. I chose to stay and spent many months attempting to persuade the chair and the power elite that I was not really a troublemaker.

Some of the faculty in our department had married upper-class women who were not disposed to be gracious to their husbands' students. These faculty would invite graduate students to their homes for social and academic occasions. I had to learn to tolerate the wives' attitudes, values, and comments about Blacks in America as yet another requirement of my graduate education.

As relationships with the families of faculty continued to develop, I learned that insensitivity from wives was only the beginning. My status among faculty children and other kin and even pets was often ambiguous. To have children who were my own children's (three sons) age address me by my abbreviated first name was disconcerting to me. I am often reminded of my graduate student experiences when I observe how the offspring of dominant parents among social animals treat the subordinate members of their group. In my household, I felt in control of the family pets. In the households of certain professors, I felt that the family pets were in control of me. I am not yet convinced that my faculty did not enjoy this process of subordination which I discuss below.

I will never forget how shocked two of my faculty were when I passed my comprehensive examinations on Africa. The senior member of the examination committee was the most powerful faculty member in our department. He was a Connecticut-born Yankee and an internationally known elitist. The two junior faculty members were sycophants of the senior member, who was an internationally recognized expert on Africa, and they could not effectively oppose his assessment of my examination. So they were anxiously awaiting the examination committee meeting to discover what he would say. For years, he had developed a reputation for discriminating against women, Catholics, and Jews. He considered Blacks so "disadvantaged" that they did not deserve his attention. The junior members, who supported me, feared that he would dismiss my examination without a fair evaluation. They knew that I was sensitive to discrimination and prone to act to defend myself. As the examinee, I was stressed by all of these factors as well as by the examination itself and the known history of the difficult comprehensive examinations given by the senior member of the committee for many years at another elite university. My department included faculty members who had taken their examinations from him, and they knew fellow students who had failed them. For years, I had been told about these famous and "impossible" exams. To the surprise of the junior committee members, however, the senior member voted a strong pass for my examination. Why were they surprised? As a reader, you might be able to guess; the author has several explanations. None of them reassures me.

The same senior faculty member had caused me some anguish in a seminar course. He, as most of my faculty, believed that my race and my "disadvantaged" background would not allow me to excel in my graduate work. They felt that if I worked very hard I could pass my courses, but none of them expected me to become a major scholar. Unfortunately, most of the fellow students whom they did expect to excel disappointed them. It became clear to me after only one semester that most of the faculty would rationalize one reason or another why my work was not excellent, regardless of its actual quality. In one course with a particular senior faculty member, all of the graduate students were trying to impress him because we realized that he could make or break graduate students if he chose. Each of us was required to present four oral reports in the seminar. I made a special effort to research well the four scholars that I had selected for my reports. This was my opportunity to use my age and the speech experience I had gained in the business world. I presented four rousing reports, and the professor and students reacted with enthusiasm. My final grade in the course, however, was not a reflection of these reports. Against the advice of my fellow students and some other faculty members, I went to the professor and questioned him about my grade. His response was that some of my reports were excellent but that some were not as good as others. Baffled by his comments, I continued to pursue the issue with others until I discovered that my fellow students and the professor had allowed me to choose two scholars (Ruth Benedict and Margaret Mead) that the professor held in contempt. No one had warned me that the only way that I could do a favorably received report about them was to discredit their work in its entirety. The balanced reports that I had attempted did not fulfill that requirement.

In another course, a junior faculty member recorded a final grade for me that I felt was below what I had actually earned. I visited him and discussed my work. He advised me that my problem had been the final examination which he had not returned for me to review. I requested my examination to determine why I had not done as well as I believed I would. After a thorough review of the examination, I discovered that he had not returned all the pages to me. I visited him again and requested the missing pages. He responded that there were no missing pages. That was the complete examination as he had received it. I asked him to review the pages with me to determine that the writing itself revealed that some answers were unreasonably abbreviated without the missing pages. He promised to look for the missing pages. A few days later, he called me to say that he had found the missing pages and that my grade would be changed to an A.

Another senior professor recorded a final grade of B+ for me in a seminar in which I thought I had earned an A. In fact, I had received an A in the only written assignment for the course, and in that paper, the professor had written comments that suggested that he was very impressed with my work. I visited the professor to discuss the grade, and he informed me that he would have given me an A if I had compared the society that I had researched with another society. This would have given my work a comparative framework. I reminded him that nowhere in the requirements of his assignments to the class was there any indication that the students should work within a comparative framework. He responded that since our discipline was a comparative one, all graduate students should know that this was the way to proceed. The B+ would be recorded as a B because of the limitations of the recording system. I lost that battle as well as many others.

Many senior professors encouraged confrontational learning in their seminars. So the "best and brightest" students earned their grades and relationships with the professor by demolishing other students' ideas and class presentations. I was often the target of these humiliating attacks. On one such occasion, my attacker was so aggressive that another female student, full of indignation at what seemed excessive criticism, came to my defense. She supported my thesis with evidence that was unknown to me and silenced my attacker with ten minutes of rebuttal that I will never forget. My defender was Lebanese, and although we had no personal relationship, she was sensitive to abuse in any form. She found the environment intolerable and left to complete her graduate work at another elite university.

Many of my professors had experienced tortured humiliations in their own graduate schools. Some of them had been converted to believe that the pain and suffering were just another rite of passage that their own students would experience to test their endurance and as a part of the professional initiation. Being older, Black, already exposed to enough pain and suffering, and believing that intelligent behavior was reasonable, I had many adjustments to make to the senseless cruelty of academic life. Some professors seemed to enjoy demolishing a paper that one had spent several months researching and writing. The final advice was "now rewrite it with my strictures in mind." I was often amazed that the paper could be demolished again after one had followed all of the instructions carefully. This time, on a second reading, the professor discovered flaws that he had overlooked during the first reading. This process can be endless, especially if it involves a chapter in a larger thesis. For a Black who already felt persecuted, it can be difficult to appreciate that this process may make his work a better product. It is especially difficult to believe that this is the professor's motivation.

My final comments are for the ubiquitous cocktail parties to which the graduate student is often the reluctant invitee. Many professors invited the graduate students instead of hiring servants or having an affair catered. They expected us to come early to help prepare and to remain late to clean. They pretended to be doing most of the work themselves and even expected us to be grateful for the privilege of mingling with their "distinguished" guests. Cocktail parties were held for new faculty, departing faculty, interviewing faculty, faculty on external evaluation teams, and visiting faculty. They were held to reciprocate, cheaply, all of the dinner parties the hosts had attended. They were held when a new chair took office, and for the old chair when he left office. They were held for holidays, birthdays, retirements, to thank God for Fridays, or just for a change of pace.

Most cocktail parties are similar and require no description here. My reason for discussing them is to describe my personal feelings on these occasions in order to reflect on my reactions in many group contexts of my graduate school experience.

In a group, conversations were usually directed to someone other than me, and people would often position themselves to avoid eye contact with me. It seemed that I was not expected to speak, and when I did, it was frequently as if I had not spoken because the conversation continued without reference to what I had contributed. If we were standing, I had constantly to reposition myself as the movements of others, leaving and returning, tended to exclude me from the group.

For a long period, I felt that these cocktail parties were simply torture chambers. I was obliged to be friendly and talkative when no one seemed interested in talking to me. When I approached people who were talking to each other just to listen unobtrusively and to wait to see if they would include me, their body kinesis seemed designed to exclude me. I moved from one scene of rejection to the next until most people were relaxed from their drinks and only then willing to include me. Even late in the evening, I could be abruptly disillusioned when I wholeheartedly welcomed someone to my conversation, sensitive to my own recent rejection, only to have them communicate that they had walked over to talk to another person in the group. Last, when my wounds were just about healed, my hosting professor or his wife would communicate that I had stayed too long.

These cocktail parties are examples of social gatherings where some insecure people attempt to reach and maintain their mythological social levels. Their ubiquitous inferiority complexes coerce them to repel any symbol of perceived inferiority.

I have survived all of this. Perhaps I am stronger because of it. I am grateful for the strength as my profession and my society seldom allow me to forget that I am Black.

ANOTHER QUEST

The documentary approach causes discomfort among anthropologists who see in the discipline's past an all-too-frequent tendency to adopt *a colonialist attitude toward "exotic" others,* or, in the words of one young visual anthropologist, "the dark, the naked, the breasted, and the feathered." (Raymond 1991: A5)

The human inferiority complex that I have struggled with personally, professionally, and anthropologically is difficult to observe or describe. This chapter will narrate the personal relationships of another anthropology professor whose inferiority complex may become so clear as to ease some of the difficulty of description.

This is the story of Aud Procterman. As I have stated, many of those who enter the profession of anthropology seem to have a more-severe inferiority complex than others. They seek to study people who are "inferior" to themselves. They enjoy associating with such people in a professional role that precludes contamination by these "inferiors." Cultural and social anthropologists enjoy the company of human "inferiors" who are the objects of their scholarly interest. Procterman had an unusual inferiority complex even for an anthropologist. His seemed pathologically severe.

Procterman was reared in Brooklyn, New York, by Jewish parents who immigrated there from the Soviet Union. He had one older brother, and his father worked as a skilled tradesman. The family was poor and the parents often argued about financial matters. These arguments contributed to Procterman's feelings that he was not loved by either parent but was merely a pawn who was frequently used in their disputes. For example, Procterman says that he was accepted into a prestigious art school with tuition assistance after he graduated from high school. His father protested that to attend would be a waste of family resources. He insisted that Procterman join the work force and provide some income to the household. But the mother was firm: Procterman would continue his education. The disagreement was not that the mother placed such a high value on her son's education, but as Procterman says, "It was that she hated my father and that was her way of torturing him." And Procterman's father was, indeed, tortured as he watched his unemployed son engaged in art projects which required his own earnings to be spent on art supplies. Procterman claims that his mother enjoyed this torture, as I listened to Procterman recall the experiences, he seemed to enjoy the torture as well. What he seemed especially to enjoy were the tactics that his mother devised to "get at" his father. She was a strategist in torture. He was an unloved child who seemed to be fascinated to be a pawn in his father's misery.

After graduation, Procterman drove a bakery truck and delivered the bakery goods over a large area of the state of New York. His artistic abilities were not sufficient to earn a living. He recalled how the long hours and the tedium of that job taxed his endurance. For him, the occupation was inferior. But he persevered as he has done most of his life. He married a Scottish woman (in three "marriages" he has never married a Jew) and released his frustrations on her by engaging in dangerous camping expeditions with her in areas where wild bear were common. He would recall with pleasure how the bears would enter his camps and tents and threaten their lives. He tested a member of this "superior" race until they were divorced.

Procterman decided to improve his life chances and escape his job by continuing his education. He matriculated at an elite university as a graduate student of anthropology. He was not considered a good student and was reported to develop catastrophes in his personal life whenever he had academic deadlines. He had difficulties passing his examinations and had a reputation for not enjoying the company of other students. Soon the students began to refer to him as "Murphy's madness" and "Murph's mistake" because Murphy was his advisor and no one could understand why or how Procterman could remain at the university with such performances. But he persevered and finally passed his examinations after more than one attempt, and he went off to the field in West Africa to rid himself of his "superiors" and to enjoy the company of his "inferiors."

Procterman's fieldwork consisted primarily of inviting men to his home in a west African city and interviewing them. Even in the field, Procterman avoided prolonged contamination with the "inferior." He did not do his research in the bush as most anthropologists in Africa do. While there, Procterman met another anthropologist from the United States. She was an African American who assisted him with his fieldwork. They married and had two children. On a trip back to the United States when she was pregnant with their second child, Procterman informed her that he could never allow his mother to meet her because she was Black. He chose to torture the bride rather than have his mother torture him. They divorced and went their separate ways. She discovered that her career was delayed and negatively affected as a single parent abandoned at such a crucial moment. Procterman did not see or support his abandoned family.

Back in the United States, Procterman began his teaching career as a single man. He claimed expertise in social structure because his department was dominated by Bigbabb (a world-renowned anthropologist) and Bigbabb's theoretical area, in urbanization because he had done his fieldwork in a city, and in "primitive art" because he had studied art and "primitives." Procterman was promoted to associate professor with tenure in 1967, supposedly aided by spreading rumors about his Jewish "rival" (a social anthropologist), namely that his rival was teaching that Bigbabb's theoretical orientation was faulty and that the rival was performing poorly in the department's required experimental course. Procterman was also aided in his bid for tenure because he was bowing to every whim and directive of Bigbabb. This was in spite of Bigbabb's history as an anti-Semite, including membership in several clubs that prohibited Jews. He insisted on calling Procterman's Jewish rival a "New York Jew," notwithstanding the many times that he was told that this colleague had been reared in Connecticut where Bigbabb himself was born and reared. Bigbabb believed that Jews were inferior, especially New York Jews. He called Procterman's research and his book "claptrap." Another distinguished, more gracious departmental professor and friend of Bigbabb called it "journalism." Bigbabb was oppressive to colleagues and to graduate students. But to Procterman, who always supported him, he was an academic pater who tortured "inferior" people.

As soon as Procterman became a full professor and chair, his expertise changed from social structure to social stratification. He was beginning to oppose being dominated. Notwithstanding his lack of research among African Americans and his failure to list African Americans as one of his areas of expertise, Procterman began to teach and behave as if he were an expert on "Negroes in the New World." His best friend was Black and the only Black graduate student in the department was his advisee. Procterman dated Black women and considered himself an expert on Blacks at a time when such expertise was valued in the university where Black student revolts were common in the late 1960s.

These behaviors changed too when Procterman became a full professor and chair. Procterman had a hostile separation from his Black friend. He ceased to date African-American women, and he lost interest in his Black graduate student. He began to date a German graduate student in anthropology, the daughter of a wealthy "old" family. They married and traveled worldwide on "departmental business" and reportedly at departmental expense. At the wedding site, the home of the bride's parents, Procterman, leading a line of cars containing his anthropology colleagues, drove over the large lawn of the estate in a rite of degradation that was costly to the parents.

In the department, he began to recruit exclusively from "the best anthropology department in the world," where he had graduated. He assumed, erroneously, that as fellow alumni these recruits would support him. He also assumed, erroneously, that as full professor and chair he could begin to dominate the department, notwithstanding the presence and power of Bigbabb. But his newly found status made him overconfident. He ceased to associate with the "socially inferior" and began ambivalently to identify with the "socially superior."

This overconfidence led to Procterman's ouster from the chair after two years and some months. He began to be less sensitive to Bigbabb's wishes and to those of his other colleagues. Some of these colleagues were quantitative anthropologists who represented a threat to the humanist anthropologists within the department. Procterman was considered a humanist anthropologist. He waited too long to accommodate one of them, Robustus, the recently appointed Mellon Professor, with a new office. He attempted to seduce another from Bigbabb's research into his own project. Ultimately, he was trying to ease Bigbabb into retirement. All of these factors enabled some hostile departmental faculty members to maneuver him into declaring that he would resign. Of course, he thought that no one would offer to replace him. The most eligible person had just received a free vacation at Procterman's largess. But he made the declaration, an acting chair was assigned, and the most eligible person agreed to accept the position at a later date, notwithstanding the vacation.

Few understood the personal impact of this upon Procterman. With his deep-seated inferiority complex he had struggled to prove that he was "superior." He published a reputable book on his African research. He maneuvered his way into an early promotion to full professor by serving Bigbabb. He was the chair of one of the major anthropology departments in the world, one that could boast of having three past presidents of the American Anthropological Association on its faculty simultaneously. He had married a wealthy "W.A.S.P." from a Revolutionary War family, and he had purchased a grand house in one of the exclusive areas where academics and professionals resided. As one of his close friends and colleagues described him after he threatened to call the police on the friend's graduate student about overdue library books, "He was drunk with power." Of course, this was a graduate student that Bigbabb had found wanting. Now, Procterman was ousted from the chair. He could not write and publish because of his despair. He could not rise in academic administration because he had failed at administration. He had a young wife who had married him because of his prominence, which was now fading. He was distraught.

As his pain began to grow old, he attempted to salvage his reputation by becoming a connoisseur of foods, African art, and wines. With his background in art, he tried to be a gentleman and a scholar. He gave dinner parties for distinguished scholars, athletes, and community leaders. But without any recent publishing feats, his behavior became a source of amusement in his department. This period was aggravated by the presence of his young children whom he tortured in response to his own pain. He had a habit of pinching the babies until they burst into cries, and their mother would rush into the room and complain about these acts. She knew what had happened because of his history with them. This was a painful period for his household.

One of the benefits of all this was Procterman's renewed interest in his Black graduate student. Procterman had more time to supervise. It demonstrated to his wife that he yet had some academic authority. The student had continued to collect his data and was beginning to write his dissertation. Procterman had more time and interest in the work now, in spite of not being impressed with the student or his work. He had collected him during a period when it was fashionable to have a Black student. He had tortured the student as he must have been tortured during his graduate-student days. He would make promises to the student and later claim that he did not remember the promises. He would allow his sharp-clawed cat to climb over the student's lap, digging it's claws into his skin, and laugh when the student responded to the pain. The student did not dare to dispatch the cat or cease to return to Procterman's home for the torture. Procterman would tell the student that the cat was "mean" and that was why he enjoyed her. He would return dissertation chapters that had been revised according to his directions with new directives that contradicted the old. He behaved as if the student would never be able to complete the work. The student believed him. Procterman had lost confidence in himself as a scholar, and he was projecting this onto the student.

Something occurred to break this impasse. The student took one of his dissertation chapters to an anthropological conference. The audience was very responsive. In the audience, there was an editor of an anthropological journal. He requested the chapter for his journal. Procterman had published in this same journal, and the editor conferred with Procterman to get his approval. Procterman was ecstatic. Anthropology was giving him approval through his student. He assisted the student to prepare the manuscript for publication. He worked with the student until the dissertation was completed, and he sought out his own book publisher to review the dissertation for publishing in revised form. The publisher accepted with some major revisions. The student was ecstatic.

During this period of renewed interest in the student's work after it had been validated elsewhere, Procterman and the student spent many hours together working and relaxing. They became close friends, and the student became close to Procterman's wife and children. After the manuscript had been accepted for publication, Procterman told the student that the student's career would soar after the book was published. He seemed to be happy for himself and the student. After the book was published, he gave a large party at his home for the student and invited those whom he held in high esteem. The party was obviously as much for Procterman as for the student. Procterman believed that this disadvantaged Black student had succeeded beyond all other students in the department because he had Procterman as his major advisor.

Later, when Procterman had calmed, he changed his perspective about the future of the student. He told him that he should be satisfied with his present position at a small college, especially since he would one day be chair of the very small department there. Procterman was reevaluating what he desired for his student, but the student did not accept the message.

Approximately one year later, Procterman's university called his student and told him that they wanted to consider him for a position in the anthropology department. This was a major shock to Procterman. His student was considering joining his own department. During the following weeks, Procterman never seemed enthusiastic about this development, but he did not display hostility until the final hour.

By this time, quantitative and humanist factions had been in close combat in the department for almost three years. A major question, now, was whether the quantitative faction was going to accept a student of Procterman, a humanist. This would mean another vote for the humanists in the department. The leader of the quantitative faction, Robustus, was to evaluate the student and report back to his quantitative colleagues. The chair of the department arranged for a meeting, in which the student won the admiration and quelled the fears of the leader. To the student, all was ready for the vote. But on the night before the vote, Procterman surprised his protege by announcing, "I will not lift a finger to help you." Procterman was angered by how little his help was needed and by the support from the other faction. The student panicked and called his humanist supporters for fear that Procterman would attempt to rally the vote against him. They reassured the student that he had their support, but they were worried that opposition from Procterman would "open the door" for other hostile expressions. No one could explain Procterman's behavior to the student to the student's satisfaction.

The vote passed, and the student entered the department as a nontenured associate professor. Procterman immediately began to behave as if he had done nothing unreasonable. On the contrary, he announced, without consulting the student, that they would be team teaching a course together. Procterman's attitude seemed to be "As long as you win, it is because you are my student and my client, but if you fail, you have lost a good battle and that is fine with me too." This egocentric position is, paradoxically, one that is frequently taken by those with severe inferiority complexes. The student tactfully declined the invitation to team teach the course and taught his own courses. He also maintained good relationships with his quantitative colleagues, to the chagrin of Procterman. The student was maintaining support for tenure in two years, and he needed the votes of the quantitative members. Procterman never complained about his student's behavior, and he had plenty of opportunities because the student visited Procterman's home two or three times a week. The student continued to be grateful for Procterman's assistance and continued to need his support.

Yet, approximately two years later, Procterman voted against the tenure of his student without ever giving any indication that he would. For the first year of this period, the student had been away as a distinguished visiting professor at another university. He had returned and continued to maintain good relationships with his colleagues.

On the day of the departmental tenure vote, the student learned that he had one negative vote—Procterman's. He went to Procterman's house in disbelief. Procterman and his wife were waiting in anticipation. They both attempted to explain that the student had enough votes to get tenure in any case. Procterman's vote was supposedly a strategic maneuver to help the next candidate for tenure avoid comparison with a recent unanimous affirmative vote. That candidate had asked Procterman to lead her through the process. Procterman knew that she could not get all of the votes of the quantitative faculty. He claimed that he was protecting her with his negative vote for his student. Was he?

I do not believe that he was. Once again, Procterman was angry that his client did not need him. He was convinced that if the student did not need him then the student had no basis to care about him. How could he be the student's patron if the client continually proved that he did not need him? In the heat of the discussion, he even told the student that if one member of the quantitative faction (whom he especially hated) "had voted against you I would have voted for you." But when everybody voted for the student, Procterman saw himself as insignificant, and he struck out against the student-client who had allowed this revelation. After all of this, Procterman still tried to convince the student that he was a decent human being: "Do you have any doubt that the university is going to give you tenure? I don't!" But even while the decision was being debated at the higher university level, Procterman was allegedly spreading the rumor that he, not the student, had written the student's book. This was reportedly discussed at the university tenure review meetings. All during this period, Procterman and his wife were pretending to be the friend of the student.

Even if Procterman had voted for the reasons that he offered, the vote was unethical and unprofessional. A tenure vote is one of the most important votes in a professor's life. It is a vote on one's scholarly achievements and prospects and not a vote for the voter's political agenda. This should have been especially true for Procterman, who constantly proclaimed his ethics, honesty, and professionalism to anyone who would listen.

While Procterman was a departmental colleague of the student, he never entered his student's office. They were friends during all of this period, but Procterman never came in and sat to talk. There were other faculty who never entered that "polluted" office, but the student understood their behavior. He was Black, a junior member of the faculty, and was doing research on African Americans. He was supposed to be avoided and especially not given the deference of being approached. But Procterman was his friend, his major advisor, his mentor, his patron, and, ironically, someone who wanted him to fail if he did not succeed by Procterman's assistance. Over the years, the student's office was ritually purified by the frequent gatherings of senior and distinguished colleagues. But in all those years, Procterman never came in to sit and talk. Even when the student invited Procterman and his wife to the student's home with other guests for dinner, Procterman attempted to dominate the affair by lecturing the student on how the drinks should be served. Later, the other guests commented on Procterman's odd behavior.

Finally, the year the student (now a tenured associate professor) left the university, Procterman voted against his promotion to full professor in a vote that was in response to another full professor's offer from a major research university. The student departed. Procterman never explained that vote. Perhaps there was no need. Years later, Procterman commented to a fellow advisee and mentor of the student about the student's continuing success: "We created a monster." The fellow advisee attempted to explain to Procterman that the student had entered graduate school at a mature age and was already "created" when they got him. A Black student who went further than Procterman was surely a monster; for once again, Procterman discovered his own feelings of inferiority documented and reinforced.

At one point, the student had been seduced into believing that there was a real friendship between him and Procterman. But Procterman was not capable of having a friend, a wife, or children who were African American. His inferiority complex was too severe. He had spent most of his life trying to become less inferior, and his student and others continued to document that he had failed. It is not the inferiority complex itself that is so devastating in this case, although we have stated that this complex leaves its devastation everywhere (Williams In Press b). But it is the drive (for example, in Hitler, Stalin, Nixon, and Napoleon) to "wipe out that damned spot" with the lives of other people that was the terrible affliction of Procterman. Unfortunately, there are many others like him in academia.

Procterman's student did not understand that just as the loyal soldier is expected to die if necessary without questioning the general, the cause, or the command, the pathological patron expects the loyal client's support regardless of the personal consequences to the client. This kind of patron cannot tolerate an "inferior" client questioning his judgment or his motives. The patron, like the general, must be right because he is "superior." As all of the soldiers who have died in lost, forgotten, and erroneous causes, the client will be out of sight and out of mind when and if the patron realizes his folly. Generals, like despots and pathological patrons, expect the destruction of lives to achieve their own successes. They have little doubt about the respective values. The value of "inferior" people is well understood by those who exploit them. What is power if not the capacity to decide your "inferior's" fate? Any "inferior" who grows to challenge his "superior's" power has, indeed, become a monster to him.

Somehow Procterman's student had never learned how to be an appropriate "inferior" for Procterman. Procterman never realized that the student was not challenging his status or his authority. The student just did not understand Procterman's kind of patronage—the kind that Procterman had learned from his mother, from his own graduate student experiences, and from his years as a close observer and sycophant of Bigbabb.

I emphasize the example format of the descriptions in this chapter. The pervasive feelings of inferiority are one of the fundamental problems of our time. These feelings make the rich, powerful, educated, famous, and exalted insecure with all their privilege, entitlement and empowerment. These wealthy greedily reach for more. Great scholars seldom believe that they are great enough. They plagiarize material, falsify scientific data, undermine their colleagues, and envy their scholarly awards. Jealousy runs rampant in the halls of the rich, powerful, and famous. I have met many "great" men and women, and none of them have felt that they were great enough. None of them had the capacity of personal security to be comfortable in association with that perceived to be inferior. No amount of upward mobility seems to make people comfortable with their inadequacies as well as with those of others. No amount of personal aggrandizement and embellishment allows them to accept their animal selves and those of all their species and kingdom.

As Baritz observes:

> Freed from civilization's shalt-nots, and from poverty's constraints, the new Americans, especially those born in the late forties and fifties, may now enjoy the perquisites of status, and liberation from the obligations and limitations imposed by love. While a rose, an infant, or a sonata does not produce advantageous cost-benefit ratios, this cold new world evidently does. Although extreme individualism necessarily shades into isolation, although a hypertropied rationalism must become callous, although commodity fetishism can never be satisfied, all nevertheless apparently justify the abandonment of place and intimacy. The cost of success, then, is a redefinition of pleasure, and thus also of pain. The fathers knew there was risk and pain in love and life. Fleeing this human adventure, the children calculated their progress toward a better life—the contemplation of all that success may produce, life as work, the happiness produced by objects, the envy of strangers, and the freedom to float above the struggles of others, in warmth and comfort, alone. (1989:318)

Conclusion

BELMAR

I have attempted to bring us from Belmar 1976 to Belmar 1991. I have tried to show the process of admitting American Blacks to Belmar and the ethos surrounding that process. We have seen Belmar—old, sapped of its commercial vitality, and economically abandoned—when Blacks were finally welcomed from their old homes which were destroyed in the Hill. We have observed some of the people who live here and some of the fiery trials and agonies that economic deprivation creates when combined with ritual pollution and racial discrimination. Exposed to the limited alternatives for viable existence in the ghetto, these residents use this entire range of opportunities. Such opportunities happen to be primarily expressive rather than instrumental.

Belmar, like many urban neighborhoods, has been almost abandoned by its white residents and its white "leaders." African-American "leaders" have operated there for almost 25 years. And when they leave or retire, their names can be found on streets, buildings, and parks. But the people of these neighborhoods and the neighborhoods themselves are usually in a worse condition when these Black "leaders" retire than when they arrived. They bring much rhetoric, symbol, charisma, and expressiveness but little or no substance and accomplishment, except for themselves and their families. They will leave Belmar with great reputations and wealth for themselves and their families, but there will be little left behind for the remaining residents who are forced to stay because of poverty and phenotype. Belmar must have African-American leaders with different aspirations if these neighborhoods are to grow and prosper. Such leaders must do more work for the people they represent and less for themselves, their families, and their co-conspirators.

Chapter 5, "Landlords and Tenants," focused directly upon American values and left little doubt that defiance, discrimination, and oppression have a corrosive effect upon the people of Belmar. Despite all this, the spirit, faith, and determination of this population bursts forth in their world view, their subsystem of symbols, and their intense appreciation of the nature of their victimization by society. Their expressive activities are consistent and congruent with this approach; they use what they have in all the ways they can. They create meaning and substance in the streets, taverns, limited open spaces, lighted areas, the few stores, churches, and, above all, themselves. Nevertheless, the wider society sees only the instrumental failures imposed upon these exploited people.

The whites escaped from Belmar in the 1960s but took with them their attitude that African Americans are the scum of the earth. Few understood that the Black newcomers were fighting for their lives. The elderly and welfare Blacks were frightened to think that their checks would not be forwarded to their new locations. They were housed with strangers in makeshift apartments because their incomes were too meager to afford better. Unfamiliar with their neighbors, they worried about the security of their checks when and if they did arrive. Extended families were forced to move into one-family dwellings because they had nowhere else to go. Children were forced to attend schools where teachers, staff, and administration resented their intrusion. And Blacks throughout the neighborhood felt the hostility of the white coalition mentioned in Chapter 3. Once again, the failure of the system was laid to rest upon the shoulders of its most exploited victims.

The impact of technology, the ethos of production, the energy crisis, population changes, and the resulting unemployment are thrusting many white Americans— educated and skilled—into the economic deprivation which they have always tolerated for the poor Black. Perhaps this, like the presence of drug abuse in the suburbs, will bring some attention to the problems that have beset and continue to plague poor Blacks in the United States.

Regardless of the future, however, I have tried to illustrate the complexity in the nature of some poor Black Americans in Belmar. Simple subcultures and simple societies do not exist, and simple explanations survive only because they are unchallenged. The simplicity in my examination of Belmar merely awaits the next analysis.

I echo the call of other Americans (see Clark 1967, Commoner 1971 and 1976, Harrington 1976, Heilbroner 1976, Lekachman 1976, and others) who say what the world needs now is "love." Developing countries must ask, "Develop to what?" "Mainstreamers" must wonder, more, "Why?" All of us must be concerned about the limited resources of our world, the wanton waste, and the concerted denial of our poor Black brothers. Otherwise, Belmar will probably go the way of the Hill and be another chapter in the story of neighborhood extinction. In a tight job market, more and more Blacks will be jobless. The rich will get richer, as the profits of big business continue to be our priorities. Organized crime will continue to be a major component of our society and the world. White-collar crime will flourish and be less often penalized. Business will be conducted as usual, and Sunday will be the Sabbath. This reminds me of the expression of the young woman in Belmar, "knowing deep down in your Black soul that the white man all over the world is going to get payback one of these days." I am afraid, however, as I have tried to express throughout these pages, that such retribution cannot be administered to such a theoretically distinct population without destroying us all.

I have found it difficult to describe the poor Black and simultaneously give a meaningful approximation of their life styles. Many words that must be used to discuss poverty have built-in connotations of degradation. This task further defined the overwhelming bias against the poor Black in this culture and society. So I ask the reader to understand that some of this struggle may have surfaced in these pages.

One may never be able to describe poor Black behavior or "lower-class culture" (Berger 1973) adequately for the minds or attitudes of "mainstream" European Americans. This is partially because the language that must be used to describe

Black life styles is pervaded with the "standard pejorative stereotypes projected upon Afro-Americans" (Valentine and Valentine 1970). Thus, depending upon our perspectives, any description of Black neighborhoods can provide the raw material to reinforce such stereotypes. I am even more fatalistic: Perhaps no amount of description or explanation will change the attitudes of those who are contemptuous of poor Blacks.

It is difficult, indeed, to strike the desired balance when attempting to put poverty in its proper perspective after millennia of myths about it and prejudice against it. My objective is not to make poverty appear attractive, for life is often an ordeal for all economic classes, but rather to cast it in a proper frame of reference to demonstrate that the poor are equal to any class in terms of potential for meaningful living.

Thus, we see the contradictory values in American life. We also see that for Black Americans, striving for American success means abandoning the symbol subsystem of many "genuine" Blacks in America. The nature of success in America requires that if "genuine" Blacks reach for it, they must become "spurious" and deny "genuine" values. Most who reach must fail and be doomed to a subcultural purgatory or a "spurious" existence. Those who succeed usually grip "mainstream" values to their bosoms and abandon their poor Black brothers and their respective expressive styles and symbols, notwithstanding their rhetoric to the contrary (Wilson 1978). This is the Black-American dilemma.

Somehow, we must bridge these cultural chasms. We, Americans, must learn to live with one another in spite of American propaganda that teaches that who and what we are depends upon our position on the economic and social ladder. We must expose ourselves to all facets of Black-American life and, though disillusioned, champion our common causes against a system that would divide and exploit us. We must go into Belmar and see the truth, the beauty, and the goodness there. We must be exposed to the suffering there, for it is our values that torture these fellow human beings. Until we become a part of the solution, we are part of the problem. Nonviolence is not only a form of social protest, but as practiced by Ghandi, it is also a way of life. The American way does violence to the poor masses just as the present human way does violence to the earth and most of its people. We must understand their plight so that we may improve their life chances as well as those of all humankind.

We see that Belmar Blacks live in an area which is economically abandoned and ravaged. They understand that they are perceived as the flotsam of humankind, and they are herded into places like Belmar that reflect such attitudes. The "genuine" Black is not far removed from chattel slavery. His "masser" is his "boss," "the man," his "welfare worker," and his many creditors whom he cannot pay. The overseer no longer beats him; the police do. The "masser" still rapes the woman and separates members of families by prostitution and poverty. Therefore, the ghetto is the new slave quarters, and the city is the plantation where the "genuine" Black has restricted access, participation, and utilization. Notwithstanding the propaganda and rhetoric to the contrary, he has never been free. He has "progressed" from chattel slavery to economic slavery, and his caste and class have remained the same.

Thus, the expressive styles and creative techniques for locking horns with life in the ghetto have persisted and evolved from the days of slavery. It requires the persistent efforts of social scientists to approximate the tangle of bicultural value orientations and concomitant behavior that are the result of the peculiar history of "genuine" Blacks in Belmar. This initial effort is only a beginning. There is far more to do.

The "genuine" Black does not believe that if he works hard, saves, and gets and education he will be successful in American society. On the contrary, he believes that "a workin' man never gets ahead." Or "hard work is a lifetime job." He seeks his salvation in leisure time—weekends, holidays, "party time," "liquor flowing like water," and "lettin' the good times roll." He enjoys himself—laughter, "rap," sex, and forms of intensive interaction—because that is all he has. In the process, he violates most middle-class standards. Such standards he has not learned well, purposefully defies, cannot afford, or cannot integrate into his life style. But he is an American, and these standards are exposed and enforced in behavior and attitudes in the wider society. So, he must be aggressive and deny, defile, and defy them to survive with his own perception of the world.

This is the social context in which he rears his children, protects his masculinity, grows old, and dies. It is a constant struggle between "sin" and "righteousness"; between success in failure and failure in success ("Whites never accept you no matter how you prove yourself"); between being Black while living, sleeping, talking, and acting white and being Black while knowing that no matter what your friends call you (for instance, "money bags"), you are the "invisible man" (Ellison 1952) and "nobody knows my name" (Baldwin 1963). He might be able to contend with the struggle if not for the perpetual reminder that in America everybody can "make it," and the "freak" (successful "mainstream") in the neighborhood is the realization of that dream. The final ironic deprivation is that he has so little contact with the "successful" in this society that he seldom realizes that this competitive, materialistic system makes failures of us all (see Coles 1977, Grinker 1978, Johnson 1978, Nisbet 1975, Simon and Gagnon 1976, Stone and Kestenbaum 1975, and Wixen 1973).

Again, I point out that there are many kinds of Blacks in Belmar, and I restrict my major account to the poor who do not opt for the system but maintain a consistent subcultural philosophy and value orientation in spite of that system—they are "genuine." We need to know them better. Neither one particular perspective nor the conceptualizations of a few informants will ever tell us what Belmar is. It is many different things to different people at various times under an array of circumstances.

These pages cannot define Belmar, only provide glimpses of a complex process, compiled with the hope that the composite reflects the human substance and content of which my informants and I have been a part. That picture contains blight; the dirty and abandoned buildings and lots attest to a process of economic decay. Yet, beneath the sands of this urban desert, there is life—people who feel a sense of belonging and who participate in the vivid life styles of this economic dumping ground, this ecological niche where poor Blacks in America are herded and confined. The young and old men keep a constant vigil on the street corners, the avenues, and the commercial establishments (Chapter 3). A few local patrons visit these enterprises and enjoy their informal relationship with their proprietors. The "genuine" atmosphere pervades the local bank, where one transacts business as well as meets and interacts with one's neighbors (often including Black tellers) and the peddlers who block the entrance. There is a distinctive relaxed cadence here that few, if any, Pittsburgh banks can claim. The restaurants seem poor and inelegant to outsiders, but that same appearance is a significant symbol of belonging to the people who eat there. The plumber's shop with its sparse supplies, the fruit and vegetable shop with more display space on the sidewalk than inside, the busy justice of the peace office, and many civic and social welfare storefronts are evidence that there is life in Belmar, although the life styles are peculiar to this ecological niche.

The night life, jitney services, and domestics going to work early in the morning contrast vividly with scenes in other Pittsburgh neighborhoods. These scenes and neighborhood characteristics are part of the socialization fabric that make it difficult for these Blacks to compete with whites who are socialized elsewhere and who are articulate and glib in the expression of "mainstream" abstractions. Such middle-class whites can express such ideas in written form, organized so that it is "readable." They can collect the necessary information for such organization. As such, they are part of the "intellectual" scene. They can enjoy the experience. It is not so for those who grow up in Belmar. They have never adapted to the nature of scholarly routine and research confinement. They are ignorant of the processes of allocating scarce time among pressing duties. Such processes project responsibility, dependability, and maturity.

The few Blacks in Belmar who do labor consistently and conscientiously for scholarly achievements do it with an emotional resistance that becomes tension as they execute such academic duties and obligations. The anxiety is nourished by the attitude that "what I do is good but is not living" and "what I do is not consistent with what I am." All of this results in an ambiguity that undermines resolve and enhances emotional strain. The middle-class white does not experience this. He does not have to tolerate this kind of discomfort, self-doubt, and identity crisis.

I have tried to offer the reader a sense of what it is like to live in a neighborhood that has been abandoned by many of those who can afford to leave. This neighborhood is perceived by the wider society as a ghetto, a slum, undesirable, polluted with crime, violence, dirt, and poor Blacks. I have attempted to demonstrate that residents who live and grow up here create and execute life styles and adaptive patterns of behavior that are partially determined by the ecological niche in which they are often forced to live. Some (the "genuine") learn to live here and get the most from the meager resources available. But at the same time, that very learning process diminishes their chances to function, achieve, and be accepted in the wider society and wider world.

This is the American dilemma. We create the environment, the ecological niche, and then restrict this poor population within it. We condemn the people and their adaptive strategies because of where and how they live. "Genuine" Blacks deny, defile, and defy some of the duties, obligations, and responsibilities with which the wider society burdens them while depriving them of concomitant material and institutional resources. They discover their salvation within intensive social interaction and let others (their critics) count the costs. The cost of being forced to live in this restricted ecology with its associated life styles is high. Such styles and patterns of behavior are not tolerated outside of neighborhoods like Belmar; on the contrary, they are symbols and cues of downward mobility and social inferiority within the wider society. Such symbols and cues produce appropriate responses, if and when they are exhibited.

We come to the conclusion of my attempt to describe the life and times of a select portion of Blacks in Belmar. Perhaps we can now begin to appreciate how distinctive socialization in a peculiar ecological niche (the ghetto) often dooms the "genuine" Black to a level of instrumental inadequacy in the affairs of the wider world. The nature of being "genuine" tends to create incompetency in the codes, cues, stimuli, and response—the standards of mobility—in "mainstream" America. The process of articulating "genuine" life styles, witnessed here in these pages, is the very process which restricts growth in "mainstream" proclivities.

It is as if learning, articulating, and valuing bodily rhythm is the antithesis of bodily poise. If the one requires a lack of inhibition in bodily expressiveness and a facile articulation of such interactional movements which often contain sexual codes, then the other requires control of such movements and the inhibiting of such expressiveness to create an artificial balance in demeanor of the human animal for cultural standards. The time, energy, and enthusiasm used by the "genuine" in acquiring rhythm undermines the potential for acquiring the poise which sells in the American marketplace.

This process is repeated many times by the "genuine" Black who grows up inept at participating in the exclusive institutions of the wider society. He learns to live well in his restricted milieu. He is in this American society, but he is seldom a part of it. He is a member of a different subculture (see Lewis 1964 and 1967, Rodman 1971).

The "spurious" are not members of the "genuine" subculture. Their behavior is situational (see Lewis 1967, Liebow 1967, Rodman 1971). They make a serious effort to avoid the patterns of behavior of the "genuine" around them, but the devastation of the urban desert has its crucial impact upon them. Even the "mainstream" Black suffers from the economic wasteland and the racial discrimination that he is forced to live with in America. Thus, even though these mainstream African Americans share little of Black culture, there is enough shared history, consensus, and commonality to perpetuate the myth. That myth and the continued persecution in this society may someday create a united Black front. Meanwhile, the economic interests in the society continue to undermine and destroy Blacks' subcultural traditions and defy their quest for community. Similar economic interests continue to undermine and destroy the earth. Thus, we will either save these African Americans or lose the whole human enterprise. That is the human dilemma.

THE WORLD

By their general affinity with man—they move, utter sounds, manifest emotions, have bodies and faces like him—and by their superior powers—the birds fly in the open, the fishes swim under water, reptiles renew their skins and their life and can disappear in the earth—by all this the animal, the intermediate link between man and nature, often his superior in strength, agility, and cunning, usually his indispensable quarry, assumes an exceptional place in the savage's view of the world. (Malinowski 1954:45)

Belmar is in the world and in American society. Thus, to understand Belmar, we must comprehend the global and structural contexts of its people. Its people are humans and their behavior is human behavior. I conclude the volume with a discussion of the world, American society, and the human theoretical framework that makes behavior in Belmar more clear to me.

Anthropologists study their "villages" to attempt to understand human behavior. When that study leads to a theory of all mankind, it constitutes the maximum reward for the research endeavor. Living and studying in Belmar and in other "villages" small enough for me to attempt to comprehend them has led me to hypothesize about all humankind. My hypotheses come at a time in human history when modern societies seem to be endangering the earth (see Goldsmith et al. 1990), and dddav seems to be endangering Belmar. The "cold war" seems to be thawed between the United States and the Soviet Union. So, the threat of nuclear war may be past if small wars (for example, Iraq) do not escalate into massive nuclear confrontations. But the threats to our world environment seem more insidious.

As Malinowski (1954:45) suggests, the human obsession with his animal kin determines his perception of the world. He perceives that world through the mediums of myth and power. The animal is the "intermediate link between man and nature," as well as between man and God. The "lower" animals separate us from meaninglessness as well as from our images of God. So we mythologize our relationship with those animals to avoid nature and to reach God. In our most creative moments, we tinker with the forbidden (the beast) and the divine. Our obsession with such a relative is no wonder. Such an obsession has impeded the social scientist from comprehending the nature of man and prompted Floyd H. Allport (1967:24) to exclaim ". . . we are at a loss to understand our origin or our essential nature."

That other human plague—materialism—is a major factor in endangering Earth. The world can no longer afford the wasted energy and pollution that accompany the manufacture and distribution of junk to provide the illusion of luxury for those with the money and need for such illusions. At a time of world crisis (in energy, pollution, and warming), this plague is spreading to the Far East and Eastern Europe. So the prognosis for the earth and the human race is poor. But the treatment remains the affirmation of human dignity without the need for the myths of superiority, the accumulation of power to support those myths, and the trapping of goods to bolster both. Such an affirmation will liberate humans who are slaves to DDDAK and free the "genuine" African American who has relied on dddav. Both have been valuable adaptive emotions and behavior. But what the world needs now is an Ecological Revolution in which humans accept themselves as a small part of the web of life dependent on the ecosystems of the world.

DDDAK is a simple approach to a massive human problem. These valuable adaptive emotions and behaviors that are the basis for culture in humans have become obsolete in modern society. The simplicity of the concept may doom it in a society where complexity has prestige. But the concept attempts to show that the direction of human history is on a terminal course. The Earth may be compared to a closed system. Humans cannot conceptualize themselves and behave as if they are above, free, and independent of all other life and even the Earth itself. The time has ended when we could rationalize the ownership of resources that we could not possibly use merely to restrict the access of others and accrue the status and prestige of such property.

In this century alone, political "leaders" have squandered resources that could have sustained the world for hundreds of years. These "leaders" have colluded with the rail, steel, auto, aviation, and oil industries. Andrew Mellon as Secretary of the U.S. Treasury, openly distributed the nation's treasure to his fellow business people under one pretext or another. He believed, as many business leaders do today, that the government had no reason to have wealth because the free enterprise system would provide for all of the worthy economic needs of the people. Later, F.D.R. was hated by these same business people because he distributed a pittance to the poor.

The military-industrial complex of which President Eisenhower warned is nothing more than a continuing conspiracy to use the resources of the United States for a few, even when the country does not have those resources. The conspirators merely force the taxpayers to borrow the money that they can never repay. The Wall Street and savings and loan scandals are just further examples of political "leaders" giving away the nation's resources in exchange for favors for themselves, their families, and friends. As a result, the United States is bankrupt. Japan, Germany, and other rich countries will soon put us into Chapter Seven and Eleven, and then, they may behave just as we have taught them. The next world war may be fought over this dilemma. Or the new rich countries may refuse to accept the conditions of the Ecological Revolution without war.

Is it any mystery that within such a value system we have places like Belmar? We desperately require a new and different human value system—the Ecological Revolution. Princeton University is establishing a center, funded by the Mellon Foundation, to study values. The idea is a timely one, but in the hands of Princeton philosophers it may never reach the outside world. If it does, perhaps it will contribute to the urgent solution for a commonwealth of humanity.

As C. Wright Mills (1959:28) reminds us, the twenty-first century will be one in which the world's most pressing problem will be to understand human behavior. That comprehension will be required to transform the "uneasiness" and "indifference" to the endangered Earth. Humans, fascinated with power, have glorified the research and scholarship of those who work to control the Earth, its energy and resources (the physical sciences). Now that we have such control, we lack the wisdom and the will to protect the Earth and its web of life. The study of mankind has its predicaments for humans, for it attempts to see us as we are rather than as we see ourselves. We would rather celebrate and glorify the human animal than know it. So societies grudgingly accept those who study mankind except within isolated confinements (for example, ivory towers) that insulate their direct impacts upon social institutions. In the twentieth century, the celebration of humans and their accomplishments (for example, the humanities) and the quest for innovative power (the physical sciences) will reach their zenith at the dawn of the Ecological Revolution. Even the selective exploitation of the social sciences (for example, economics with its vested business interests and political science with its vested governmental interests and its propensity to accept, rationalize, protect, and participate in bureaucratic agencies of power) will wane because none of these disciplines is able to adequately address the required discourse and social transformations in an age of social and ecological revolution. Those social sciences that once addressed the larger questions of human behavior and have been eclipsed by the comfort, rapidity, and prestige of technological, statistical, and mathematical paradigms in their disciplines will be revived. As one former president of the American Anthropological Association said of the scholars in anthropology, "everybody is doing trivia." We are preparing our students for a world that will be "Gone with the Wind."

The victims are not to blame for social problems in American cities. It is DDDAK, dddav, and the social system that results from the history of humans and of American society. The study of the victims keeps the focus of attention away from the problem and allows those who create and profit from the problem to oppress without notice. Studies of the poor, the underclass, the culture of poverty, the ghetto poor, are all designs of the oppressive system that directs attention upon the victims and avoids the spotlight on the "power elite." It is like males studying pornography and for centuries examining all the graphic details of female and child abuse. They repeatedly conclude how women and children must be protected and how they must help to protect themselves. But they rarely discuss the billion-dollar industry in movies, television, magazines, and videos that are subsidized by the taxpayers and protected by the government. We know that cigarettes kill, and African Americans are especially affected, but the Black media and tobacco industry profit from the deaths through their advertisement sales and cigarette sales, respectively.

Social problems are pervasive. Our culture-bound approaches to them have reflected the social system while protecting itself and its sacred inner circle (see Figure 1.3). We need a blameless approach to the social problems that plague the peoples of the world and of the Earth upon which they live. Such an approach will give us insight even into little neighborhoods like Belmar. We will discover the common denominators of oppression and discrimination as well as the panhuman characteristics that accompany them. Human oppression and discrimination are normal human behavior associated with myths and accumulated power. Discrimination is the nature of man, a nature that the Earth itself can no longer tolerate. With the malleable character of human culture, we must change that nature.

Public-policy decisions that attempt to treat discrimination must be consistent with human values. Equal opportunity is mythological as long as race is polluted with inferiority. If large numbers of "inferior" people are given access to high-status positions, then the positions lose their prior status and become as "inferior" as the people who occupy them. So many middle-class Blacks secretly enjoy being token African-American employees and subtly resist the recruitment and hiring of others for "Fear of Falling" (see Ehrenreich 1989). We have described the conspiracy of successful Black women in an attempt to include them in our discussions, but that description is not intended to exclude the Black men who also conspire with whites to discriminate against African Americans. Middle-class African Americans can be conceptualized both as a socioeconomic status and as a level of integration into "mainstream" (white) society. Middle-class rank is often articulated by associations and clientships with powerful whites. Such "prestigious" associations and clientships are ambivalently appreciated by all classes of African Americans. Thus, Black "leaders" can be pawns of the white power structure while simultaneously manipulating Black cultural symbols of language, style, and ethos. These "leaders" maintain the loyalty of the Black masses because they are Black, charismatic, and appear powerful because of the white company they keep. These Black "leaders" articulate Black aspirations and manipulate African-American symbols. But they are also full participants in the white power structure that is designed to keep African Americans in their "place."

My students are often shocked when I describe the "mainstream" preacher who is quoted in Chapter 7 ("World View in Belmar") as "he speaks before a neighborhood audience to celebrate Black Solidarity Week." It is difficult for them to imagine that an African-American "leader" who speaks with such commitment to Black people can live where he does, with whom he does, and how he does. He is much symbol and little substance in the service of his church and its community. He is a poor role model and mentor to African Americans in Belmar. But he rationalizes all of that as being "mainstream" and a member of the Black middle class. He would defend to his death his inheritance and possession of "soul." But his basic interests and his values lie elsewhere. His wife, neighborhood, grocer, barber, dry cleaner, physician, dentist, broker, and even his car are white. Yet, on the basis of his education, charisma, and success, he believes that he should be an African-American leader. He has a cosmetic commitment and a rhetorical expressiveness to all but his own selfish interests. Nothing reflects the plight of the Black middle class more tragically than the fact that at the close of this century more African-American political energy is directed toward gaining the White House than toward creating a viable Black community. African-American "leaders" spend more time on the lucrative lecture circuit than among their poor "followers." After all, they are just "The Middle-Class Negro in the White Man's World" (Ginzberg 1967). They believe, as did the Jews in Germany in the 1920s, that if they integrate themselves into the society they will be accepted as full Americans.

All of this is to say that African Americans are just another artificial category of humans (for example, the Ibo of Nigeria, the Luo of Kenya, the Blacks, Colored, and Hindu of South Africa, the Tamil of Sri Lanka, the Hutu of Ruanda, the Kurds of Iraq, the Ukranians of the Soviet Union, the Armenians of Turkey and the Soviet Union, the Jews of Nazi Germany, the Eta and Ainu of Japan, the Indians of the Americas, the barbarians in China, the Catholic Irish in Britain, and the Hispanics in the United States) that have similar problems worldwide. As we approach a new century, we must have new leadership. Race, class, sex, ethnicity, religion, and imperialism must cease to divide the peoples of the world. The words of Lincoln continue to ring true almost 150 years later. Region against region, class against class, race against race—"a house divded against itself cannot stand." That house has become a global one. This is an exciting period in the history of mankind. We will soon test the malleability of human culture, for we must discover a new approach to living on Earth or, like the dinosaur, we will end our time on Earth.

The next decade must bring profound transformations—the Ecological Revolution. Education in this country must be reevaluated as our present ways of life are swept away in the winds of change. Leadership must have vision. Former communist countries of the world must learn that materialism is not democracy. Prisons must cease to be social solutions. Wildlife must be respected as a viable component of life on Earth. Drugs, garbage, oil spills, pollution, greed, immorality, racism, sexism, classism, imperialism, and abortion must cease to be the subject of television's nightly news. Most of us alive today will live to see these changes because it will soon be evident that we have no alternatives. These transformations will eliminate the plight of the people who live in Belmar.

Until such times as these changes occur, humans will discriminate against other humans on whatever basis that they can create or discover—standards of beauty, wealth, body size, body proportions, personality, physical fitness, hair characteristics, age, sexual preferences, eye color, skin color, facial features, phenotype, religion, geographic origin, political preferences, moral predilections, speech characteristics, education, standards of intelligence, athletic ability, class, race, occupation, and professionalism. The challenge is not to continue to demonstrate the occasions of such behavior as we do with death and sexual and physical violence in the media, but to recognize the long and continuing history of such phenomena and commit ourselves to the transformation of the character of humans. This provides us with hope and discourse for the future.

With the present character of mankind, we will not distribute the resources of the Earth equitably. We will not maintain the infrastructure of our cities adequately. We will not provide shelter, health care, education, and related social services for those without power. The Rubicon is that we will not save the biosphere and the world's ecosystems. Humans must change.

Let me end this volume with some final thoughts on the "genuine, spurious, and mainstream" African American. It is not facile to communicate the values of one population to another population with different values. The translation attempts are distorted notwithstanding precautions. My approach here is to illustrate by the analogy of an invading army. The analogy is only suggestive.

It is difficult to occupy a people's territory for long without their own complicity and corruption. Approximately 30 million African Americans experience discrimination as a result of American values which posit all African Americans as inferior and deprive many of them economically.

The "genuine" African Americans can be depicted as cultural resistance fighters who attempt to demoralize the occupying army. In their sabotage, they have many casualties, take great risks, and are the objects of the enemy's relentless roundups, hostage taking, firing squads, and other persecutions. But these "freedom fighters" never allow the enemy to forget that they are occupying another people's territory. The sufferings of the "genuine" keep the truth before us and benefit all African Americans when the propaganda of the enemy would have us believe that his rule and control will create a better world for African Americans. The enemy teaches us that his values are best for everybody, notwithstanding that those values create the perception that African Americans are inferior. The enemy selects only the cultural traitors as his collaborators and gives them limited economic opportunities. But he does not share power with them. The enemy "props up" these collaborators as "leaders," role models, scholars, business people, and politicians. He gives them a dubious status and the illusion of power and pretends that they are important, but allows them limited association among the enemy as long as they provide useful information and perform activities vital in the control of their own people. Like the accused "Vichy French," these collaborators court power. They have sex, friendship, and conspiracies with their enemy, the occupying army. They do the enemy's bidding in scholarship, in business, education, and politics. In this analogy, the "spurious" and "mainstream" Blacks are the collaborators. Every occupying army depends upon collaborators to oppress and control the conquered peoples. The collaborators rationalize that if you have no power or courage, then you must live by the myths of those who do. The resistance fighters say that the will and courage to resist is power. We have heard the stories of the enemy burning the books of the conquered people, but there is no need to burn books that were never allowed to be published, or if published are not distributed, promoted, and used in the schools. One does not have to be concerned with the truth if one controls most of the means of communication.

The freedom fighters prefer to die in the resistance movement rather than acquiesce to perpetual "inferiority" and servitude. Like Harriet Tubman, they come from a long line of African-American resistance fighters. They are being labeled as "gangs," "crack dealers," "roving packs" (note the animal imagery), and the "underclass." They are not only victims, but "inferior" devils as well. But perhaps many of them are just members of the resistance movement who are saying in their own subcultural way, "Give me freedom or give me death." Perhaps Ahad Ha-'Am (1912:193) says it better.

But alas! I shall doubtless be dead and buried before then. To-day, while I am still alive, I try mayhap to give my weary eyes a rest from the scene of ignorance, of degradation, of unutterable poverty that confronts me here in Russia, and find comfort by looking yonder across the border, where there are Jewish professors, Jewish members of Academies, Jewish officers in the army, Jewish civil servants; and when I see there, behind the glory and the grandeur of it all, a twofold spiritual slavery—moral slavery and intellectual slavery—and ask myself: Do I envy these follow-Jews of mine their emancipation?—I answer, in all truth and sincerity: No! a thousand times No! The privileges are not worth the price! I may not be emancipated; but at least I have not sold my soul for emancipation. I at least can proclaim from the housetops that my kith and kin are dear to me wherever they are, without being constrained to find forced and unsatisfactory excuses. I at least can remember Jerusalem at other times than those of "divine service": I can mourn for its loss, in public or in private, without being asked what Zion is to me, or I to Zion. I at least have no need to exalt my people to Heaven, to trumpet its superiority above all other nations, in order to find a justification for its existence. I at least know "why I remain a Jew"—or, rather, I can find no meaning in such a question, any more than if I were asked why I remain my father's son. I at least can speak my mind concerning the beliefs and the opinions which I have inherited from my ancestors, without fearing to snap the bond that unites me to my people. I can even adopt that "scientific heresy which bears the name of Darwin," without any danger of my Judaism.

Looking toward the future—the old scene

In a word, I am my own, and my opinions and feelings are my own. I have no reason for concealing or denying them, for deceiving others or myself. And this spiritual freedom—scoff who will!—I would not exchange or barter for all the emancipation in the world.

Almost one hundred years ago (1903), W. E. B. DuBois said:

We feel and know that there are many delicate differences in race psychology, numberless changes that our crude social measurements are not yet able to follow minutely, which explain much of history and social development. (DuBois 1961:123)

DuBois was expressing a sentiment that has continued until today. That sentiment is that African people from sub-Saharan Africa have a distinctive cultural contribution. Leopold S. Senghor described it as Negritude. Asante (1987) described it as "Afrocentric." And recently, Leonard Jeffries (see Blum 1990) at the City College of the City University of New York called it "humanistic, communal, and caring."

My own suggestions are motivated by the resistance to modernity in sub-Saharan Africa. We can yet find hunters and gatherers among the Bushman, Pigmy, Sandawe, Hatsa, and Dorobo. The endurance of the African American during slavery, the Civil War, and Reconstruction are noted. My explanations are that the quality and intensity of the human inferiority complex that is created by DDDAK (see Williams 1989 b) may vary among human populations. These variations determine the extent to which people perceive themselves as a part of the web of life, a component of the biosphere rather than as a separate species designed to control the Earth and other species. Populations such as those in sub-Saharan Africa and women generally seem to have less drive to manipulate, control, and exploit the

Looking at the future: the same male a decade later—the new scene

environment. A popular American perspective on some individual ramifications which may result from the human inferiority complex are discussed by Kinder in his book *Going Nowhere Fast* (1990) as well as by Baritz in his volume *The Good Life* (1989). Thorstein Veblen (1987) discussed some of these same behavioral dynamics almost 75 years ago.

If my suggestions have some validity, then humans will have some selective populations to examine when it finally becomes evident that we can no longer survive with the quality and intensity of inferiority complexes that have created modern society. After the Ecological Revolution no child may lack love, food, shelter, clothing or health care. No child may be coerced into a career or may fear the final rite of passage—the natural transformation of death. Such children may grow and develop to accept their animal kinship, to embrace the family of man (humankind) and the mother of all families, the Earth. They may live peacefully in the global village and as adults teach their own children of another historical era—the Ecological Revolution.

POSTSCRIPT

It is now the social scientist's foremost political and intellectual task—for here the two coincide—to make clear the elements of contemporary uneasiness and indifference. It is the central demand made upon him by other cultural workmen—by physical scientists and artists, by the intellectual community in general. It is because of this task and these demands, I believe, that the social sciences are becoming the common denominator of our cultural period and that the sociological imagination is becoming our most-needed quality of mind (Mills 1959:28).

REFERENCES CITED

Abrahams, R. D., 1964, *Deep Down in the Jungle: Negro Narrative Folklore from the Streets of Philadelphia*. Hatboro, Pa.: Folklore Associates.

Agar, Michael H., 1986, *Speaking of Ethnography*. Newbury Park, Calif.: Sage Publications.

Allport, Floyd H., 1967, "A Theory of Enestuence (event-structure theory): Report of Progress." *American Psychologist*, 22:24.

Anderson, C. H., 1976, *The Sociology of Survival: Social Problems of Growth*. Homewood Ill.: Dorsey Press.

Anderson, E., 1978, *A Place on the Corner*. Chicago: University of Chicago Press.

Asante, Molefi K., 1987, *The Afrocentric Idea*. Philadelphia: Temple University Press.

Aschenbrenner, J., 1975, *Lifelines: Black Families in Chicago*. New York: Holt, Rinehart and Winston.

Baldwin, J., 1963, *Nobody Knows My Name*. New York: Dell.

Baritz, Loren, 1988, *The Good Life*. New York: Knopf.

Becker, Ernest, 1962, *The Birth and Death of Meaning*. Glencoe, Ill.: Free Press.

————, 1973, *The Denial of Death*. New York: Free Press.

Bennett, J., 1976, "Anticipation, Adaptation, and the Concept of Culture in Anthropology." *Science*, 192:847–853.

Berger, B. M., 1973, "Black Culture or Lower Class Culture." In L. Rainwater (ed.), *Soul: Black Experience*. New Brunswick, N.J.: Transaction Books.

Berreman, G., 1968, "Ethnography: Method and Product." In J. Clifton (ed.), *Introduction to Cultural Anthropology*. Boston: Houghton Mifflin.

Berreman, Gerald D., 1972, "Race, Caste, and Other Invidious Distinctions in Social Stratification." *Race* 13:(No. 4, April 1972).

Bett, H., 1929, *The Games of Children: Their Origins and History*. London: Methuen.

Beuf, Ann Hill, 1990, *Beauty is* the Beast: Appearance-Impaired Children in America*. Philadelphia: University of Pennsylvania Press.

Blackwell, J. E., 1975, *The Black Community: Diversity and Unity*. New York: Wiley.

Blum, Debra E., 1990, "Inquiry Prompts Professor to Sue College and Panel." *The Chronicle of Higher Education* (10-10-90) page 17.

Branch, Taylor, 1988, *Parting the Waters: America in the King Years 1954–63*. New York: Simon and Schuster.

Breton, Raymond et al., 1990, *Ethnic Identity and Equality: Varieties of Experiences in a Canadian City*. Toronto: University of Toronto Press.

Brown, Donald E., 1991, *Human Universals*. New York: McGraw-Hill.

Burghart, G. M., and H. A. Herzog, Jr., 1989, "Animals, Evolution, and Ethics." In R. J. Hoage (ed.) *Preceptions of Animals in American Culture*. Washington D.C.: Smithsonian Institution Press. pp. 129–151.

Caillois, R., 1961, *Man, Play, and Games*. New York: Free Press.

Campbell, Joseph, 1973, *The Hero with a Thousand Faces*. Princeton: Princeton University Press.

———, 1959–67, *The Masks of God*. Princeton: Princeton University Press.

Chronicle of Higher Education, 1978, "John Hope Franklin: "I Try to Wear It with Some Grace." January 9.

Clark, K. B., 1967, *Dark Ghetto: Dilemmas of Social Power*. New York: Harper Torchbooks.

———, 1978, "No. No. Race, Not Class Is Still at the Wheel." *New York Times*, Wednesday, March 22.

Coles, R., 1977, *Privileged Ones: The Well-Off and the Rich in America*. Boston: Little, Brown.

Commoner, B., 1971, *The Closing Circle: Nature, Man and Technology*. New York: Knopf.

———, 1976, *The Poverty of Power: Energy and the Economic Crisis*. New York: Knopf.

Cooley, C. H., 1922, *Human Nature and the Social Order*. Charles Scribner and Sons: New York.

Crook, J. H., 1980, *The Evolution of Human Consciousness*. Oxford: Clarendon Press.

Davis, A. et al., 1941, *Deep South*. Chicago: University of Chicago Press.

Degler, Carl N., 1991, *In Search of Human Nature*. New York: Oxford University Press.

Demott, Benjamin, 1990, *The Imperial Middle:* New York: Morrow.

Dobzhansky, T., 1966, *Mankind Evolving: The Evolution of the Human Species*. New Haven, Conn.: Yale University Press.

Dougherty, M. C., 1978, *Becoming a Woman in Rural Black Culture*. New York: Holt, Rinehart and Winston.

Douglass, N., 1931, *London Street Games*. London: Chatto and Windus.

Drake, St. C., 1965, "The Social and Economic Status of the Negro in the United States." *Daedalus*, 94:771–814.

———, and H. R. Cayton, 1962, *Black Metropolis: A Study of Negro Life in a Northern City*. New York: Harper Torchbooks.

DuBois, W. E. B., 1896, *The Philadelphia Negro: A Social Study*. New York: Benjamin Blom.

———, 1961, *The Souls of Black Folk*. Greenwich, Conn.: Fawcett.

Dubos, R., 1976, "Symbiosis between the Earth and Humankind." *Science*, 193:459.

Ehrenreich, Barbara, 1989, *Fear of Falling: The Inner Life of the Middle Class*. New York: Pantheon.

Ellison, R., 1952, *Invisible Man*. New York: Random House.

Epstein, A., 1969, *The Negro Migrant in Pittsburgh*. New York: Arno Press.

Erikson, E., 1970, *Childhood and Society*. New York: Norton.

Fetterman, David M., 1990, *Ethnography: Step by Step*. Newbury Park, Calif.: Sage Publications.

Frazier, E. F., 1965, *Black Bourgeoisie*. New York: Free Press.

———, 1968, *Black Bourgeoisie*. New York: Collier Books.

Freedman, D. H., 1971, "An Analysis of the Institutional Capability of the City of Pittsburgh to Provide Effective Technical Assistance to Black Businessman." Unpublished Ph.D. dissertation in Public and International Affairs, University of Pittsburgh.

Gazaway, Rena, 1969, *The Longest Mile*. Garden City, N.Y.: Doubleday.

Geertz, C., 1973, *The Interpretation of Culture*. New York: Basic Books.

Gensch, D., and R. Staelin, 1970, "An Analysis of Shopping Patterns and Shopping Attitudes for the Residents of Homewood-Brushton." Pittsburgh: Graduate School of Industrial Administration, Carnegie-Mellon University.

Ginzberg, Eli, 1967, *The Middle-Class Negro in the White Man's World*. New York: Columbia University Press.

Goldsmith, Edward et al., 1990, *Imperiled Planet: Restoring Our Endangered Ecosystems*. Cambridge: MIT Press.

Green, V. M., 1970, "The Confrontation of Diversity within the Black Community." *Human Organization*, 29:267–272.

Grinker, R. R., Jr., 1978, "The Poor Rich: The Children of the Super-Rich." *American Journal of Psychiatry*, 135:913–916.

Griot, The, 1990, 9(Number 1):15–19.

Gulick, J., 1973, "Urban Anthropology." In J. Honigmann (ed.), *Handbook of Social and Cultural Anthropology*. Chicago: Rand McNally.

Gump, P. V., and B. Sutton-Smith, 1955, "The 'It' Role in Children's Games." *Group*, 17: 3–8.

Ha—'Am, Ahad, 1912, "Slavery in Freedom." In Ahad Ha—'Am (ed.) Selected Essays. Philadelphia: The Jewish Publication Society of America.

Hall, E. T., 1976, *Beyond Culture*. Garden City, N.Y.: Doubleday.

Hannerz, U., 1969, *Soulside: Inquiries into Ghetto Culture and Community*. New York: Columbia University Press.

Haraway, Donna, 1989, *Gender, Race, and Nature in the World of Modern Science*. New York: Routtledge.

Hare, Nathan, 1970, *The Black Anglo-Saxons*. New York: MacMillan.

Harrington, M., 1976, *The Twilight of Capitalism*. New York: Simon and Schuster.

Hartley, R. E., L. K. Frank, and R. M. Goldenson, 1952, *Understanding Children's Play*. New York: Columbia University Press.

Health and Welfare Association of Allegheny County, 1963, *A Social Plan for Homewood-Brushton*. Pittsburgh: Health and Welfare Association of Allegheny County.

Heilbroner, R. L., 1976, *Business Civilization in Decline*. New York: Norton.

Hippler, A. E., 1974, *Hunter's Point: A Black Ghetto*. New York: Basic Books.

The Homewood Needle, November 13, 1942.

Honigmann, J. J., 1976, "The Personal Approach in Cultural Anthropological Research." *Current Anthropology,* 17:243–261.

Horwitz, T., and Forman, C., 1990, "Clashing Cultures: Immigrants to Europe from the Third World Face Racial Animosity." *Wall Street Journal,* 71:1 (no. 211) August 14.

Huizinga, J., 1955, *Homo Ludens: The Play Element in Culture*. Boston: Beacon.

Jet Magazine, 1977, "Black Named to Head Largest University System." November 17.

Johnson, A., 1978, "In Search of the Affluent Society." *Human Nature*, 1 (9):50–60.

Johnson, N., and P. Sanday, 1971, "Subcultural Variations in an Urban Poor Population." *American Anthropologist*, 73:128–143.

Kapsis, R. E., 1978, "Black Ghetto Diversity and Anomie: A Sociopolitical View." *American Journal of Sociology*, 83:1132–1153.

Kardinar, Abram and Lionel Ovesey, 1962, *The Mark of Oppressions: A Psychological Study of the American Negro*. New York: World Publishing.

Keil, C., 1966, *Urban Blues*. Chicago: University of Chicago Press.

Keiser, L. R., 1979, *The Vice Lords: Warriors of the Streets*, fieldwork ed. New York: Holt, Rinehart and Winston.

Kennedy, T. R., 1980, *You Gotta Deal with It: Black Family Relations in a Southern Community*. New York: Oxford University Press.

Kerri, J. N., 1974, "'Sciencing' in Anthropology: Toward Precision in the Sciences of Applied Anthropology." *Human Organization*, 33:359–366.

Kinder, Melvyn, 1990, *Going Nowhere Fast*. New York: Prentice Hall.

Kozol, J., 1967, *Death at an Early Age*. Boston: Houghton Mifflin.

Kroeber, A. L., 1935, "History and Science in Anthropology." *American Anthropologist*, 37:539–569.

Kunkel, P., and S. S. Kennard, 1971, *Spout Spring: A Black Community*. New York: Holt, Rinehart and Winston.

Ladner, J. A., 1971, *Tomorrow's Tomorrow: The Black Woman*. Garden City, N.Y.: Anchor.

Landy, D., 1974, "Role Adaptation: Traditional Curers under the Impact of Western Medicine." *American Ethnologist* 1:103–127.

Lehman, H. C., and P. A. Witty, 1927, *The Psychology of Play Activities*. New York: A. S. Barnes.

Lekachman, R., 1976, *Economists at Bay: Why the Experts Will Never Solve Your Problems*. New York: McGraw-Hill.

Lemann, Nicholas, 1991, *The Promised Land*. New York: Knopf Publishing Co.

Lewis, Bernard, 1990, "The Roots of Muslim Rage." *The Alantic* (September) 266 (No. 3): 47–69.

———, 1990, *Race and Slavery in the Middle East: On Historical Enquiry*. New York: Oxford University Press.

Lewis, H., 1964, *Blackways of Kent*. New Haven, Conn.: College and University Press.

———, 1967, "Culture, Class and Family Life among Low Income Urban Negroes." In A. M. Rose and H. Hill (eds.), *Employment, Race and Poverty*. New York: Harcourt.

———, 1971, "Culture of Poverty? What Does It Matter?" In E. B. Leacock (ed.), *The Culture of Poverty: A Critique*. New York: Simon and Schuster.

Liebow, E., 1967, *Tally's Corner: A Study of Negro Streetcorner Men*. Boston: Little, Brown.

Lorant, S., 1975, *Pittsburgh: The Story of an American City*. Lenox, Mass.: Published by author.

Lowe, J. R., 1968, *Cities in a Race with Time*. New York: Random House.

Lubove, R., 1969, *Twentieth Century Pittsburgh*. New York: Wiley.

Lynd, R. S., and H. M. Lynd, 1937, *Middletown in Transition*. New York: Harcourt.

———, 1956, *Middletown: A Study in Modern American Culture*. New York: Harcourt.

Malinowski, Bronislaw, 1954, *Magic, Science, and Religion*. New York: Anchor.

Majors, Gerri, 1976, *Black Society*. Chicago: Johnson Publishing.

Maquet, J., 1973, *The Sociology of Knowledge*. Westport, Conn.: Greenwood.

McHarg, I., 1972, "Man: Planetary Disease." In R. V. Guthrie, and E. J. Barnes (eds.), *Man and Society: Focus on Reality*. Palo Alto, Calif.: James E. Freel and Associates.

McLellan, J., 1970, *The Question of Play*. New York: Pergamon.

Mead, M., 1975, *World Enough: Rethinking the Future*. Boston: Little, Brown.

Mills, C. W., 1959, *The Sociological Imagination*. New York: Oxford University Press.

Montagu, M. F. Ashley, 1952, *Man's Most Dangerous Myth: The Fallacy of Race*. New York: Harper and Brothers.

Montagu, M. F. Ashley (ed.), 1968, *Man and Aggression*. New York: Oxford University Press.

———, 1968b, "The New Litany of Innate Depravity or Original Sin Revisited." In M. F. A. Montagu (ed.) *Man and Aggression*. New York: Oxford University Press, pp. 3–17.

Myrdal, Gunnar, 1944, *An American Dilemma*. New York: Harper and Brothers.

Nader, L., 1974, "Up the Anthropologist: Perspectives Gained from Studying Up." In D. Hymes (ed.), *Reinventing Anthropology*. New York: Vintage Books.

New York Times, 1977, "Chinese Report Success in Effort to Turn Deserts into Vineyards." August 31:A12.

Nisbet, R. A., 1975, *Twilight of Authority: The Redecline of the West*. New York: Oxford University Press.

Norbeck, E. (ed.), 1974. *The Anthropological Study of Human Play*. Rice University Studies 60, No. 3. Houston: Rice University Press.

Noske, Barbara, 1989, *Humans and Other Animals: Beyond the Boundaries of Anthropology*. London: Pluto Press.

Ogbu, J. U., 1974, *The Next Generation—An Ethnography of Education in an Urban Neighborhood*. New York: Academic Press.

Orwell, George, 1946, *Animal Farm*. New York: Harcount Brace Jovanovich.

Pelto, P. J., and G. Pelto, 1975, "Intra-Cultural Diversity: Some Theoretical Issues." *American Ethnologist* (Special Issue), 2:1–18.

Phillips, Kevin, 1990, *The Politics of Rich and Poor: Wealth and the American Electorate in the Reagan Aftermath*. New York: Random House.

Piaget, J., 1951, *Play, Dreams, and Imitation in Childhood*. New York: Norton.

Piers, M. W., 1972, *Play and Development*. New York: Norton.

Powdermaker, H., 1939, *After Freedom*. New York: Russell and Russell.

Rainwater, L., 1967, "The Lessons of Pruitt-Igoe." *Public Interest*, 8 (Summer): 116–126.

———, 1974, *Behind Ghetto Walls: Black Family Life in a Federal Slum*. Hawthorne, N.Y.: Aldine.

Raymond, Chris, 1991, "Increasing Use of Film by Visually Oriented Anthropologists Stirs Debate Over Ways Scholars Describe Other Cultures." *The Chronicle of Higher Education* XXXVII (No. 28):A5.

Riezler, K., 1941, "Play and Seriousness." *Journal of Philosophy,* 38:505–517.

Robbins, F. G., 1955, *The Sociology of Play, Recreation and Leisure Time.* Dubuque, Iowa: William C. Brown.

Roberts, J. M. et al., 1959, "Games in Culture." *American Anthropologist,* 61:597–605.

Roberts, J. M., M. D. Williams, and G. C. Poole, 1982, "Used Car Domain: An Ethnographic Application of Clustering and Multidimensional Scaling." In H. C. Hudson (ed.), *Classifying Social Data.* San Francisco: Jossey-Bass, pp. 13–38.

Rodman, H., 1963, "The Lower-Class Value Stretch." *Social Forces,* 42:205–215.

———, 1971, *Lower-Class Families: The Culture of Poverty in Negro Trinidad.* New York: Oxford University Press.

———, 1977, "Culture of Poverty: The Rise and Fall of a Concept." *Sociological Review,* 25:867–876.

Rose, Dan, 1990, *Living the Ethnographic Life.* Newbury Park, Calif.: Sage Publications.

Sahlins, Marshall D., 1960, "The Origin of Society." *Scientific American* 204:76–87 (September, 1960).

Sapir, E., 1966, *Culture, Language and Personality.* Berkeley: University of California Press.

Sennet, Richard and Jonathan Cobb, 1973, *The Hidden Inquiries of Class.* New York: Vintage Books.

Simon, W., and J. H. Gagnon, 1976, "The Anomie of Affluence: A Post-Mertonian Conception." *American Journal of Sociology,* 82:356–378.

Singer, P., 1981, *The Expanding Circle: Ethics and Sociobiology.* New York: Farrer, Straus and Giroux.

Smith, M. G., 1965, *The Plural Society in the British West Indies.* Berkeley: University of California Press.

———, 1969, "Institutional and Political Conditions of Pluralism" and "Some Developments in the Analytical Framework of Pluralism." In L. Kuper and M. G. Smith (eds.), *Pluralism in Africa.* Berkeley: University of California Press.

Spindler, G. D., 1955, *Sociocultural and Psychological Process in Menomini Acculturation.* Berkeley: University of California Press.

———, and L. Spindler, 1971, 1990, *Dreamers without Power: The Menomini Indians.* New York: Holt, Rinehart and Winston.

Spindler, L. & G. 1990, *The American Cultural Dialogue and Its Transmission.* New York: The Falmer Press.

Spurlack, J. and C. B. Robinowitz (eds.), 1990, *Women's Progress: Promises and Problems.* Plenum: New York.

Stack, C. B., 1974, *All Our Kin.* New York: Harper and Row.

Steele, Shelby, 1990, *The Content of Our Character.* New York: St. Martin's Press.

Stone, M., and C. Kestenbaum, 1975, "Maternal Deprivation in the Children of the Wealthy." *History of Childhood Quarterly,* 2:79–106.

Suttles, G. D., 1970, *The Social Order of the Slum: Ethnicity and Territory in the Inner City.* Chicago: University of Chicago Press.

Sutton-Smith, B., and J. M. Roberts, 1963, "Game Involvement in Adults." *Journal of Social Psychology,* 60:15–30.

Szwed, J. F., 1972, "An American Anthropological Dilemma: The Politics of AfroAmerican Cultures." In D. Hymes (ed.), *Reinventing Anthropology*. New York: Pantheon.

Tabb, William K., 1971, "Race Relations Models and Social Change," *Social Problems* 18: (Spring).

Time Magazine, 1977, "The American Underclass: Destitute and Desperate in the Land of Plenty." (August 29):1427.

Torgovnick, Marianne, 1990, *Gone Primitive: Savage Intellects, Modern Lives*. Chicago: University of Chicago Press.

Tylor, E. G., 1958, *The Origins of Culture*. New York: Harper and Row.

———, 1960, *Anthropology*. Ann Arbor: University of Michigan.

Umoja, 1978, 2(Number 3):169–82.

Valentine, B., 1978, *Hustling and Other Hard Work: Life Styles in the Ghetto*. New York: Free Press.

Valentine, C. A., and B. L. Valentine, 1970, "Making the Scene, Digging the Action, and Telling It Like It Is." In N. E. Whitten and J. F. Szwed (eds.), *Afro-American Anthropology: Contemporary Perspectives*. New York: Free Press.

Valentine, Charles H., 1971, "Deficit, Differences and Bicultural Models of Afro-American Behavior." *Harvard Educational Review* 41:137–157.

Van Trump, J. D., 1973, "Valley of Memory and Decision." *Carnegie Magazine:* 240–247.

Veblen, Thorstein, 1987, *The Theory of the Leisure Class*. New York: Penguin Books.

Warner, W. L. et al., 1963, *Yankee City*. New Haven, Conn.: Yale University Press.

Wengle, John L., 1988, *Ethnographers in the Field*. Tuscaloosa: University of Alabama Press.

West, J., 1945, *Plainville, U.S.A.* New York: Columbia University Press.

Whyte, W., 1955, *Street Corner Society*, 2nd ed. Chicago: University Chicago Press.

Williams, M. D., 1973a, "The Black Community: A Social Prognosis: A Brief Note on the Black Quest for Community in Pittsburgh." *Pastoral Institute Newsletter* (Special Hillman Issue), 2:12–13.

———, 1973b, "Food and Animals: Behavioral Metaphors in a Black Pentecostal Church in Pittsburgh." *Urban Anthropology*, 2:7479.

———, 1974, *Community in a Black Pentecostal Church: An Anthropological Study*. Pittsburgh: University of Pittsburgh Press.

———, 1975, *Selected Readings in Afro-American Anthropology*. Lexington, Mass.: Xerox College Publishing.

———, 1978, "Childhood in an Urban Black Ghetto: Two Life Histories." *UMOJA*, 2: 169–182.

———, 1980, "Belmar: Diverse Lifestyles in a Pittsburgh Black Neighborhood." *Ethnic Groups: An International Journal of Ethnic Studies* 3:23–54.

———, 1981, *On the Street Where I Lived*. New York: Holt, Rinehart and Winston.

———, 1984, *Community in a Black Pentecostal Church: An Anthropological Study*. Paper Edition. Prospect Heights, Ill: Waveland Press.

———, 1989a, "Children's Games and Play of the Straits Salish Indians of Vancouver Island." In R. Bolton (ed.), *The Content of Culture*. New Haven, Conn.: HRAF Press, pp. 19–32.

————, 1989b, *Culture and Extinction: Man, Myth, and Modernity*. Ann Arbor, Mich.: Published by the author.

————, 1990, "The Afro-American in the Cultural Dialogue of the United States." In G. and L. Spindler (eds.), *The American Cultural Dialogue and Its Transmission*. New York: Falmer Press.

————, In Press, "The Black Church in a Midwestern University Twin City." In R. Dennis (ed.) *Race and Ethnic Relations Research*. Greenwich: JAI Press.

————, In Press b, *The Black Middle Class and Social Transformations*. Newbury Park, Calif.: Sage Publications.

Wilson, W. J., 1978, *The Declining Significance of Race: Blacks and Changing American Institutions*. Chicago: University of Chicago Press.

————, 1987, *The Truly Disadvantaged*. New York: MacMillan.

Windell, P., 1975, *Homewood South: The Redevelopment of an Urban Subarea*. Pittsburgh: University Center for Urban Research, University of Pittsburgh.

Wixen, B. N., 1973, *Children of the Rich*. New York: Crown.

Wolman, A., 1976, "Ecologic Dilemmas." *Science*, 193:740.

Young, V. H., 1970, "Negro Community." *American Anthropologist*, 72:269–288.